HERMENEUTICS: STUDIES IN THE HISTORY OF RELIGIONS

Kees W. Bolle, Editor

Richard Marks, The Image of Bar Kokhba in Traditional Jewish Literature: False Messiah and National Hero

Joanne Punzo Waghorne, The Raja's Magic Clothes: Re-Visioning Kingship and Divinity in England's India

Devin DeWeese, Islamization and Native Religion in the Golden Horde: Baba Tükles and Conversion to Islam in Historical and Epic Tradition

Gregory D. Alles, The *Iliad*, the *Rāmāyaṇa*, and the Work of Religion: Failed Persuasion and Religious Mystification

Arvind Sharma, The Philosophy of Religion and Advaita Vedānta: A Comparative Study in Religion and Reason

The Philosophy of Religion and Advaita Vedānta

The Philosophy of Religion and Advaita Vedānta

A Comparative Study in Religion and Reason

Arvind Sharma

The Pennsylvania State University Press
University Park, Pennsylvania

Library of Congress Cataloging-in-Publication Data

Sharma, Arvind.
The philosophy of religion and Advaita Vedanta : a comparative study in religion and reason / Arvind Sharma.

p. cm.—(Hermeneutics, studies in the history of religions)
Includes bibliographical references and index.
ISBN 0-271-01032-0
1. Religion—Philosophy. 2. Advaita. 3. Śaṅkarācārya. 4. Hick, John. I. Title. II. Series: Hermeneutics, studies in the history of religions (1980–)
BL51.S497 1995
200′.1—dc20 93-25526
CIP

Printed in the United States of America

Published by The Pennsylvania State University Press,
University Park, PA 16802-1003

It is the policy of The Pennsylvania State University Press to use acid-free paper for the first printing of all clothbound books. Publications on uncoated stock satisfy the minimum requirements of American National Standard for Information Sciences—Permanence of Paper for Printed Library Materials, ANSI Z39.48–1984.

Contents

For
K. Satchidananda Murty

Preface

The philosophy of religion, as it is known in the West, and Advaita Vedānta, as it evolved in India, represent two solitudes, as it were. If in this book I cannot make them talk to each other, I shall at least make them sit on the same bench.

Yet the philosophy of religion and Advaita Vedānta each represent a tradition not only different from the other but also diverse within itself as well, so that once the decision to present them together has been made, a concomitant question inevitably arises. If neither tradition, though cohesive and cumulative, is monolithic or static, then what points within them should be compared?

One has no choice but to choose. And though all choices are in some sense arbitrary they need not on that account be unreasonable. I decided to take John H. Hick as representative of the philosophy of religion and Śaṅkara (I have in mind here especially his commentary on the Upaniṣads, the Brahmasūtra, and the Bhagavadgītā) as representative of Advaita Vedānta. These choices certainly require clarification and perhaps some justification.

I have chosen John Hick as representative of the "philosophy of religion" primarily in his capacity as the author of a book of the same title. In order not to be misunderstood I would like to distinguish John Hick as a philosopher of religion in his own right from John Hick as a representative of the current state of the philosophy of religion in this book. I engage the latter. I use not him but rather his book on the philosophy of religion as representative of the current state of the field. There are, of course, many other general surveys of the philosophy of religion, and in principle any one of them could have served my purpose as well; however, it is equally obvious to me that perhaps one must focus on a single book, and I chose John Hick's for the simple reason that it was the one I was most familiar with. I must emphasize that I do not compare John Hick's philosophy with Śaṅkara's. I leave that task to his other admirers. I compare the philosophy of religion as known in the West, and as epitomized in the book on it by John Hick, with Advaita Vedānta.

I have, in the same spirit, chosen Śaṅkara to represent Advaita Vedānta. Śaṅkara, however, flourished in the ninth century and has had many interpreters. Since 1800 many Indian thinkers have written on Śaṅkara in English. Prominent among them are M. Hiriyanna, S. Radhakrishnan, K. C. Bhattacharyya, K. Satchidananda Murty, and T.M.P. Mahadevan. This is a vital point for two reasons. First, these scholars were already familiar with at least some of the issues in the philosophy of religion current in the West and therefore tended to take them into intellectual account in their own discussions of Advaita Vedānta. They thus anticipated what I often try to elucidate, and I naturally gravitated toward them. Second, their participation in the larger intellectual life of the globe left them faithful to the tradition but not bound to it, as someone whose knowledge is solely confined to classical Advaita and the other schools of Indian thought alone might be. They enlarged the tradition hermeneutically and critically, and I have not hesitated to accept their enlargement of the tradition as authentic. Although I offer evidence from Advaita sources themselves, how these scholars have deployed the Advaita tradition has as much significance for me as my own study. Thus my understanding of Śaṅkara as a representative of Advaita Vedānta incorporates theirs.

How I chose to present the material of this book was governed as much by the intended audience as by the intention of the author. My book is for those who know Western philosophy of religion and are interested in what the Hindu school of thought called Advaita Vedānta has to offer in the field and those who are familiar with Advaita Vedānta and want to know what light it can shed on issues in the Western philosophy of religion. Unfortunately, the readers of this book are likely to be more conversant with one pole of comparison than the other. I therefore try to present material from both the philosophy of religion and Advaita Vedānta so that neither side is shortchanged. To accomplish this I have often had to cite at considerable (but I hope judicious) length. I regret trying the patience of those who are familiar with that material. This situation could not be avoided, for if one wants to ensure that no side is shortchanged, one has to put up with a bit of loose change lying around. I have arranged the material here to follow the order of presentation in John Hick's textbook on the philosophy of religion, not to aggregate or integrate the two streams of thought, but rather to coordinate them. If covering both streams accounts for the length of this book, I hope it also accounts for its value.

Western philosophy has long regarded Indian philosophy as its Other; perhaps the family resemblances reflected in these pages will lead to the recognition that the two are now neighbors and may be, just may be, also brothers. As for the amount of sibling rivalry this provokes, I let the sagacious reader be the judge.

1

The Advaitic Conception of God

The word "God" is an ambiguous term. I use it here in its traditional Judeo-Christian sense as that unique being who is "the infinite, eternal, uncreated, personal reality, who has created all that exists and who is revealed to human creatures as holy and loving."[1] Each of these attributes merits examination in turn.

God as Unique Being

It is a point of some interest that although Hindu thought by and large accepts monotheism,[2] Advaita Vedānta hesitates to do so on *logical* grounds. (I discuss this point in more detail in Chapter 2.) At this stage another aspect of Advaitic thought on God must be highlighted. In the Western philosophy of religion, when God is described as 'one', it is also presumed that God is the one ultimate reality. Advaita demurs on this point.[3] It

1. John H. Hick, *Philosophy of Religion*, 3d ed. (Englewood Cliffs, N.J.: Prentice Hall, 1983), 14.

2. Haridas Bhattacharyya, ed., *The Cultural Heritage of India* (Calcutta: The Ramkrishna Mission Institute of Culture, 1969), vol. 3, chap. 33.

3. Passages such as the following seem to contradict this statement; however, here the word "God" is used to mean *nirguṇa brahman:* "If God connotes, among other things, the Supreme Reality, Śaṅkara's theory is not surely atheism, but rather the logical perfection of the theistic faith. Indeed, whereas atheism believes only in the world and not at all in God, and ordinary theism believes in both, the world and God, Śaṅkara believes only in God. For him God is the only Reality" (Satischandra Chatterjee and Dhirendramohan Datta, *An Introduction to Indian Philosophy* [1950; reprint, Calcutta: University of Calcutta, 1968], 395).

distinguishes two aspects of Brahman, the ultimate reality: the Absolute and God. As the Absolute (*nirguṇa*) it is "pure unqualified consciousness," "without quality or distinction," "undifferentiated being."[4] But alongside this "there is also the teaching about *saguṇa Brahman. Saguṇa Brahman* means *Brahman* endowed with attributes. According to this latter teaching *Brahman* is the cause or ground of the universe. It is from that which all beings spring into existence, in which they live, and into which they return at the end. As thus related to the world, *Brahman* is also called *Īśvara* (God)."[5] One of the problems of Vedantic thought has been "how to reconcile the two views of *Brahman*[?] For solving this problem, Śaṅkara postulates two standpoints: the absolute (*pāramārthika*) and the relative (*vyāvahārika*). The supreme truth is that *Brahman* is nondual and relationless. It alone is; there is nothing real beside it. But from our standpoint, which is the empirical, relative standpoint, *Brahman* appears as God, the cause of the world."[6]

But if God is the ultimate reality only from the relative point of view, and only a relative or empirical ultimate reality from an absolute point of view, are we then, on the basis of the above distinction between *nirguṇa* and *saguṇa* or *pāramārthika* and *vyāvahārika* to "assume that Brahman has a double nature? No, because the *saguṇa* aspect has no transcendental validity. 'Hence Īśvara's being Īśvara, His omniscience, His omnipotence, etc. all depend on the limitation due to the adjuncts whose self is nescience, while in reality none of these qualities belong to the Self whose true nature is cleared, by right knowledge, from all adjuncts whatever.' "[7]

Thus Advaita accepts one God as the ultimate *empirical* reality but not as the ultimate *absolute* reality.

The God of Advaita, however, otherwise functions analogously to the God of the Judeo-Christian tradition, although with important differences.

The important similarity is that God is one, that the "world is not self-explanatory; it refers back to an intelligent cause as its creative ground,"[8]

4. Eliot Deutsch and J.A.B. van Buitenen, *A Source Book of Advaita Vedānta* (Honolulu: The University of Hawaii Press, 1971), 308.

5. T.M.P. Mahadevan, *Outlines of Hinduism* (1960; reprint, Bombay: Chetana, 1971), 147.

6. Ibid.

7. Bhattacharyya, ed., *Cultural Heritage,* 3:540. See also Deutsch and van Buitenen, *Source Book,* 310. It should be added that Śaṅkara has been criticized by some for drawing such a distinction and by others for not drawing it clearly enough (S. Radhakrishnan, *Indian Philosophy* [London: George Allen & Unwin, 1927], 2:554), although it is the standard Advaitic position. See S. Radhakrishnan, ed., *The Principal Upaniṣads* (London: George Allen & Unwin, 1953), 64.

8. Deutsch and van Buitenen, *Source Book,* 309.

which is one. Important differences will emerge in the discussion of God in his role as creator. It should be noted here, however, that God's *oneness* is not compromised by the plurality of God's creation.

God as Infinite and Self-Existent

When the Absolute becomes God, God does not lose all aspects of infinity. In fact, one of the arguments used by Advaita against inferring a creator from the existence of the world is that we "can infer only a finite creator from a finite world,"[9] whereas God is to be regarded as infinite. This infinity also distinguishes God from a *jīva* (individual soul),[10] for in this case God "cannot be any finite consciousness in the sense in which a Jīva is, for it must know the contents of the entire universe."[11]

At this point we face a philosophical problem. A God that is infinite *per se* "could only act in one way, or rather, Śaṁkara would say, . . . could not act at all. [Such a God] could only be and not become,"[12] but the world comes to be so that "the only way is through the recognition of a saguṇa Brahman or changing Brahman, an Īśvara who combines within himself the natures of both being and becoming."[13] This God or Īśvara is "the home of all finite existence."[14]

From the point of view of infinity in relation to God, Śaṅkara "attempts to combine the ideas of the negation of the finite and the presupposition of the finite in his conception of Īśvara."[15] This leads to the following result—God possesses infinite consciousness vis-à-vis the universe, but because God exists only in relation to the universe God possesses qualified rather than infinite being. Infinity by itself may be postulated of *nirguṇa* (unqualified) Brahman,[16] whereas "qualified Brahman, if personified, becomes God." This is why God, though holy, is not self-existent. Yet it is to God that the

9. S. Radhakrishnan, *Indian Philosophy* (London: George Allen & Unwin, 1962), 2:543.
10. Ibid., 554.
11. M. Hiriyanna, *Outlines of Indian Philosophy* (London: George Allen & Unwin, 1964), 363.
12. Radhakrishnan, *Indian Philosophy* (1927), 2:559 n. 1.
13. Ibid., 555.
14. Ibid., 559.
15. Ibid., 558.
16. S. Radhakrishnan, trans., *The Brahma Sūtra: The Philosophy of a Spiritual Life* (London: George Allen & Unwin, 1960), 31. But see Chatterjee and Datta, *Introduction*, 391.

universe owes its own existence, for God creates the universe by God's own power (*śakti*). *Māyā* (cosmic appearance) as wielded by God becomes *śakti*, and God becomes the material as well as the efficient cause of creation. In this context God's role in creation is often compared to that of a magician. In fact God is called the Great Magician. This comparison is significant in two respects. First, a magician produces magical objects out of his own sleeves and is both the efficient and material cause of his magical creations. Second, and this is an important point, the magician is not deceived by his own magic, the onlookers are. God remains free from delusion and evil consequent to it, whereas the beings in the universe fall prey to it. Nevertheless God, as qualified Brahman, is not identical with the Absolute.[17]

As with infinity, God's self-existence has to be understood carefully. Both the Absolute and God are infinite, but the Absolute is infinite in the sense of being all-comprehensive, whereas God *possesses* infinity. Similarly, both the Absolute and God are self-existent, but God is self-existent from the point of view of the universe. As S. Radhakrishnan puts it, "Since nothing superior to Īśvara can be conceived, therefore Īśvara exists uncaused."[18] But as pointed out in the passage cited above, the situation from the point of view of the Absolute is different. This point is not unconnected with the issue of infinity. "Īśvara is the creator of the world when Brahman is the locus of all superimposition: when we confound the infinite and the finite, and it is natural that we do this, Brahman, as Īśvara, is the material and the efficient cause of the world."[19]

The confusion over the uses of infinity for both *nirguṇa* Brahman and Īśvara arises from the "limitations on the infinity of God" resulting from the existence of co-eternal matter. However, because matter is comprised within God and is subject to God, the limitation is itself of a very limited nature. One must not forget that Brahman in relation to the world is Īśvara. It is not the case that the world emerges as an emanation from Īśvara and Īśvara in turn from Brahman.[20] It should also be borne in mind that whereas *nirguṇa* Brahman is the ground of the universe, Īśvara is its source.

17. M. Hiriyanna, *The Essentials of Indian Philosophy* (London: George Allen & Unwin, 1948), 164. See also Hiriyanna, *Outlines*, 366–67. Despite God's "non-identity" with the Absolute, God and the Absolute are not "two corresponding realities" but "*one* reality."

18. Radhakrishnan, *Indian Philosophy* (1927), 2:546 n. 4.

19. Deutsch and van Buitenen, *Source Book*, 309.

20. "Śaṁkara does not regard the infinite as something which exists in itself first and then feels itself under a necessity to get out into the finite" (Radhakrishnan, *Indian Philosophy* [1927], 2:551).

God as Creator

In relation to God's rule as creator the Advaitin and Christian understandings diverge sharply. Consider the following points:

In Advaita, ontology is more important than cosmology. As Satischandra Chatterjee and Dhirendramohan Datta put it, "There are two problems that appear in the human mind as to the world. One of them is: What is the ultimate ground, substance, or reality *logically presupposed by* the world? The other is: *why or how* the world originates from what is accepted as the ultimate?" Advaita is much more concerned with the former than the latter, and Śaṅkara is even prepared to suggest that the creation stories should not be taken literally.[21]

In Christianity God is the efficient cause of the universe, but in Advaita "Brahman, as Īśvara, is [both] the material and the efficient cause of the universe." Or, "That out of which the universe is made is the same as that which makes it."[22]

Christianity in general subscribes to *creatio ex nihilo,* but Advaita sees creation (effect) as preexisting within the creator (cause).[23]

Unlike Christianity, in Advaita "the world is without an absolute beginning in time." This possibility was entertained but rejected by Thomas

21. Chatterjee and Datta, *Introduction,* 396; N. K. Devaraja, *Hinduism and the Modern Age* (New Delhi: Islam and The Modern Age Society, 1975), 70 n. 2. Some descriptions of the process of creation were developed, however, on physiological or botanical analogies. From the idea of the states of consciousness—of deep sleep, dreaming, and waking—a cosmic vision of the emergence of the universe was formulated. Three terms are important in this respect: Īśvara, Hiraṇyagarbha (or Sūtrātmā or Prāṇa), and Vaiśvānara or Virāṭa. As Īśvara, Brahman possesses the power of creation or māyā; as Hiraṇyagarbha, the power of "subtly differentiated Māyā," that is, "the totality of all subtle objects"; and as Vaiśvānara, the power of "Māyā differentiated further into gross or perceptible objects." "Sometimes this gradual process of evolution is compared to the three states of the individual, namely, deep sleep, dream and wakefulness. Īśvara is God in deep slumber. Hiraṇyagarbha is God in dreaming state, and Vaiśvānara is God fully awake. It should be remembered that whereas ordinarily Īśvara implies the entire immanent aspect of God, that is, Brahman associated with Māyā in all stages, the word is used in the present context in a narrower sense, and confined only to the first stage" (Chatterjee and Datta, *Introduction,* 395–96). On the botanical analogy the three stages may be compared to (1) seed, (2) germination, and (3) plant (ibid., 395).

22. Deutsch and van Buitenen, *Source Book,* 309; T.M.P. Mahadevan, as cited in Herbert Herring, *Reflections on Vedānta* (Madras: University of Madras, 1978), 10.

23. Deutsch and van Buitenen, *Source Book,* 309. This is commonly known as *satkāryavāda* (effect preexists in material cause) but as S. N. Dasgupta suggests, it may more properly be called *satkāraṇavāda* in this context, since only the "cause" really exists (Surendranath Dasgupta, *A History of Indian Philosophy* (Delhi: Motilal Banarsidass, 1975), 1:468.

Aquinas because "Christian revelation asserts a beginning." Hindu revelation, as interpreted in Advaita, asserts no such beginning.[24]

On account of the sharp distinction involved between the creator and the created in the doctrine of *creatio ex nihilo* "any thought of human beings becoming God is thus ruled out as meaningless by the Judaic-Christian conception of creation." In Advaita, however, the "selves or Jīvas differ from the common objects of experience in being coeval with time and not in it like them," and each is "assumed to have been there from beginningless time." Thus the idea of man becoming God is not precluded in Advaita—but has to be understood cautiously. For only as considered apart from their adjuncts "the Jīva and Īśvara are one, or more strictly, are not different, that is the significance of tat tvam asi" or That Thou Art.[25]

The most significant difference, however, between Judeo-Christian thought and Advaita Vedānta is that from the ultimate point of view in Advaita Vedānta there is neither creator nor creation: "From the standpoint of Reality, though, there is no creation and there is no creator god. The effect is really only an *apparent* manifestation of the cause (*vivarta*); in reality, there is only Brahman."[26]

According to Śaṅkara this position offers a "more rational view of creation." The issue to be resolved is the nature of the relationship between God and creation. If creation is the outcome of God acting on a substance then one has to admit another reality beside God. If, however, God brings about creation out of something within, then it means that God or some part within God is subject to change, and to that extent God's immutability is compromised. The doctrine of phenomenal or apparent change is more rational in the sense that it avoids these difficulties.[27]

24. Deutsch and van Buitenen, *Source Book,* 309; Hick, *Philosophy of Religion,* 9; see Śaṅkara on Brahma Sūtra 2.3.16–17.

25. Hick, *Philosophy of Religion,* 9; Hiriyanna, *Outlines,* 362, 364 (see also Hiriyanna, *Essentials,* 163–64, 172); Radhakrishnan, ed., *The Principal Upaniṣads,* 460.

26. Deutsch and van Buitenen, *Source Book,* 310.

27. Chatterjee and Datta, *Introduction,* 374. An Indian scholar has suggested that the Christian doctrine of absolute creation may not be as antagonistic to the Advaitic doctrine of no creation as might appear at first sight: "In fact, we may venture to say that the doctrine of absolute creation is a religious version of the doctrine of *vivarta,* because absolute creation amounts to the view that the world comes out of God without in any way affecting Him; God creates the world without becoming the world which is wholly dependent on Him. But the trouble is that Christianity regards the created world as real and not as appearance. How can the real be *created* and that too out of nothing? To be consistent, theism whether of the Indian variety or of the western type, must give up its realism and accept absolutism with its implication of māyāvāda [the doctrine of māyā]" (R. K. Tripathi, *Problems of Philosophy and Religion* [Varanasi: Banaras Hindu University, 1971], 78).

Another question arises at this point in relation to the fact of creation. Why does it occur? Why, in the Christian case, does God create the universe? And why, in the Advaitic case, does creation periodically recur?

Let the Christian case be examined first. According to some scholars one of the problems with *creatio ex nihilo* or absolute creation is that "it is an unfathomable mystery as to why God should indulge in the act of creation; there is no problem and no motive for creating the world."[28] This is so, however, only if the personal nature of God in Christianity is ignored, for God can really be a person only in relation to persons, and objects or the "other." This point is recognized even by Śaṅkara who "holds that even before creation [in the Hindu context] the personal Īśvara has an object in 'the names and forms which are neither to be defined as beings nor as their opposites, which are not evolved though striving towards evolution.' "[29]

On this argument the motive for creation is to be found within God.[30] But in Advaita the motive for creation is provided by the souls of *Jīvas.* "The problem is the existence of bound souls whom God out of . . . infinite goodness wants to lead to freedom and therefore creates a world in which such facilities as are necessary for the spiritual evolution of every soul [exist]. But for this gracious act of God no soul could hope to attain freedom."[31] Thus God the creator cannot be blamed for creating an imperfect universe because it has to be created in accordance with the karma of the *jīvas.*[32] Sometimes this creative activity of God is referred to as *līlā* (sport). "Līlā avoids thereby any problem of evil of the sort associated with Judaeo-Christian theism, and it sets aside as meaningless any question of why Īśvara creates in the first place. There can be no 'why' to creation."[33]

28. Tripathi, *Problems,* 73.

29. Radhakrishnan, *Indian Philosophy* (1927), 2:557. It should be noted, however, that in Advaita "the universe as emerging from Īśvara is not around but within him" and that "the exercise of this potency gives rise to 'the other' " (Hiriyanna, *Outlines,* 365).

30. For a Hindu parallel of sorts, see the Chāndogya Upaniṣad 6.2.

31. Tripathi, *Problems,* 74.

32. See Swami Gambhirananda, trans., *Brahma-Sūtra-Bhāṣya of Śrī Śaṅkarācārya* (Calcutta: Advaita Ashrama, 1977), 504–6.

33. Eliot Deutsch, *Advaita Vedānta: A Philosophical Reconstruction* (Honolulu: East-West Center Press, 1969), 39. See also Radhakrishnan, *Indian Philosophy* (1927), 2:550–51: "The conception of līlā conveys a number of suggestions. The act of creation is not motivated by any selfish interest. It is the spontaneous overflow of God's nature (svabhāva), even as it is the nature of man to breathe in and out. God cannot help creating. The work of the world is not the result of chance or thoughtlessness, but is simply the outcome of God's nature. Out of the fullness of his joy, God scatters abroad life and power. Śaṁkara does not regard the infinite as something which exists in itself first and then feels itself under a necessity to go out into the finite. He creates out of the abundance of his joy and

God as Personal

The God of Advaita is definitely personal, though not ultimate: "not pure consciousness (Caitanya) but a self-conscious personality." It should be noted, however, that just as *saguṇa* Brahman is an aspect of Brahman, so is Īśvara one way of looking at *saguṇa* Brahman. Or as Hiriyanna explains it in terms of the distinction between religion and philosophy, "Such a conception naturally lends itself to a two-fold presentation, and that is why it is described not only as Īśvara or 'the Lord' but also as the saguṇa Brahman. The former being personal may be taken as the ideal of advaitic religion—standing for the Absolute which explains the world-system as it is."[34]

Surendranath Dasgupta argues that "in the Vedānta system," by which here is meant Advaita Vedānta, "Īśvara has but little importance, for he is but a phenomenal being; he may be better, purer, and much more powerful than we, but yet he is as phenomenal as any of us."[35] Although it is true that God is not the ultimate reality in Advaita, it plays a much more significant role in Advaita than Dasgupta suggests. Philosophically, God is not subject to *māyā* like the *jīvas; māyā* is subject to him. He wields *māyā* whereas the *jīvas* yield to *māyā.*

> For understanding this higher aspect of God as He is really in Himself (without relation to the world) along with the lower aspect, Śaṅkara constantly draws on the analogy of the magician (māyāvī) as suggested in the *Śvetāśvatara* [Upaniṣad]. The magician is a juggler only to those who are deceived by his trick and who fancy that they perceive the objects conjured up. But to the discerning few who see through the trick and have no illusion, the juggler fails to be a juggler. Similarly, those who believe in the world-show think of God through this show and call Him its Creator, etc. But for those wise few who know that the world is a mere show, there is neither any real world nor any real Creator.[36]

---

for the fulfilment of the demands of morality. By looking upon creation as the cosmic game in which the Supreme indulges, Śaṁkara brings out the purposiveness, rationality, ease and effortlessness with which the creation is sustained."

34. Radhakrishnan, *Indian Philosophy* (1927), 2:556; Hiriyanna, *Outlines,* 366–67.

35. Dasgupta, *History,* 1:477.

36. Chatterjee and Datta, *Introduction,* 389.

It should also be added that the magician is not taken in by his own tricks: "As the magician is not affected by the māyā which he has himself created, since it is unreal, so also the supreme is not affected by the māyā of saṁsāra."[37]

Even more significant is the role of God as an object of worship. Two points need to be noted here. The first is that though final release only results from knowing the Absolute, a devotee of God "gets into *brahma-loka* [the world of Brahmā] where he dwells as a distinct individual enjoying great power and knowledge. When he gains knowledge of *Brahman* he obtains final release. Until the final redemption of all takes place, release can take the form of the attainment of the nature of *Īśvara* and not identity with [*nirguṇa*] *Brahman*."[38]

The second is that there are numerous hymns to a personal God believed to have been written by Śaṅkara. Some of these attributions may be erroneous, but the tradition in this respect seems too strong not to be taken into account. Radhakrishnan seems to be just in his assessment that "while the Absolute is beyond words human nature brings it within the limits of its comprehension by making it into a personal God" and that Śaṅkara "adopts a catholic view with regard to these personal conceptions."[39] The following illustrations of his hymns to Śiva and to Viṣṇu are well worth citing in this context.

To Śiva

> Forgive me, O Śiva, my three great sins. I came on a pilgrimage to Kāśī forgetting that you are omnipresent; in thinking about you, I forget that you are beyond thought; in praying to you I forget that you are beyond words.[40]

To Viṣṇu

> O Lord, even after realising that there is no real difference between the individual soul and *Brahman* I beg to state that I am yours and not that you are mine. The wave belongs to the ocean and not the ocean to the wave.[41]

37. See Radhakrishnan, *Indian Philosophy* (1927), 2:558.
38. Radhakrishnan, trans., *Brahma Sūtra,* 38–39.
39. Ibid., 38.
40. Ibid.
41. Ibid. Recent textual scholarship regarding Śaṅkara's works tends to doubt the authenticity of the ascription of such hymns to Śaṅkara. The secure place of theism in Śaṅkara's system,

Martin Buber is often remembered for having "pointed to two radically different kinds of relationship, I-Thou and I-It."[42] A little reflection will suggest that the relationship of the spiritual aspirant toward *nirguṇa Brahman* is likely to be of the I-It type and that toward Īśvara is likely to fall into the I-Thou category. One must avoid the assumption here that the human personality is capable of only one of these; indeed Buber himself had experiences of both types, though he rejected the I-It type.[43]

God as Loving

Can the God of Advaita be a loving God—with the impersonal Brahman lurking in the background? Many modern writings on Advaita tend to generate the impression that the God of Advaita is a mere construct and only reluctantly accepted within the system. Eliot Deutsch and J.A.B. van Buitenen, who go on to emphasize the theistic character of the Bhagavadgītā,[44] remark that as "even Śaṅkara to whom the *text is not at all congenial*" should have to comment on it is an indication of its popularity.[45] In Radhakrishnan's elaborate discussion of the Advaita Vedānta of Śaṅkara love enters the discussion in the following form: "He who does nothing and stands aloof from the world is not God, not at any rate a God of love. Love lives in the life of its objects, exhibiting the sorrow though not the guilt of wrong-doing and sin and the joy of righteous living."[46] But Hiriyanna's description of God in Advaita evokes more a God one emulates rather than a God one loves or is loved by.[47]

R. K. Tripathi, however, considers it unfortunate that the "place of Īśvara in Advaitism is not adequately appreciated,"[48] and he addresses himself to the question of God as both loving and good. His views are refreshing as well as cogent. On the question of love he makes the point that only meta-

---

however, which these verses serve to illustrate has not been questioned. See also Śaṅkara's introduction to his gloss on Bhagavadgītā 11.55.

42. Hick, *Philosophy of Religion,* 11.
43. *Encyclopedia Britannica,* 14th ed., Macropaedia, s.v. "Religious Experience."
44. Deutsch and van Buitenen, *Source Book,* 35–36.
45. Ibid., 34; emphasis added.
46. Radhakrishnan, *Indian Philosophy* (1927), 2:557.
47. Hiriyanna, *Outlines,* 366.
48. Tripathi, *Problems,* 81.

physical equals can truly love and that the nondualism of Advaita provides precisely such a foundation. He writes:

> Consider the question of love. Apparently love requires duality but really is it possible for one being to love another who is completely different? Love requires some kind of unity and tends to realize that unity which is obscured by apparent difference. Love is the merger of one into the other. The Biblical sentence "Not my will but Thy will be done" means just such an achievement of unity with the Lord; self-will or self-identity is inconsistent with love. Only that can be really loved which is our self or only that which is ourself can be really loved. If God is the wholly other, one may stoop to Him and fear Him but one cannot love Him. This is the significance of the famous saying of the Bṛhadāraṇyaka Upaniṣad that everything is dear to us for the sake of self: even God is dear to us just for that reason. If we love God it only means that we want to make Him our very self and this can be done only if He is already our self, not the present self but the deeper or the higher self; the distinction between the lover and the beloved is there, but it is of levels only; love is the attraction felt by the lower self for the higher self; prayer and worship also should be understood in the same way. No real communion is possible between man and God so long as a real gap between the two is admitted.[49]

The reference here is to a famous passage in the Bṛhadāraṇyaka Upaniṣad:

> Verily, not for the sake of the husband is the husband dear but for the sake of the Self is the husband dear. Verily, not for the sake of the wife is the wife dear but for the sake of the Self is the wife dear. Verily, not for the sake of the sons are the sons dear but for the sake of the Self are the sons dear. Verily, not for the sake of wealth is wealth dear but for the sake of the Self is wealth dear. Verily, not for the sake of the cattle are the cattle dear but for the sake of the Self are the cattle dear. . . .[50]

49. Ibid., 76–77.
50. Radhakrishnan, trans., *The Principal Upaniṣads,* 282–83.

Some comparative comments might be helpful here. One is the distinction in Christian thought[51] of the kind of love God has for human beings (*agape*) from the love one human being may have for another (*eros, philia*). No such distinction is drawn here. Indeed, the Advaitin would be strongly tempted to interpret the statement about man being made in God's image along the lines of the above passage.[52]

For Tripathi, in order for God to be fully good he must (1) teach, (2) create, (3) incarnate, and (4) be present within one's self. The Advaitin then would want to know how well God as depicted in other religions fares in the light of these criteria.

Western philosophers of religion identify another problem concerning God and goodness: Is goodness as a value intrinsic or extrinsic to God? If it is intrinsic to God and God is "good by definition," then the criterion of goodness becomes arbitrary. Whatever God decides becomes good; even murder, for instance, would become good should God so change his mind. But if it is extrinsic, then this implies a point of reference external to God and God ceases to be, at least axiologically, the ultimate reality.[53]

This seems to be a particularly Christian dilemma. In Advaita, God clearly possesses goodness and is not goodness,[54] but there is nothing external to God, and therefore there is no moral standard external to God.

God as Holy

In Advaita Vedānta "truth is impersonal and absolute and not relative and personal. This is why in Advaitism, Brahman the impersonal absolute is regarded as superior to Īśvara or the personal. Īśvara knows himself as Brahman or the impersonal truth; He does not consider himself to be a person. . . . That Īśvara knows Himself as Brahman implies two things: that Brahman and Īśvara are not different, and also that Īśvara cannot be the ultimate (Brahman)."[55]

Advaita may then deny the holiness of *ultimacy* to God, but it cannot deny him the holiness of *intimacy*. For in Advaita

51. Hick, *Philosophy of Religion*, 11–12.
52. Ibid., 12.
53. Hick, *Philosophy of Religion*, 12–13.
54. Tripathi, *Problems*, 78.
55. Ibid., 150. Although God does not, the jīvas do consider God to be a person.

> God is conceived of as an Almighty Person, the Ruler or niyanta, the Protector, the raksaka; and the devotee enters into diverse relations with Him determined by the manner in which he conceives Him, as father, son, mother, friend, guardian, lover, beloved, etc. An emotional bond connects the devotee and the Deity and the whole situation partakes essentially of a human nexus. All this is framed in the alphabet of human relationships in the sphere of the vyavaharic world.[56]

Most systems of philosophy and religion tend to terminate in a personal God. Advaita does not, but one must not on that account rush to the conclusion that God is dispensed with. Advaita distinguishes two orders of reality: the relative (*vyāvahārika*) and the ultimate (*pāramārthika*).[57] Keep in mind that "it is wrong to say that God has an inferior place in Advaita." One could argue that "God is a fact of reality in the vyāvahārika stage; but [of course] in the pāramārthika stage, the question of the reality of God does not arise."[58] But such an argument overlooks the following: God's "*inapplicability* in the pāramārthika stage does not mean *invalidity* in the vyāvahārika."[59] Indeed devotion to God may pave the way to the knowledge of *nirguṇa* Brahman. (This is a common sentiment[60] but one also meets with the sentiment that "it is only by the grace of God that man will be drawn to Advaita"!)[61]

The holiness of God on the empirical level is attested to in several ways in Advaita. In the Dakṣiṇāmūrti Stotra, for instance, attributed to Śaṅkara,[62] one finds the following tribute to God: "All that is moving or unmoving in the universe—earth, water, air, fire, ether, the sun, the moon and the spirit—is but the eightfold form of Him, and there is nothing whatever which on reflection is other than the Supreme Lord."[63]

56. P. Sankaranarayanan, *What Is Advaita?* (Bombay: Bharatiya Vidya Bhavan, 1970), 68.

57. Sometimes a third, the *prātibhāsika* (subjective illusion) is also added (Hiriyanna, *Essentials,* 167).

58. Sankaranarayanan, *What Is Advaita?* 67.

59. Ibid., 68.

60. Ibid. See also Chatterjee and Datta, *Introduction,* 390, 392–93.

61. Appaya Dīkṣita, quoted in Sankaranarayanan, *What is Advaita?* 69. See also the explanation cited by him of Bhagavadgītā 18.55 and compare it with Śaṅkara's (Alladi Mahadeva Sastry, trans. *The Bhagavad Gita with the Commentary of Sri Sankaracharya* [1979; reprint, Madras: Samata Books, 1985], 492–95).

62. See Sankaranarayanan, *What Is Advaita?* 212–42.

63. Radhakrishnan, *Indian Philosophy* (1927), 2:558 n. 2.

Two aspects of the treatment of theism in Advaita Vedānta must be singled out in concluding this chapter. The first is that in emphasizing the priority of *nirguṇa* Brahman in Advaita Vedānta, the systemic necessity of positing Īśvara within it, in accordance with its theory of knowledge, often gets overlooked. The second is related to the first and also has to do with the priority just alluded to. Sometimes we lose sight of the fact that while one might speak of two Brahmans, *nirguṇa* and *saguṇa* as it were, there *is* only one Brahman, and that the two—*nirguṇa* and *saguṇa*—are aspects of the same Brahman, like two sides, one bare and the other embossed, of the *same* coin.

2

Grounds for Belief and Disbelief in God

As I pointed out earlier, Advaita accepts the existence of God, but *not on rational grounds*. It takes into account many of the so-called proofs of God and concludes that the existence of God cannot be established on their basis.

The Ontological Argument

In Advaita Vedānta the ontological argument, or its analogues, proceed in one of three ways: through etymology, epistemology, or yoga.

The first Brahmasūtra states: "Now therefore the desire to know Brahman (the Ultimate Reality)"[1] or "now, therefore, the inquiry into Brahma (should be taken up)."[2] Because the next *sūtra* refers to the world in relation to Brahman, as Śaṅkara states in his gloss,[3] it will not be off the mark to analyze the commentary here for potential theistic proofs. After all, if one wishes to inquire into Brahman in the context of the universe, one should first establish that Brahman exists. Advaitin commentators attempted to do exactly that, arguing from the etymology of the word "Brahman" (which is formed from a root signifying expansion). According to the argument, it is said that we "find 'greatness' predicated of persons who excel others in

1. S. Radhakrishnan, trans. *The Brahma Sūtra: The Philosophy of a Spiritual Life* (London: George Allen & Unwin, 1960), 227.
2. V. M. Apte, trans., *Brahma-Sūtra Shānkarabhāshya* (Bombay: Popular Book Depot, 1960), 5.
3. Ibid., 7.

genius or power and are free from the shortcomings of others. Brahman, being the greatest thing of all, cannot have any defects such as 'limited substantiality,' 'inertness' [and so on]."[4] These commentators, however, never develop the argument into a proof, because they acknowledge that "a conception so arrived at through etymology only shows that the existence of such a thing is possible" and "does not establish that there is such a thing."[5]

Epistemologically, Advaita Vedānta accepts the doctrine of the self-validity of knowledge, namely, "that truth (*pramā*) is intrinsic to knowledge (*jñāna*). The causes which account for the rise of knowledge yield truth also."[6] In other words, epistemology implies a corresponding ontology. One could then invoke this view in support of the assertion that "as Brahman is not entirely unknown"[7] one *presumes* that it exists. This point does not seem to have been developed in Advaita in relation to God.

An argument given in Yoga, which is sometimes connected with[8] but is different from the ontological argument,[9] is also considered by Advaita. As Ninian Smart puts it:

> A passage in the *Yogabhāṣya* (i.24) (i.e. the commentary on the Yoga aphorisms or Yogasūtra) has sometimes been seen as reminiscent of the Ontological Argument of Anselm and others. It is this. "The Lord's pre-eminence is altogether without anything equal to it or excelling it. For . . . it cannot be excelled by any other pre-eminence, since whatever might seem to excel it would itself turn out to be that very pre-eminence. Therefore that is the Lord wherein we reach this uppermost limit of pre-eminence." Further, two equals are impossible, for when they simultaneously desire the same thing, one will necessarily be frustrated and thus will be inferior to the other.[10]

The Advaitins counterargued that "there might be a number of deities, who possess knowledge, glory, power etc., to an equally great degree."[11] This "polytheistic" argument will be used by them again.

4. K. Satchidananda Murty, *Revelation and Reason in Advaita Vedānta* (New York: Columbia University Press, 1959), 54.

5. Ibid.

6. T.M.P. Mahadevan, *Outlines of Hinduism* (1960; reprint, Bombay: Chetana, 1971), 134.

7. Murty, *Revelation and Reason*, 55.

8. Ninian Smart, *Doctrine and Argument in Indian Philosophy* (London: George Allen & Unwin, 1964), 157.

9. Ibid.

10. Ibid.

11. Murty, *Revelation and Reason*, 142.

The Causal Argument

According to the causal argument the universe as an effect points to a cause, which is God.

The Advaitins find the causal argument unconvincing on the following grounds: First, the "concept of cause, which is not adequate even in the empirical world," is not very helpful when applied to "the world of the experience of ultimate reality, which is said to manifest itself through it."[12] Second, a finite world would lead one to infer a finite creator even if the concept of cause is accepted as applicable.[13] Third, even if the world's cause is inferred, "it cannot be established that there is *only* one such cause." When parsimony was adduced as an argument in support of one cause it was argued that the "principle of parsimony cannot establish that the world has only one author, because in experience we see that many wonderful and complex things like palaces are made by the co-operative effort of several persons."[14] (In other words, the universe could as well have been produced by a committee and to the cynic shows every sign of having been so.) And fourth, even if inquiry into the nature of causation is not pushed to the point of radical skepticism, the world as an effect cannot establish Brahman "because having never perceived Brahman we cannot be sure that a particular effect is related to Brahman."[15]

The Five Arguments of Aquinas

Thomas Aquinas tries to establish the existence of God on rational grounds in five ways: "The first Way argues from the fact of motion to a Prime Mover; the second from causation to a First Cause; the third from contingent beings to a Necessary Being; the fourth from degrees of value to Absolute Value; and the fifth from evidences of purposiveness in nature to a Divine Designer."[16]

12. S. Radhakrishnan, *Indian Philosophy* (London: George Allen & Unwin, 1962), 2:543. See also M. Hiriyanna, *The Essentials of Indian Philosophy* (London: George Allen & Unwin, 1949), 158–59.

13. Radhakrishnan, *Indian Philosophy* (1962), 2:543.

14. Murty, *Revelation and Reason,* 141.

15. Ibid., 143.

16. John H. Hick, *Philosophy of Religion,* 3d ed. (Englewood Cliffs, N.J.: Prentice Hall, 1983), 20.

Advaita considers all these lines of argument suspect. Movement, in order to be imparted, involves a relationship between the moved and the mover, namely God. What then is the nature of the connection between God and these things? Śaṅkara points out "that there cannot be conjunction of one with the other, nor can God inhere in them nor they in him"[17] on account of the spiritual nature of God. Moreover, if we take perceptual experience as our test of the real,[18] "Advaita says that since we nowhere see an unembodied person doing something, we have to think of God as one having a body and subject to all the consequent limitations."[19] If it be argued that "atoms, being material entities, are in themselves inert, and their combination, after a period of cosmic dissolution, can only be explained by reference to an intelligent being capable of volitions," such motion could also as well be ascribed, as Ninian Smart goes on to add, "*to many intelligent beings.*"[20]

Aquinas's First Cause argument is difficult to fit into a system like Advaita in which the universe, the *jīvas*, *karma*, *māyā*, *avidyā* (ignorance), and so on, are all *anādi* or "without beginning."[21] As John Hick presents the First Cause argument, according to Aquinas, "Everything that happens has a cause, and this cause in turn has a cause, and so on in a series that must either be infinite or have its starting point in a first cause. Aquinas excludes the possibility of an infinite regress of causes and so concludes that there must be a First Cause, which we call God." John Hick points out that "the weakness of the argument as Aquinas states it lies in the difficulty (which he himself elsewhere acknowledges) of excluding as impossible an endless regress of events, requiring no beginning."[22]

The argument from Absolute Value is sometimes subsumed under the ontological argument that "whatever admits of degrees must have a maximum." Thus God must possess the highest degree of omniscience, and so on. One Advaitic response, among others, is to argue that "why should not the middle term be used to infer that bulk, hatred, pain, etc. are also found to the greatest possible degree in the same being?"[23]

The purposiveness of a divine designer may be considered next. Advaita

17. Murty, *Revelation and Reason,* 144–45.
18. Ibid.; Hick, *Philosophy of Religion,* 105–6.
19. Murty, *Revelation and Reason,* 144–45.
20. Smart, *Doctrine,* 156; emphasis added.
21. Eliot Deutsch, *Advaita Vedānta: A Philosophical Reconstruction* (Honolulu: East-West Center Press, 1969), 85; Radhakrishnan, *Indian Philosophy* (1962), 2:549; M. Hiriyanna, *Outlines of Indian Philosophy* (London: George Allen & Unwin, 1964), 369.
22. Hick, *Philosophy of Religion,* 20–21.
23. Murty, *Revelation and Reason,* 142.

raises several objections here. Not only is the question of design in creation raised, the whole idea of designing a creation is called into question. The Advaita critique would then run as follows: "All activity is admitted to be purposive, and so must creation be. What then is the purpose of creation? If it is purposeful, whose purpose does it serve? God cannot have any end, which he seeks to achieve; nor can he serve the purpose of others. Some schools of thought say God is a person and that a person is one who is indifferent (*udāsīna*). It is incoherent to say that one who is indifferent has created this world."[24]

Next the question arises, What does God forge the universe from (what is that which is designed)? If on the one hand it is created out of nothing, "it is absolutely unintelligible" to Advaita "how any power, even the almighty, can create existence; Indian philosophy finds it absolutely repugnant to believe that even souls can be created. As Spinoza realized, no substance could be created out of nothing."[25] On the other hand, if the world is moulded by God out of primal matter, "Śaṅkara says that if this matter is visible and gross, there is no need to further mould something which has already a form and shape. If the primal matter has no form at all and so imperceptible, how can we conceive God working on it? Nobody can work materially upon an invisible thing, for no potter made a pot out of invisible clay."[26]

Aquinas's third argument, temporarily passed over, concerned Necessary Being. It has been suggested that the Advaitins actually use this argument. Eliot Deutsch writes:

> The most common Advaitic argument for Brahman has to do with "necessary existence." Reminiscent of (but differing in many interesting and obvious ways from) Thomas' "third proof," the Advaitin argues that there must be a ground or substratum to experience, for otherwise it would be impossible to deny or negate the existence of anything. Śaṁkara puts it this way: "Whenever we deny something unreal, we do so with reference to something real; the unreal snake, e.g. is negatived with reference to the real rope. But this (denial of something unreal with reference to something real) is possible only if some entity is left. If everything is denied, no entity is left, and if no

24. Ibid., 144.

25. R. K. Tripathi, *Problems of Philosophy and Religion* (Varanasi: Banaras Hindu University, 1971), 73.

26. Murty, *Revelation and Reason*, 144.

> entity is left, the denial of some other which we may wish to undertake, becomes impossible, i.e. that latter entity becomes real and as such cannot be negatived."[27]

A little reflection will show, however, that from an Advaitic point of view this is an argument for *nirguṇa* Brahman as the ground of being and not for God, as understood in Advaita, who is contingent.[28] Deutsch's position is weakened further by several related points. First, the Advaitic argument above is for *existence*, not so much the existence *of God.*[29] Second, a distinction must be drawn between the absolutistic proofs in Advaita[30] and theistic proofs of the type being discussed here. Third, the possibility that "there might be an infinite series of finite contingent events overlapping in the time sequence so that no moment occurs that is not occupied by them" should not be overlooked in the context of the Advaitic view of a beginningless creation. Finally, as Radhakrishnan puts it, if "we say God has determinations, like personality, perfection, etc., it is difficult to conceive how they can coexist with absoluteness. The attempt to conserve the characters of personality (*guṇa*) and absoluteness (Brahman) seems to be well nigh impossible for logic."[31]

Moral Arguments

Some schools of Hindu thought argue that action by itself is inert. Therefore one cannot presume karma operates automatically, which implies God. The Advaitic answer is that such a "bestowal of happiness and unhappiness in proportion to virtue and vice might be done even by a plurality of Gods."[32]

27. Deutsch, *Advaita Vedānta,* 12.
28. Hick, *Philosophy of Religion,* 22.
29. See Satischandra Chatterjee and Dhirendramohan Datta, *An Introduction to Indian Philosophy* (1950; reprint, Calcutta: University of Calcutta, 1968), 375–82, 393–94.
30. Mahadevan, *Outlines of Hinduism,* 146.
31. Radhakrishnan, *Indian Philosophy* (1962), 2:544.
32. Murty, *Revelation and Reason,* 142. Radhakrishnan presents another facet of the argument in modern terms: "The moral argument that the context of things is adapted to the soul of man and shows the workmanship of a benevolent God is quite unsatisfactory. However the matter be turned, in a real world the responsibility for sin and evil falls on God. If, to relieve him of the authorship of evil, we accept something like the mythology of Persia and make Satan responsible for it, then the oneness of God disappears and we reinstate a dualism between God and Satan" (*Indian Philosophy* [1962], 2:544).

Normally the doctrine of karma is seen as safeguarding God from getting enmeshed in the problem of evil, as evil can be attributed to individual souls according to this doctrine. But on the issue of theism the Advaitins press the argument further to the point of a thoroughgoing critique of theism, the doctrine of karma notwithstanding. K. Satchidananda Murty summarizes the Advaitin position succinctly by asking (1) how God could have created the universe in accordance with the fruits of actions of the souls if actions per se are inert and (2) why if God is omnipotent, did he allow bad karma to arise in the first place, and by pointing out (3) that if God is moved by karmas to create and if karmas produce results as moved by God, then this logical reciprocal dependence cannot be explained away by invoking a temporal reciprocal dependence that relies on the beginninglessness of the world.[33]

A moral argument *against* the type usually presented would run as follows: "Again, if the soul is a part of God, God must feel the pain of the soul also, even as, when one member of the body suffers, the whole body suffers with it. It follows that the sufferings of God are much greater than those of the individual souls, and it is better for us to remain self-enclosed individuals with our limited sufferings than rise to the level of God and take upon ourselves the burden of the whole world."[34] If it is further argued that evil is evil only in relation to creatures and not in relation to God, just as the poison is not deadly to the serpent but to the one bitten by one, then the question arises: Doesn't God know what is evil for the creatures even if it is not evil for God?

Advaita thus arrives at the conclusion that "the 'existence' of Īśvara as such cannot be demonstrated rationally,"[35] but to "set aside the logical proofs is not to deny the existence of Īśvara."[36] Rather, what is argued is that the case for the existence of God cannot be based on reason alone. Advaita maintains that the case must rest on the scriptural authority of revelation. This, from the point of view of modern philosophy of religion, appears rather retrograde; the case for revelation, therefore, must be examined more closely. An appeal to scriptural authority, in the Hindu world, constitutes an appeal to

33. Murty, *Revelation and Reason,* 143–44. For a similar effort to put the question of suffering beyond karma, see Robert Payne, *The Life and Death of Mahatma Gandhi* (New York: E. P. Dutton, 1969), 125.

34. Radhakrishnan, *Indian Philosophy* (1962), 2:544.

35. Deutsch, *Advaita Vedānta,* 43.

36. Radhakrishnan, *Indian Philosophy* (1967), 2:545.

religious experience. This interpretation of scriptural authority is identifiable in Śaṅkara[37] and made quite explicitly in modern Advaita.[38] Eliot Deutsch states that "scriptural authority is derived from spiritual experience"[39] and cites with approval Krishnachandra Bhattacharyya's statement: "For purposes of philosophy, we may generally substitute in place of faith in scriptures, spiritual experience,"[40] so that ultimately "to say that God exists means that spiritual experience is possible. The possibility of the experience of God constitutes the most conclusive proof of the reality of God."[41]

37. Radhakrishnan, trans., *Brahma Sūtra,* 243–44.

38. Hiriyanna, *Essentials,* 42–45, and *Outlines,* 182 n. 4, and 380 n. 1; Mahadevan, *Outlines of Hinduism,* p. 144.

39. Deutsch, *Advaita Vedānta,* 75.

40. Ibid.

41. S. Radhakrishnan, *Eastern Religions and Western Thought* (New York: Oxford University Press, 1959), 22.

3

The Problem of Evil in Advaita Vedānta

One may begin by restating the problem of evil to make it amenable to consideration within the framework of Advaita Vedānta. John H. Hick offers a classical formulation of the problem, but rejects a solution in Christian terms. His formulation is a useful starting point for our investigation: "As a challenge to theism, the problem of evil has traditionally been posed in the form of a dilemma: if God is perfectly loving, God must wish to abolish all evil; and if God is all-powerful, God must be able to abolish all evil. But evil exists; therefore God cannot be both omnipotent and perfectly loving."[1] (It should, of course, be borne in mind that in Christianity God creates the world.)[2]

An Advaitic formulation of the issue—far less succinct—is found in the *pūrvapakṣa* (preliminary view) in Śaṅkara's gloss on Brahmasūtra 2.34. It basically argues that a loving and good God[3] could not have created the universe:

> For that would lead to the possibility of partiality and cruelty. For it can be reasonably concluded that God has passion and hatred like some ignoble persons. . . . Hence there will be a nullification of God's nature of extreme purity, (unchangeability), etc., that are declared in the Vedas and Smṛtis [sacred tradition]. And owing to infliction of misery and destruction on all creatures, God will be

1. John H. Hick, *The Philosophy of Religion,* 3d ed. (Englewood Cliffs, N.J.: Prentice Hall, 1983), 41.
2. Ibid., 9–10.
3. Ibid., 11–12.

> open to the charge of pitilessness and extreme cruelty, abhorred even by a villain. Thus on account of the possibility of partiality and cruelty, God is not an agent.[4]

The Absolutist Standpoint

The issue of the problem of evil is thus set up at the level of Īśvara—that is, the *saguṇa* Brahman or Absolute *in relation to the world.* But before we examine this point further I should point out, even if only in passing, that from the standpoint of the Absolute (as distinguished from the relative) evil does not exist. Neither does good, for the Absolute is a unity, and good and evil represent dualities, which cannot exist in the ultimate. Modern philosophy of religion rejects this position as vigorously as Advaita asserts it. As John Hick puts it:

> One possible solution (offered, for example, by contemporary Christian Science) can be ruled out immediately so far as the traditional Judaic-Christian faith is concerned. To say that evil is an illusion of the human mind is impossible within a religion based upon the stark realism of the Bible. Its pages faithfully reflect the characteristic mixture of good and evil in human experience. They record every kind of sorrow and suffering, every mode of "man's inhumanity to man" and of our painfully insecure existence in the world. There is no attempt to regard evil as anything but dark, menacingly ugly, heartrending, and crushing. There can be no doubt, then, that for biblical faith evil is entirely real and in no sense an illusion.[5]

By contrast a popular Advaitic manual (Vivekacūḍāmaṇi) describes the liberated one as beyond both good and evil in the following terms:

> 503. How can there be merits and demerits for me, who am without organs, without mind, changeless, and formless—who am the realisation of Bliss Absolute? . . .

4. Swami Gambhirananda, trans., *Brahma-Sūtra-Bhāṣya of Śrī Śaṅkarācārya* (Calcutta: Advaita Ashrama, 1977), 362.
5. Hick, *Philosophy of Religion*, 41.

> 504. If heat or cold, or good or evil, happens to touch the shadow of a man's body, it affects not in the least the man himself, who is distinct from the shadow.[6]

The point might baffle the Western reader—that Brahman is often described as good, yet stated to be beyond good and evil. In the Advaitic frame of reference this is not hard to explain with the help of an analogy. The earth is characterized by the duality of day and night, but day and night on earth are made possible by something beyond them: the sun, which itself knows neither night nor day. Yet if one were pressed to describe the sun in terms of either day or night, one would surely prefer to call it more like day. Just as the sun is beyond day and night, Brahman is beyond good and evil; just as the sun's existence accounts for the existence of both day and night on earth, the existence of the Absolute accounts for the relative existence of both good and evil; just as the sun in relative terms is best identified with the day, the Absolute is best identified with the good.

It is clear, then, that the problem of evil has no place on this plane of nondualism, a plane from which we must now descend.

The Relative Standpoint

On the level of Īśvara the issue of evil is real, as the earlier reference to the Brahmasūtra indicated. How is the problem solved, once its existence is accepted at the empirical level?

The answer, briefly, is that in creating the world, God takes "other factors into consideration," which absolve God from any blame. These factors are the karmas of the *jīva*s. As Śaṅkara comments in the course of his gloss on Brahmasūtra 2.1.34:

> What factors does He take into consideration?
>
> We say that these are merit and demerit. No fault attaches to God, since this unequal creation is brought about in conformity with the virtues and vices of the creatures that are about to be born. Rather,

6. Swami Madhavananda, *Vivekachudamani of Shri Shankaracharya* (Calcutta: Advaita Ashrama, 1966), 193–94.

> God is to be compared to rain. Just as rainfall is a common cause for the growth of paddy, barley, etc., the special reasons for the differences of paddy, barley, etc., being the individual potentiality of the respective seeds, similarly God is the common cause for the birth of gods, men, and others, while the individual fruits of works associated with the individual creatures are the uncommon causes for the creation of the differences among the gods, men, and others. Thus God is not open to the defects of partiality and cruelty, since he takes other factors into consideration.[7]

This could lead to an objection: If this karma is performed by *jīva*s *after* creation, how can it be invoked to explain the justness of creation itself along karmic lines? According to Advaita, this problem is no problem because the process of birth-death-rebirth characterized by karma has no beginning.[8] *Saṁsāra* is *anādi.*

How, then, does one establish the beginninglessness of karma? Śaṅkara offers the question, "Which came first, the chicken or the egg?" as the answer. The Advaitic version of the chicken-egg paradox is the seed-sprout paradox, which appears at the end of Śaṅkara's gloss on Brahmasūtra 2.1.36:

> And it is logical for the transmigratory existence to have no beginning; for had it emerged capriciously all of a sudden, then there would have been the predicament of freed souls also being reborn here, as also the contingency of results accruing from non-existing causes, for the differences in happiness and misery would have no logical explanation. It has been pointed out already that God is not the cause of inequality, nor is ignorance by itself a source of this, it being homogeneous. Ignorance can at best become the creator of inequality in consequence of the fruits of work, which are acquired as a result of the influence of past impressions of the three infatuations—love, hatred, and delusion. The fallacy of mutual dependence does not arise from the impossibility of bodies, being created without *karma* and *karma* being performed without bodies; for if creation is beginningless, all this becomes reasonable on the

7. Gambhirananda, trans., *Brahma-Sūtra-Bhāṣya,* 363.
8. Ibid., 364.

> analogy of the seed and the sprout, and hence there will be no defect.[9]

Opinions could be divided on how fair or sound the idea of a beginningless *saṁsāra* is. Some regard it as a vicious regress, but most Advaitins would side with Arthur L. Herman, who holds that though a regress is involved, "it is not vicious for the simple reason that at each stage the nature of existence can be explained by previous existences—there is no case of a no-explanation-until-the-regress-is-completed-and-it-can't-be-completed conclusion. That would indeed be a vicious regress. Here, on the contrary, at each stage we have an answer to the question, Why do I suffer the evil that I do when God is so perfect? There is no postponement of an answer until the incompletable series is completed. The answer, however vague, is there: Because of karma, my karma."[10]

Evil and Līlā

The problem of evil—if it may still be considered a problem—presents at least two further difficulties: one of a general philosophical nature and one of a peculiarly Advaitic nature.

The general problem is this. Even if it is granted that there is justice within creation and evil is not arbitrary, it is still the case that, arbitrary or not, evil *does* exist. And it would not exist if creation did not exist. Therefore creation is a cause of evil.

Śaṅkara argues in his gloss on Brahmasūtra 2.1.33 that the process of creation per se is not evil because it does not result from any extraneous motive. He uses two examples: (1) *līlā* (sport) and (2) breathing. The first is spontaneous, the second natural, and neither has an extraneous motive underlying it.

> As in the world it is seen that though a king or some councillor of the king who has got all his desires fulfilled, may still, without any aim in view, indulge in activities in the forms of sports and pastimes, as a

9. Ibid., 364–65.

10. Arthur L. Herman, *The Problem of Evil and Indian Thought* (Delhi: Motilal Banarsidass, 1976), 263–64.

> sort of diversion, or as inhalation, exhalation, etc. proceed spontaneously without depending on any external motive, so also God can have activities of the nature of mere pastime out of His spontaneity without any extraneous motive.[11]

Śaṅkara proceeds to emphasize the "pastime" aspect of creation in relation to God.[12]

Arthur L. Herman argues that the *līlā* solution, as he calls it, is uncalled for. According to him all objections can be handled "rather neatly by the rebirth solution"[13] and he proceeds to criticize the *līlā* solution.[14] He does not clearly distinguish, however, between Śaṅkara's two examples of playing and breathing and lumps them both under the *līlā* solution. This seems to be a mistake as the two examples are qualitatively different. The failure to recognize the difference leads him to make the following farcical comments:

> Śaṁkara's example of breathing is curious, but the same question raised above can be applied to it. Some people are poor breathers—"shallow breathers" my physician calls them. They breathe at the very top of their lungs; their respiration, in place of the normal sixteen per minute, runs twenty-five to thirty: They must breathe faster, for only one-fourth to one-third of their full lung's capacity is being used. They are bad breathers—but they can be taught to breathe better. Looking at the creation, one could ask of Brahman, "Why didn't He learn to breathe out or in better?" Once more, we are back to T. P. E. [the theological problem of evil]. Thus the *līlā* ploy solves nothing.[15]

Two points need to be emphasized. First, the problem remains: even if the evil in creation is karmically just, why should there be a creation (which however includes more than just evil) at all? Second, treating creation as *līlā* can be very suggestive but treating it as a natural expression of God's existence, as breathing is of human existence, seems philosophically more sound. It has no motive because it is automatic—or natural to God.

11. Gambhirananda, trans., *Brahma-Sūtra-Bhāṣya,* 361.
12. Ibid.
13. Herman, *Problem of Evil,* 268.
14. Ibid., 268–71.
15. Ibid., 270–71.

Evil and Destruction

One peculiarly Advaitic objection remains to be discussed. This natural process of breathing—inhalation, retention, exhalation—has its cosmic correlates in creation, preservation, and destruction. The question arises, Is the destruction of the universe by God justified? A. L. Herman gets theodicial mileage out of Śaṅkara's statement of the opponent's position in his gloss on Brahmasūtra 2.1.32 by analyzing the passage, cited earlier, as containing three arguments against God: (1) a discrimination argument, (2) a cruelty argument, and (3) a destruction argument.[16] By identifying the destruction-of-the-world argument as separate, Herman shows the influence of Western thought[17] but he suggests an answer in keeping with Hindu thought: "Final cosmic dissolutions can be accounted for by a form of rebirth solution that stresses the downright unregenerated state of the creation immediately preceding and even during that dissolution."[18]

Evil and Creation

When it is argued that the creation is evil because there is evil in creation, Advaitins like to point out that the problem of evil does not so much pertain to creation as such but to how one *relates* to creation. Sri Ramana Maharshi presents this position clearly and forcefully as follows:

> Creation is neither good nor bad; it is as it is. It is the human mind which puts all sorts of constructions on it, seeing things from its own angle and interpreting them to suit its own interests. A woman is just a woman, but one mind calls her "mother," another "sister," and still another "aunt" and so on. Men love women, hate snakes, and are indifferent to the grass and stones by the roadside. These value-judgments are the cause of all the misery in the world. Creation is like a peepul tree: birds come to eat its fruit, or take shelter under its branches, men cool themselves in its shade, but some may hang themselves on it. Yet the tree continues to lead its quiet life, uncon-

16. Herman, *Problem of Evil,* 274.
17. Ibid., 272–73.
18. Ibid., 283.

cerned with and unaware of all the uses it is put to. It is the human mind that creates its own difficulties and then cries for help. Is God so partial as to give peace to one person and sorrow to another? In creation there is room for everything, but man refuses to see the good, the healthy and the beautiful. Instead, he goes on whining, like the hungry man who sits beside the tasty dish and who, instead of stretching out his hand to satisfy his hunger, goes on lamenting, "Whose fault is it, God's or man's?"[19]

General Assessment

The points made above in a somewhat rapid-fire fashion may now be assessed in a more relaxed manner, as a general might analyze his strategy once removed from the heat of battle. Such an exercise can uncover some remarkable features in the deployment of the intellectual forces of Advaita Vedānta on the problem of evil.

To begin with, the problem of evil is not directly confronted. This is not to say that it is not engagd, only that it is not engaged head-on. Sri Ramana Maharshi's reflections in the previous section have their source in an ancient Advaitic attitude that makes the question, Why is there evil in creation? secondary to, even a subset of, the questions, Why is there creation at all? and What is the nature of creation? In other words, since all evil is evil in creation, the source of evil cannot be sought outside creation, and for the Advaitin the central issue is not the question of evil but the question of creation.

This point emerges in clear relief when M. Hiriyanna tries to decide whether the conception of God can be considered "satisfactory enough to be final."[20] He adds right away: "The conclusion of Advaita is that it is not whether we judge it from the standpoint of practical religion or from that of speculative philosophy."[21] He identifies the standpoint of practical religion with the "theistic ideal." As he proceeds to demonstrate its inadequacy he begins by referring to the problem of evil and points out that "there is the well-known difficulty—to mention only one—of reconciling God's assumed

19. David Godman, ed., *The Teachings of Sri Ramana Maharshi* (London: Arkana, 1985), 210.
20. M. Hiriyanna, *Outlines of Indian Philosophy* (London: George Allen & Unwin, 1964), 368.
21. Ibid.

goodness and power with the presence of physical and moral evil in the world."[22] In this context he cites Brahmasūtra 2.1.34–36, but adds: "Even supposing that *evil exists only from our standpoint and not from that of God* or Īśvara as defined above, the theistic position does not become fully comprehensible. *We cannot, for instance, understand why God should have created the world.*"[23] He identifies the difficulty and even adds that there are "solutions to such difficulties suggested in Advaita as in theistic doctrines generally" and although he does not fail to note that "such attempts at justifying the ways of God to man are not without their appeal" he immediately invokes Śaṅkara's comment to the effect that they "have reference to the world of names and forms founded on avidyā [nescience]."[24] Thus, he concludes, "*Such solutions, like the problems they solve, keep us tied in the realm of relativity* and, as the essence of the relative is to point beyond itself for its complete explanation, the theistic conception cannot be regarded as ultimate."[25]

From such a perspective even good and evil cannot be regarded as ultimate, and the problem of evil can only retain its full vigor if it is in some sense absolute. But the problem of evil is a secondary issue at best, not only in Advaita Vedānta but in Hindu thought in general, which optimistically asserts (pace Albert Schweitzer) that "ignorance or error will . . . be superseded in the end by truth. . . . *If either evil or error were final, the world would be irrational,*"[26] which according to Hindu thought, is not the case.

To return to Advaita Vedānta, neither good nor evil in the ordinary acceptations of the terms can find a place in it. An analogy might help. The opposites of good and evil are consistent with Brahman just as heat and cold are consistent with electricity. The radiator and the refrigerator can function simultaneously with their plugs attached to the same socket! In Advaita, therefore, the problem of evil is primarily a metaphysical rather than a moral issue.

To the extent that it remains a moral issue it is tied to the doctrine of karma. The counterpart in Advaita Vedānta to the problem of evil in relation to God in the philosophy of religion is the problem of the beginning of

22. Ibid.

23. Ibid.; emphasis added.

24. Ibid. He refers here to Śaṅkara's commentary on Brahmasūtra 2.1.33 and to the famous commentary of Vācaspati Miśra (known as Bhāmatī) on Śaṅkara's commentary, especially on *sūtra* 34.

25. Ibid., 368–69; emphasis added.

26. M. Hiriyanna, *The Essentials of Indian Philosophy* (London: George Allen & Unwin, 1948), 51.

karma. The approaches to solving it may be identified as the cosmological and the logical. We discussed a cosmological solution earlier in this chapter, and may turn now to the logical approach. The usual Hindu answer to the question, When did karma commence? is that such a point is not identifiable, that karma is *anādi* or without a beginning, as elaborated earlier in a cosmological context. From a logical point of view, however, the question is either answerable or not. M. Hiriyanna asserts that it is not. As he puts it, "such a question is really inadmissable, for it takes for granted that there was a time when the self was without any disposition [karma] whatsoever. Such a view of the self is an abstraction as meaningless as that of mere disposition which characterizes no one. The self, as ordinarily known to us, always means a self with a certain stock of dispositions; and this fact is indicated in Indian expositions by describing karma as beginningless (*anādi*)."[27]

To understand Hiriyanna one must avoid the error of asking which came first, the individual who is characterized by karma or karma which characterizes the individual. As Satischandra Chatterjee and Dhirendramohan Datta put it, "Such difficulties arise only if we regard one as *preceding* the other. But we regard [karma] and individuality as but two interdependent aspects of the same fact, as a circle and circumference, or a triangle and its sides, the difficulty does not arise."[28]

27. Ibid., 27–28.

28. Satischandra Chatterjee and Dhirendramohan Datta, *An Introduction to Indian Philosophy* (1950; reprint, Calcutta: University of Calcutta, 1968), 421.

4

Revelation, Faith, and Issues of Epistemology

Grounds for Belief in Brahman

The central question in Advaita Vedānta is that of Brahman, and one might well ask what grounds we have for believing that such a thing exists. Interestingly, the question is answered in a slightly different way if we ask: On what grounds can we believe that God exists?

Let us first pursue the question of God. On this point there is a remarkable convergence in the positions of not just Advaita Vedānta but virtually all schools of Vedānta as well as the Western philosophy of religion: the existence of God cannot be established on rational grounds. Thus John H. Hick, one of the leading philosophers of religion today, clearly states after surveying the various arguments (an exercise also carried out earlier in this book from an Advaitin point of view) that "it is not possible to establish either the existence or the non-existence of God by rational arguments proceeding from universally accepted premises." He adds that "arguments to the effect that theism is more probable than naturalism, or naturalism than theism, are basically defective, since the term 'probable' lacks a precise meaning in this context." Hick goes on to say: "In spite of the immense intellectual investment that has been going into the various attempts to demonstrate the existence of God, the conclusion which many have reached that this is indemonstrable agrees both with the contemporary philosophical understanding of the nature and limits of logical proof and with the biblical understanding of our knowledge of God."[1]

1. John H. Hick, *The Philosophy of Religion*, 3d ed. (Englewood Cliffs, N.J.: Prentice Hall, 1983), 57.

The conclusion that many (including Hick) have reached about the rational indemonstrability of the existence of God is not only consistent with "the contemporary philosophical understanding of the nature and limits of logical proof" and "the biblical understanding of our knowledge of God"[2] but is also in harmony, to a degree, with the conclusions reached within the various schools of Vedānta, including Advaita Vedānta. Indeed, the theistic forms of Vedānta, despite the shared belief in God, are more concerned with establishing the rational indemonstrability of God instead of, as one would expect, offering proofs for God's existence. The explanation of this curiosity lies in the reliance they place on the testimony of revelation. They take pains to assert that knowledge of the existence of God cannot be acquired rationally in order to establish the authority of scripture on this point. That they consider revelation as not possessing either a human or a divine source has a vital bearing on the issue, for it reverses our normal expectation that scripture derives its validity from being the word of God. In most forms of theistic Vedānta belief in the existence of God derives its validity from self-existent scripture. Our normal expectation is fulfilled only by the school of Nyāya, which does derive the validity of the Hindu scriptures from their being the word of God and therefore seeks to establish the existence of God independently on rational grounds.[3]

Modern philosophical views and the views of Advaita Vedānta seem to be in *negative agreement* that the proof of the existence of God cannot be established on logical grounds but they seem to diverge when Advaita Vedānta claims that such knowledge can be gained through scripture.

This point needs to be examined with much care. The acceptance in Hindu thought of verbal testimony (*śabda*) as a means of valid knowledge and its "inclusion among the *pramāṇas*" (means of valid knowledge), along with perception (*pratyakṣa*) and inference (*anumāna*) "is a striking feature of Indian logic."[4] To establish the contrast between Indian and Western views on valid knowledge I would like to present the following statement by John H. Hick:

> Philosophy recognizes two ways in which human beings may come to know whatever there is to be known. One way (stressed by empiri-

2. Ibid.

3. Satishchandra Chatterjee and Dhirendramohan Datta, *An Introduction to Indian Philosophy* (1950; reprint, Calcutta: University of Calcutta, 1968), 373. Udayana's *Nyāyakusumāñjali* is a celebrated Nyāya text on this question.

4. M. Hiriyanna, *The Essentials of Indian Philosophy* (London: George Allen & Unwin, 1948), 43.

> cism) is through experience, and the other (stressed by rationalism) is through reasoning. The limitation of the rationalist way is that the only truths capable of being strictly proved are analytic and ultimately tautological. We cannot by logic alone demonstrate any matters of fact and existence; these must be known through experience. That two and two equal four can be certified by strict proof; but that we live in a world of objects in space, and that there is this card table and that oak tree and those people, are facts that could never be known independently of sense perception. If nothing were given through experience in its various modes, we should never have anything to reason about. This is as true in religion as in other fields. If God exists, God is not an idea but a reality outside us; in order to be known to men and women, God must become manifest in some way within their experience.[5]

This statement may now be compared with those which represent the Advaitin position on this point. Although the exact number of *pramāṇa*s (means of valid knowledge) formally acknowledged as such depend on the specific school involved, at least three are considered crucial by the orthodox schools: *pratyakṣa* (perception), for it reveals the world to us as we know it to begin with; *anumāna* (inference), which is based on perception, and reveals a fact not apparent to perception; and *śabda* (verbal testimony). Seeing a fire on a hill reveals the operation of *pratyakṣa.* Inferring the fire from seeing the smoke represents the operation of *anumāna.* Learning of the fire from someone else when both fire and smoke are beyond my ken represents the operation of *śabda.* In a religious context, however, *śabda* denotes revelation, and the prevailing view in Advaita is that although the first two means tell us what we wish to know about the world, *only* the third provides access to the supersensible realm.[6]

It is important to recognize at this point that different views are held on what revelation represents. The mainstream position within Advaita Vedānta is that revelation is a repository of propositional truths. But as Radhakrishnan explains, "There is another view of the Veda as *āpta-vacana* or sayings of the wise, those who had attained to a realization of *Brahman,*

5. Hick, *Philosophy of Religion,* 57–58.

6. Eliot Deutsch and J.A.B. van Buitenen, *A Source Book of Advaita Vedānta* (Honolulu: The University of Hawaii Press, 1971), 6.

Brahma-prāpti. This view is supported by (Ś)aṅkara who makes out that *Śruti* or scripture is *pratyakṣa* or records of the direct experiences of seers, which are of a self-certifying character."[7]

This aspect of the Advaitin position, though not identical to that of modern philosophy of religion, comes fairly close to it.

If one moves the discussion from God to Brahman *as such,* then the parallel between Hick's insistence on God becoming manifest in experience and Śaṅkara's similar stance in relation to Brahman becomes striking. The following passage appears in Śaṅkara's commentary on Brahmasūtra 1.1:

> But, it may be asked, is Brahman known or not known (previously to the enquiry into its nature)? If it is known we need not enter on an enquiry concerning it; if it is not known we can not enter on such an enquiry.
>
> We reply that Brahman is known. Brahman, which is all-knowing and endowed with all powers, whose essential nature is eternal purity, intelligence, and freedom, exists. For if we consider the derivation of the word "Brahman," from the root *brh,* "to be great," we at once understand that eternal purity, and so on, belong to Brahman. Moreover the existence of Brahman is known on the ground of its being the Self of every one. For every one is conscious of the existence of (his) Self, and never thinks "I am not." If the existence of the Self were not known, every one would think "I am not." And this Self (of whose existence all are conscious) is Brahman.[8]

7. S. Radhakrishnan, trans., *The Brahma Sūtra: The Philosophy of a Spiritual Life* (London: George Allen & Unwin, 1960), 243.

8. See Deutsch and van Buitenen, *Source Book,* 155. Śaṅkara goes on to say: "But if Brahman is generally known as the Self, there is no room for an enquiry into it! Not so, we reply; for there is a conflict of opinions as to its special nature. Unlearned people and the Lokāyatikas are of the opinion that the mere body endowed with the quality of intelligence is the Self; others that the organs endowed with intelligence are the Self; others maintain that the internal organ is the Self; others, again, that the Self is a mere momentary idea; others, again, that it is the Void. Others, again (to proceed to the opinion of such as acknowledge the authority of the Veda), maintain that there is a transmigrating being different from the body, and so on, which is both agent and enjoyer (of the fruits of action); others teach that that being is enjoying only, not acting; others believe that in addition to the individual souls, there is an all-knowing, all-powerful Lord. Others (i.e., the Vedāntins), finally maintain that the Lord is the Self of the enjoyer (i.e. of the individual soul whose individual existence is apparent only, the product of Nescience)" (ibid.).

Rationalism, Empiricism, and Advaita

In this section we shall discuss some Advaitin responses to issues pertaining to aspects of rationalism and empiricism as constituent strands of the Western philosophy of religion.

Descartes (1596–1650) has been a major factor in the pronounced emphasis on rationalism in Western philosophy. Here I am concerned with two aspects of his thought: (1) his emphasis on doubt, that we should doubt "everything that can without self-contradiction be doubted and in this way discover if anything remains immune to our skepticism"; and (2) his emphasis on "the fact that I who am now doubting exist: *cogito ergo sum* (I think, therefore I am). Building on this immovable point of certainty, Descartes tried to establish, first the existence of God and then, through the argument that God will not allow us to be deceived, the veracity of our sense perceptions."[9]

The Advaitin position on these points is instructive. Advaita Vedānta takes validity rather than doubt as its starting point. Thus it maintains, as T.M.P. Mahadevan puts it, that "all knowledge is self-valid (*svataḥ prāmāṇya*). What is meant by the self-validity of knowledge is that truth (*pramā*) is intrinsic to knowledge (*jñāna*). The causes that account for the rise of knowledge yield truth also. And, the means by which we know knowledge is presumably valid. It is only where in a particular case, knowledge fails to be valid that we seek an explanation. So, invalidity or error is extrinsic."[10]

Descartes's famous dictum—*cogito ergo sum*—and the corollary that "there is one . . . indubitable item, namely, the fact that I who am now doubting exist"[11] has its counterpart in Advaita Vedānta. M. Hiriyanna remarks (with Śaṅkara's gloss on Vedānta-Sūtra 2.3.7 in mind): "That there is a Reality at the back of all empirical things again is not a mere assertion, for it is maintained here, as we know, that the thinking subject in us is not different from it so that its being becomes an immediate certainty. If we denied it, the very fact of denial would affirm it.[12] We may not know what it

9. Hick, *Philosophy of Religion,* 58. For an approach somewhat different from the one adopted here on the issue of doubt, Descartes, and Advaita, see S. Radhakrishnan, *Eastern Religions and Western Thought* (New York: Oxford University Press, 1959), 235.

10. T.M.P. Mahadevan, *Outlines of Hinduism* (1960; reprint, Bombay: Chetana, 1971), 133–34.

11. Hick, *Philosophy of Religion,* 58.

12. See Śaṅkara on Brahmasūtra 2.3.7.

exactly is; but its presence itself, owing to the basic identity of ourselves with it, can never be doubted."[13]

Similarly, T.M.P. Mahadevan (with Śaṅkara's gloss on Vedānta Sūtra 1.1.4 in mind) remarks: "Even to say that reality is non-conscious there is required a fundamental consciousness. It is to indicate the nature of this basic consciousness that such terms as Ātman and Brahman are employed. *The ultimate reality is called Ātman in order to indicate that it cannot be denied; for it is the self of even the one who denies.* We know *that* the self is; but we do not know *what* it is."[14]

The implications of not being able "to doubt the doubter" have, however, produced different results in Western philosophy and Advaita. This "indubitable item," the "immovable pinpoint of certainty" is the *ātman* as *sākṣī* (witness) in empirical experience. It is also the "witness" of the world of our individual existence. But the world of our individual existence does not exist independently of a world of our shared experience, the objective world as it were. However, as "consistently with the eventually idealistic position of the Advaita there can be no reality outside what either knows or is known,"[15] the question arises, Who "bears witness" to this objective world? That consciousness to which the whole universe appears as an object belongs to God, a fact denoted by the term *Īśvara-sākṣī,* which is "in reality, the ground of the whole universe" and is to be identified as *svarūpa jñāna* (pure consciousness).[16]

One crucial step has been omitted. In Advaita, God and the world of sense perceptions, which were established as true by Descartes on the basis of the "cannot doubt the doubter" axiom, are *not* regarded as *ultimately* true, but as only conventionally true, for they can all be resolved into the supreme (*nirguṇa*) Brahman.

G. E. Moore (1873–1958) and others led the movement away from the rationalist assumptions of Western philosophy, of which the "still popular idea that to know means to be able to prove"[17] is a legacy. Their position on what is real is of interest from the point of view of Advaita Vedānta. The empiricist position on what it means to say that something is real may be summarized thus: "If the word 'real' has any meaning for us, we must acknowledge standard or paradigm cases of its correct use. We must be able to point to a clear and unproblematic instance of something's being real.

13. M. Hiriyanna, *Outlines of Indian Philosophy* (London: George Allen & Unwin, 1964), 373.
14. Mahadevan, *Outlines of Hinduism,* 146; first emphasis added.
15. Hiriyanna, *Outlines,* 360.
16. Ibid.
17. Hick, *Philosophy of Religion,* 58.

What can this be but some ordinary physical object perceived by the senses? But if tables and chairs and houses and people are accepted as paradigm cases of real objects, it becomes self-contradictory to suggest that the whole world of tables and chairs and houses and people may possibly be unreal. By definition, they are not unreal, for they are typical instances of what we mean by real objects."[18]

The Advaitin position on what is real is very clear and very different. According to Advaita Vedānta reality is that "which persists uncontradicted through all forms of existence in all places and times"[19]—or, as it is called, *trikāla-abādhita* (uncontradicted in all the three times—past, present, and future). Śaṅkara makes this clear in his discussion on Chāndogya Upaniṣad 6.2.2 and Vedāntasūtra 2.1.11.

This is in stark contrast to the empiricist position that "to doubt whether some particular perceived object is real is to doubt whether it is *as real as* the other sensible objects that we experience. 'Is that chair really there?' means 'Is it there in the way in which the table and the other chairs are there?' But what does it mean to doubt whether there is really anything whatever there? Such 'doubt' is meaningless. For if nothing is real, there is no longer any sense in which anything can be said to be *un*real."[20]

Here the *chair* is said to be as real as the *table*, each affirming the reality of the other, for to claim that either one of them is real is to claim that it is *as real as* the other.

Advaita Vedānta takes the opposite view, that the reality of the chair undermines the reality of the table. To grasp this apparently startling position one needs to recognize that Śaṅkara recognizes two kinds of contradiction—one experiential and the other logical.[21] In Advaita Vedānta even when "the perception of the pot is not experientially contradicted by that of a cloth, both are found logically inconsistent with the nature of reality,"[22] not mutually confirming. This is so because what is once seen as a snake may later on turn out to be a rope; that is, one experience may be contradicted by another. The existence of such experiential contradiction means that the "theoretical possibility of a change in perception"—as in the case of the snake and the rope—"and of consequent contradiction, then makes the status of every particular object precarious in respect to its

18. Ibid., 59.
19. Chatterjee and Datta, *Introduction,* 387.
20. Hick, *Philosophy of Religion,* 59.
21. Chatterjee and Datta, *Introduction,* 387.
22. Ibid., 387.

reality. We can never be absolutely certain that what appears now as pot will not appear otherwise later." This is how "different particular forms of existence, like pot and cloth, weaken and undermine each other's claim to indubitable reality."[23] The situation is further undermined when Śaṅkara shows that "change, which is actually perceived, is . . . unreal because it is found inconsistent by logical thinking." For inspection shows that "form is but a state of the material or substance, and cannot be separated from the latter even in thought."[24] We cannot therefore "interpret the perception of a change in form as a change in reality," as no "causation involves any change in substance," only in form: all pots of various forms of clay are only made of clay. "This amounts to the position that though we *perceive* changes we cannot *rationally* accept them as real. We have therefore to understand them in the same way as we do, when we perceive an illusory object. We *do* perceive a rainbow, a blue sky, movement of the sun and many other things which we cannot believe as real because reasoning proves them to be unreal."[25] "It is in the light of this logic that we can understand the somewhat puzzling assertion of Śaṅkara that a pot and a cloth which exclude each other also contradict and falsify each other."[26]

Concerning the empiricist position, which not only establishes reality in terms of objects and regards, for example, a table *as real as* a chair, but also maintains that "if tables and chairs and houses and people are accepted as paradigm cases of real objects, it becomes self-contradictory to suggest that the whole world of tables and chairs and houses and people may possibly be unreal" because by definition they are definitive of reality, Advaita Vedānta would have at least two comments. First, objects do not define reality, only a certain *order of reality*. If something is psychologically[27] or, better, phenomenologically given (*prasiddha*) it cannot thereby be said to be logically established (*siddha*). The "things of the world"[28] are claimed in Advaita Vedānta to be "though not ultimately real," "yet of a certain order of reality."[29] Second, although in terms of one level of reality it would be "self-contradictory to suggest that the whole world of tables and chairs and

23. Ibid., 388.
24. Ibid., 383.
25. Ibid., 384.
26. Ibid., 387.
27. Hiriyanna, *Essentials*, 156.
28. Ibid.
29. Ibid.

houses and people may possibly be unreal," it may not be so from another point of view or level of reality.

It seems that the empiricist argument was designed in part to rebut *subjective* idealism, which consigns all tables, chairs, and so on to unreality and encourages a "universal skepticism of the senses" by denying the extramental reality of any object. Empiricists might be interested to know that Advaita Vedānta, although it represents an idealist position, rejects *subjective* idealism. Against subjective idealism, which declares that "the world, like a dream, is only an illusory product of the imagination," Advaita Vedānta raises several objections. Chatterjee and Datta have summarized some of the main objections raised by its prominent spokesman Śaṅkara as follows:

> (a) The existence of external objects cannot be denied because they are *perceived to exist by all persons.* To deny the existence of a pot, cloth or pillar while it is being perceived, is like denying the flavour of the food while it is being eaten: it is a falsification of immediate experience by sheer force. (b) If immediate experience is disbelieved, then even the reality of mental states cannot be believed in. (c) To say that ideas of the mind illusorily appear *as external objects* is meaningless unless at least something external is admitted to be real. Otherwise, it would be as good as to say that a certain man looks *like* the child of a barren woman. (d) Unless different perceived objects like pot and cloth are admitted, the idea of a pot cannot be distinguished from that of a cloth, since, as consciousness, they are identical. (e) There is a vital difference between dream-objects and perceived objects: the former are contradicted by waking experience, whereas the latter are not. External objects perceived during waking experience cannot be said to be unreal so long as they are not felt to be contradicted.[30]

The point to be kept in mind is that Advaita Vedānta does not question the empirical reality of the world, only its ultimate reality. The reason its ultimate reality is to be questioned is that although it is true that in terms of empiricism "the mind should conform to the object and not the object to the mind," one may ask, "How are we to know that the cognition corresponds to reality?"[31]

30. Chatterjee and Datta, *Introduction,* 371.
31. Mahadevan, *Outlines of Hinduism,* 105–6.

The Role of Experience

John H. Hick has shown how the conclusions of modern philosophy of religion are in line with what he calls "the contemporary revolt against the rationalist assumptions which have dominated much of western philosophy since the time of Descartes,"[32] as well as how an empiricist approach has emerged in the present century to challenge rationalism, and how "this empiricist reasoning is in agreement with the unformulated epistemological assumptions of the Bible."[33] He goes on to say: "Philosophers of the rationalist tradition, holding that to know means to be able to prove, have been shocked to find that in the Bible, which is the basis of western religion, there is no attempt whatever to demonstrate the existence of God. Instead of professing to establish the reality of God by philosophical reasoning, the Bible takes God's reality for granted."[34]

This suggests an interesting parallel in Advaita Vedānta. The early texts of Hindu thought on which Advaita Vedānta is also based often speak of *jijñāsā* or the desire to *know* the ultimate reality. The very first aphorism of the Vedāntasūtra reads: "*Athāto brahmajijñāsā: Now therefore we desire to know Brahman* (the ultimate reality)."[35] However, the emphasis shifted, perhaps within the Hindu tradition in general but certainly within the tradition of Advaita Vedānta in particular, to liberation (mokṣa): *mumukṣā* (the desire for liberation) replaced *jijñāsā* or the desire to know Brahman. To be sure, the knowledge of Brahman was deemed to be *saving* knowledge but somehow being saved became a stronger concern than *knowing* Brahman. In the popular texts of Advaita the pupil approaches the Master to be saved rather than enlightened. Consider, for instance, the following sentiments:

> How to cross this ocean of phenomenal existence, what is to be my fate, and which of the means should I adopt—as to these I know nothing. Condescend to save me, O Lord, and describe at length how to put an end to the misery of this relative existence.
>
> As he speaks thus, tormented by the afflictions of the world—which is like a forest on fire—seeking his protection, the saint eyes him

32. Hick, *Philosophy of Religion,* 58.
33. Ibid., 59.
34. Ibid.
35. Radhakrishnan, trans., *Brahma Sūtra,* 227.

with a glance softened with pity and spontaneously bids him give up all fear.[36]

This shift from *jijñāsā* to *mumukṣā* involves a revulsion from the process of *saṁsāra*—which consists of continuous reincarnation in the phenomenal universe until one attains *mokṣa* or liberation. The point to be considered here is that just as the rationalist philosophers "holding that to know means to be able to prove, have been shocked to find that in the Bible, which is the basis of western religion, there is no attempt whatsoever to demonstrate the existence of God," modern scholars, perhaps of the rationalist persuasion, have been shocked that little effort has been made to demonstrate the truth of reincarnation on which the soteriology of the Hindu tradition and of Advaita Vedānta seems to be founded.[37] Reincarnation is taken for granted in most of Advaita Vedānta—but the attempt to demonstrate its validity is interestingly not found so much in Advaita Vedānta, as in the texts of the Nyāya school[38] and in Hindu medical texts.[39] P. V. Kane notes that apart from the three basic texts of Vedānta—the Upaniṣads, the Vedāntasūtra, and the Bhagavadgītā—"There are very few regular treatises on the doctrine of Karma and re-incarnation. One work comparatively early in date is the Vijñānadipikā of Padmapāda (said to be the same as the favorite pupil of the first Śaṅkarācārya) in 71 verses."[40] It, however, deals with achieving *mokṣa* by annihilating karma and does not demonstrate the fact of the existence of rebirth. It might be added, pace Kane, that even the treatises he mentions barely concern themselves with proving the fact of reincarnation.

Thus it seems that just as in Christianity the existence of God was accepted as a fact, in Advaita Vedānta reincarnation is accepted as a fact not requiring proof.

The next parallel is provided by the *living* experience of God on the part of the people in the Bible and the *living* experience of the knowledge of Brahman described by the Advaitins. In an eloquent passage John H. Hick writes:

36. Swami Madhavananda, *Vivekachudamani of Shri Shankaracharya* (Calcutta: Advaita Ashrama, 1966), 15–16. Śaṅkara's authorship of this text remains to be definitely established.

37. M. Hiriyanna, *Popular Essays in Indian Philosophy* (Mysore: Kavyalaya Publishers, 1952), 43.

38. Wendy Doniger O'Flaherty, ed., *Karma and Rebirth in Classical Indian Traditions* (Berkeley and Los Angeles: University of California Press, 1980), xxi.

39. R. K. Sharma and V. B. Dash, trans., *Caraka Saṁhitā* (Varanasi: Chowkhamba Sanskrit Series Office, 1976), 1:204–19.

40. P. V. Kane, *History of Dharmaśāstra* (Poona: Bhandarkar Oriental Research Institute, 1977), vol. 5, part 2, 1599.

> The biblical writers were (sometimes, though doubtless not at all times) as vividly conscious of being in God's presence as they were of living in a material environment. It is impossible to read their writings with any degree of sensitivity without realizing that to these people God was not a proposition completing a syllogism, or an abstract idea accepted by the mind, but the reality that gave meaning to their lives. Their pages resound and vibrate with the sense of God's presence as a building might resound and vibrate from the tread of some great being walking through it. It would be as sensible for a husband to desire a philosophical proof of the existence of the wife and family who contribute so much to the meaning in his life as for the person of faith to seek a proof of the existence of the God within whose purpose one is conscious that one lives and moves and has one's being.[41]

We seem to find at least in Śaṅkara what reads like a reference to a living realization of Brahman. Hiriyanna refers to Śaṅkara's statement at the end of his commentary on Vedāntasūtra 5.1.15, "which tradition views as an allusion to his own direct experience of the ultimate truth."[42] T.M.P. Mahadevan translates the passage as follows: "How can one contest the heart-felt cognition of another as possessing *Brahman*—knowledge, even though bearing a body?"[43] S. Radhakrishnan also cites it when speaking of those who have achieved direct realization thus: "How can one, Śaṅkara asks, contest the truth of another possessing knowledge of *Brahman*, vouched as it is by his heart's conviction?"[44]

It is clear, then, that both Western philosophy of religion and Advaita Vedānta offer an experiential challenge to the rationalist tradition.

The Limits of Proof and Doubt

Advaita Vedānta clearly recognizes that there is a limit to proof in the context of Brahman. Consider the following dialogue between Gārgī and

41. Hick, *Philosophy of Religion,* 60.
42. Hiriyanna, *Outlines,* 381 n. 2.
43. Mahadevan, *Outlines of Hinduism,* 143.
44. Radhakrishnan, trans., *Brahma Sūtra,* 243–44.

Yājñavalkya in the Bṛhadāraṇyaka Upaniṣad. Gārgī starts out by asking Yājñavalkya, "Since all this world is woven, warp and woof, on water, on what, pray is the water woven, warp and woof?"[45] She then goes on pressing for answers in an ascending dialectic that ultimately provokes a sharp reproof from Yājñavalkya when she asks:

> "On what then, pray, are the worlds of Brahma woven, warp and woof?"
>
> Yājñavalkya said: "Gārgī, do not question too much, lest your head fall off. In truth, you are questioning too much about a divinity about which further questions cannot be asked. Gārgī, do not over-question."
>
> Thereupon Gārgī Vācaknavī held her peace.[46]

At this point Śaṅkara remarks in effect that the limits of logic have been reached. He states that "the nature of the deity is to be gathered from scriptures and not inferred by logic."[47] The dialogue, however, is itself a part of scripture! Moreover, this should not be mistakenly regarded as concluding the dialogue for it is resumed later. Gārgī asks:

> "O Yājñavalkya, [that] which is above the sky, that which is beneath the earth, that which is between these two, sky and earth, that which people call the past and the present and the future—across what is that woven, warp and woof?"
>
> He said: "That, O Gārgī, which is above the sky, that which is beneath the earth, that which is between these two, sky and earth, that which people call the past and the present and the future—across space alone is that woven, warp and woof."
>
> "Across what then, pray, is space woven, warp and woof?"
>
> He said: "That, O Gārgī, Brahmans call the Imperishable (*akṣara*). It is not coarse, not fine, not short, not long, not glowing [like fire], not adhesive [like water], without shadow and without darkness, without air and without space, without stickiness, (intangible), odorless, taste-

45. Robert Ernest Hume, trans., *The Thirteen Principal Upanishads,* 2d ed. (London: Oxford University Press, 1968), 113.

46. Ibid., 114.

47. S. Radhakrishnan, ed., *The Principal Upaniṣads* (London: George Allen & Unwin, 1953), 223.

> less, without eye, without ear, without voice, without mind, without energy, without breath, without mouth, (without personal or family name, unaging, undying, without fear, immortal, stainless, not uncovered, not covered), without measure, without inside and without outside.
>
> It consumes nothing soever.
> No one soever consumes it.[48]

That is, however, not a proof but a statement. M. Hiriyanna, a modern Advaitin, shows that logical proof arrives at two logically irrefutable positions: materialism and solipsism. Concerning the Cārvāka (materialist) school he writes: "Naturally the denial of the ātman, which occupies an important place in the other Indian systems, provoked the keenest controversy; *but theoretically the position of the Cārvāka, it must be admitted, is irrefutable.* It cannot be *demonstrated* that the soul or atman in the accepted sense *is.* That indeed is recognized by some orthodox thinkers themselves, who accordingly lay stress in their refutation of the Cārvāka doctrine upon the indemonstrability of the opposite position that the body and the soul are not *distinct.*"[49] Concerning the solipsists he criticizes subjective idealism on the grounds that

> . . . as a consequence of rejecting external objects, the subjectivist must deny the existence of all selves besides his own, for, if there is no reason to believe in external physical objects, there can be none to believe in other people except as part of his dream. The doctrine will thus be reduced to solipsism, or the theory that there is only a solitary self and that everything else is mere fancy. It is clear that such a theory, though it cannot be logically proved to be wrong, stultifies all the presuppositions of practical life and puts an end to all philosophical controversy.[50]

Thus, according to Advaita Vedānta as presented by M. Hiriyanna, these two diametrically opposed positions—materialism and solipsism—represent the limits of logic.

48. Hume, trans., *Thirteen Principal Upanishads,* 118.
49. Hiriyanna, *Outlines,* 192; emphasis added.
50. Hiriyanna, *Essentials,* 81.

Out of these Hiriyanna perceives the latter as posing the more serious challenge to Advaita Vedānta. He accounts for materialism from an Advaitin point of view in the following manner:

> But even at its best the materialistic theory carries no conviction with it, since it tries to account for the higher principle of mind by the lower one of matter. Starting with the existence of matter, it explains mind as only a function of it. But in thus starting, the theory has already taken for granted that there is no mind, although it is as much an implication of experience as matter. In fact, we have no conception at all of matter, except as it appears to an observing mind. Believing in the existence of the one thus amounts to believing in the existence of the other. The truth that may underlie the theory is that all the things of the world can finally be brought under a single head, but it is wrong to conclude from this that that unitary source is necessarily physical.[51]

But whereas Hiriyanna is able to counter the challenge of materialism on more or less *logical grounds,* he has to meet the challenge of solipsism on broader rational grounds or even practical grounds. He writes, while explaining the Advaitic ontological position at the empirical level:

> One and the same object again may occasion different and even opposite feelings in different persons. But these worlds as given in the experience of individuals are not entirely separate. They have, as indeed we ordinarily take for granted, a common basis unlike the dream-worlds, for instance, of two or more persons. That is the world as it is; and it is termed Īśvara-sṛṣṭa ("God-created"), while the same as it exists in the medium of one's individual consciousness is described as jīva-sṛṣṭa ("jīva-created"). Such a view implies that we accept many selves. There is of course nothing preventing us from criticizing this position as a begging of the question, but the only alternative *to it is solipsism, which, though as a theory it may be irrefutable, is repugnant to thought and really stultifies all effort at philosophizing. We shall accordingly take for granted the plurality of selves so far as our present discussion goes.*[52]

51. Ibid., 59.
52. Hiriyanna, *Outlines,* 362; emphasis added.

The limits of doubt are as interesting as the limits of logic, since both possess the illuminating property of the extreme case.

Advaita Vedānta has to face the question of the limits of doubt no less than the modern philosophy of religion. Modern philosophical thought, it seems, has reached the conclusion that "really radical and thorough doubt can never be reasoned away, since it includes even our reasoning power within its scope. The only way of escaping such doubt is to avoid falling into it in the first place."[53] A reference to Descartes's demon is helpful here. When Descartes advocated an ab initio skeptical approach to sense data, he dramatized his point by introducing the possibility of a malicious demon capable of manipulating both sense data *and* the mind. This has devastating consequences, as Hick explains, "for the possibility that the 'malicious demon' exists and has power over our minds undermines all proofs, since the demon can (by tampering with our memories) make us believe an argument to be valid that is in fact not valid."[54]

Moreover, even without the demon at work, doubting can be carried too far, as Hick points out elsewhere: "It has also been argued that when doubt becomes universal in its scope, it becomes meaningless. To doubt whether some particular perceived object is real is to doubt whether it is *as real as* the other sensible objects that we experience. 'Is that chair really there?' means 'Is it there in the way in which the table and the other chairs are there?' But what does it mean to doubt whether there is really anything whatever there? Such 'doubt' is meaningless."[55]

In other words, limits of doubt have been recognized both in the rationalist and the empiricist strands of modern philosophy. It is somewhat striking that modern Advaitin thought seems to take a similar position. This is best illustrated by its response to two other schools of Indian thought that in the Indian universe of philosophical discourse may be said to represent the extreme empiricist and rationalist positions from the Advaitic standpoint. Consider the materialist (Cārvāka) school of Indian thought as an example of the extreme empiricist position and the Mādhyamika school of Buddhist thought as an example of the extreme rationalist position.

The materialists, who generally admitted perception as the only valid means of knowledge, sometimes outdid even that extreme position. A. L. Basham refers to the "one materialist philosophical text which survived" the

53. Hick, *Philosophy of Religion*, 58.
54. Ibid.
55. Ibid., 59.

ravages of time. "This is the *Tattvopaplavasiṁha* (freely "The Lion Destroying All Religious Truth") written by a certain Jayarāśi in the 8th century A.D. The author was an out-and-out Pyrrhonist denying the possibility of any certain knowledge at all, and he demolished with able dialectic, to his own satisfaction at any rate, all the basic presuppositions of the chief religious systems of his day."[56] It is surely a question worth asking that if the "possibility of any certain knowledge at all" is denied, then how can this knowledge of denial be accorded any certainty? In the case of the materialist who denies inference, it could similarly be maintained that in any strict sense such a denial "would be absurd, since the denial itself would be a generalized conclusion like those to which he objects."[57] It is clear that "this negative conclusion that inference is not valid is itself the result of induction and points to a conviction that in one case at least the relation of vyāpti [universal concomitance] holds true. It would then refute itself, for what is rejected would be admitted in the very act of rejecting it."[58]

The Mādhyamika school of Buddhism represents the limits of doubt at the other end of the spectrum. Its case for all-embracing doubt can be argued with the help of the following example from the famous Hindu text of the fourteenth century, the Sarvadarśana-saṅgraha of Mādhava. The example is particularly interesting as it employs the famous rope-snake metaphor of Advaita to elucidate the position of another school. Two points need to be recognized before the metaphor can be pressed into service. The first pertains to the mutual interdependence of the knower, the known, and the knowledge in the process of knowing. All three are implicated in this process of knowing.

> The reality of one depends on each of the other two, and if one be false, the others also must be so (just as the fatherhood of any person will be proved false if the existence of his children be proved to be false). But it must be admitted by all that when we perceive a snake, in a rope, the object perceived, namely, the snake, is absolutely false. Hence the mind or the subject which knows such an object turns out to be false and its knowledge also becomes false. Thus it may be concluded that all that we perceive within or without, along with their perception and the percipient mind, are illusory like dream-

56. A. L. Basham, *The Wonder That Was India* (New York: Grove Press, 1954), 297.
57. Hiriyanna, *Essentials*, 58. For a more elaborate treatment, see his *Outlines*, 190.
58. Hiriyanna, *Outlines*, 190.

> objects. There is, therefore, nothing, mental or non-mental, which is real. The universe is śūnya or void of reality.[59]

The Advaitin rebuttal of this position is significant and deserves to be cited at some length. Although a simpler version of it will be presented later, we must recognize the limits of doubt in the context of the *system* of Advaita Vedānta rather than in any system of plain logic. Before I present the argument, however, I would like to clarify the Advaitin description of the world as *self-discrepant.* Advaita Vedānta considers the world as self-discrepant because it is characterized by different objects, that is, by "difference." As Hiriyanna explains it, "The idea of difference between A and B (say) presupposes a knowledge of these two entities; but that knowledge, since it points to them as *two,* already involves the idea of difference. There is thus mutual dependence between the notion of difference and that of the things which differ, and neither can therefore be fully understood without the other. The Advaitins accordingly regard the idea of difference as self-discrepant, and dismiss it as but an appearance."[60] However,

> by postulating a reality behind the self-discrepant world of experience, Śaṁkara differentiates his doctrine from the śūnya-vāda of the Mādhyamika. The discrepancy characterizing the saguṇa Brahman or its relativity only degrades it to the level of appearance; it does not dismiss it altogether. If according to the Mādhyamika it is impossible for thought to rest in the relative, it is equally impossible for it, according to Śaṁkara, to rest in absolute nothing. To use the terminology of the Upaniṣads, the Advaita denies only "names" and "forms" but not that which appears under their guise. Or, as an old writer has ob-

59. Chatterjee and Datta, *Introduction,* 145–46. The same point can be made philosophically rather than metaphorically: "It may be pointed out how small, in spite of this extreme position of the Mādhyamika, is its difference from the remaining three schools [Vaibhāṣika, Sautāntrika, Yogācāra]. According to all of them alike, common knowledge contains elements which are super-imposed by the mind. Thus general features like cow-ness have no objective reality according to any of them and are entirely due to the nature of thought. In the Yogācāra school, this illusory character is ascribed to the whole of the physical world. That is, scholastic Buddhism as a whole regards the greater part of common knowledge as only conventionally true. The Mādhyamika merely extends this principle to all experience. But it may be asked whether the system is altogether devoid of the notion of a positive ultimate. Our object here being chiefly to present later Buddhism as it was understood by Hindu thinkers and is found set forth in their works, it is easy to answer this question; for they all alike agree in holding that the void is the only truth according to the Mādhyamika" (Hiriyanna, *Outlines,* 220–21).

60. Hiriyanna, *Essentials,* 187–88.

> served, while the Advaitin negates only distinction (bheda), the Mādhyamika negates it as well as the distincts (bhidyamāna). That there is a Reality at the back of all empirical things again is not a mere assertion, for it is maintained here, as we know, that the thinking subject in us is not different from it so that its being becomes an immediate certainty. If we denied it, the very fact of denial would affirm it. We may not know what it exactly is; but its presence itself, owing to the basic identity of ourselves with it, can never be doubted.[61]

The point can also be made more simply if somewhat more polemically. The Hindu thinkers describe the Mādhyamika school "as nihilistic and have no difficulty in refuting that apparently absurd position. Some even go so far as to say that such a view needs no serious refutation, because it stands self-condemned. It may appear to us that the negation of everything is inconceivable without implying a positive ground (avadhi) hereby, and that the ultimate truth cannot therefore be the void. Nothing can be proved false, if nothing is taken as true. That is the very criticism of Hindu philosophers passed on the Mādhyamika."[62]

This chapter must be concluded with a caveat. It must be clearly indicated, in the interest of fairness, that the positions ascribed herein to the Cārvākas and the Mādhyamika schools are those attributed to them in Hindu texts and may not correspond to their own self-understanding. Modern Hindu writers are aware of this.[63] They have been used here to *illustrate* the extreme implications of empiricist and rationalistic positions of these schools as per the Hindu texts, without the further implication that these positions as such were actually held by those schools. Our interest in them is not as Cārvāka or Mādhyamika positions per se, but as representing the extreme limits of empiricist and rationalistic positions, and it is the Advaitic response to these positions (and not the schools to which they were attributed) which is the focus of our interest in them.

61. Hiriyanna, *Outlines,* 372–73.
62. Ibid., 221.
63. Ibid., 188, 195; Hiriyanna, *Essentials,* 182–83.

5

Revelation in Advaita Vedānta

The concept of revelation plays a pivotal role in Advaita Vedānta. In fact, it possesses its own full-fledged theory of revelation, which differs radically from the doctrines of revelation as known in the Western philosophy of religion. In this chapter, I first present an Advaitic critique of the Western views of revelation, then the Advaitic doctrine of revelation itself.

Christian thought contains two identifiably different doctrines of revelation—usually referred to as the propositional and the nonpropositional views of revelation and faith. As Christian thought contains these "two very different understandings of the nature of revelation, and as a result, two different conceptions of faith (as the human reception of revelation), of the Bible (as a medium of Revelation), and of theology (as discourse based upon Revelation),"[1] it is best to review them in the light of Advaitic thought separately.

The Propositional View of Revelation and Faith

The propositional view of revelation asserts that "the content of revelation is a body of truths expressed in statements or propositions."[2] So long as the definition of the propositional view of revelation is restricted to this statement it is in accord with that of Advaita Vedānta. Advaita Vedānta also asserts that

1. John H. Hick, *The Philosophy of Religion*, 3d ed. (Englewood Cliffs, N.J.: Prentice Hall, 1983), 60.

2. Ibid., 60.

the content of revelation consists of propositional truths. The Upaniṣads constitute the revealed texts of the Vedānta as a school in general, as well as one of its major subschools, that of Advaita, and "The consensus of the Vedānta is that in the Upaniṣads significant and authoritative statements are made concerning the nature of Brahman."[3] However, in the Christian context such propositional statements are claimed to be "divinely authenticated," or in the words of the *Catholic Encyclopedia,* "Revelation may be defined as the communication of some truth by God to a rational creature through means which are beyond the ordinary course of nature."[4]

At this point the Advaitic view diverges from the Catholic in two ways: (1) that God communicates the propositional truths and (2) that these are received through means that are "beyond the ordinary course of nature." There is some room for discussion on the applicability of the second point to Advaita Vedānta, but not the first.

Eliot Deutsch and J.A.B. van Buitenen point out that the concept of revelation in the Western religions (which they refer to as the "Mediterranean Religions"), such as Judaism, Christianity, and Islam, differs radically from that in Advaita Vedānta—so radically that they think one should forget the implications of the term in the Mediterranean Religions if one hopes to gain a proper appreciation of it in the Advaitic context. The difference is this: in the former, revelation implies a revealer, namely God; in Advaita Vedānta, it does not.

At this point (following Deutsch and van Buitenen) the question naturally arises, If revelation does not come from God,

> Then from where does it come? The answer is stark and simple: it is given with the world. For some of the Mīmāṁsā (or orthodox, exegetical) thinkers who have addressed themselves to this problem, the world is beginningless and the assumption of a creator is both problematic and unnecessary. And even if a beginning of the world is assumed, as in later Hindu thought when it is held that the universe goes through a pulsating rhythm of origination, existence, and dissolution, it is also held that at the dawn of a new world the revelation reappears to the vision of the seers, who once more begin the transmission.[5]

3. Eliot Deutsch and J.A.B. van Buitenen, *A Source Book of Advaita Vedānta* (Honolulu: The University of Hawaii Press, 1971), 7.

4. As quoted in Hick, *Philosophy of Religion,* 60.

5. Deutsch and van Buitenen, *Source Book,* 5.

Vedānta, more specifically Advaita Vedānta, shares this concept of revelation up to a point. Like the Mīmāṁsā school, Advaita Vedānta holds that revelation is "given with the world" and that it has no author. The Mīmāṁsā school, however, rejects both the idea of God and the cyclical cosmology of much of Hinduism. It postulates a succession of teachers and pupils without beginning, and thereby dispenses with the need of an author for the Veda. As Deutsch and van Buitenen explain it, "Revelation, therefore, is by no means God's word—because, paradoxically, if it were to derive from a living person, its credibility would be impugned. It is held to be authorless, for if a person, human or divine, had authored it, it would be vulnerable to the defects inherent in such a person. It is axiomatic that revelation is infallible, and this infallibility can be defended only if it is authorless."[6] Advaita Vedānta accepts the ideas of God and a cyclical cosmology, but even according to Advaita Vedānta God is not the *author* of the revelation but only its *promulgator* at the beginning of each aeon. A cyclical cosmology only seems to interrupt the transmission of the Veda; in fact, the Veda is reproduced verbatim at the beginning of each aeon.

The Advaitic view is thus apparently radically different from the propositional view of revelation. The only point of agreement is the propositional nature of the statements. The other point of possible convergence is provided by the mode of reception. Although the Veda is revealed with the world and God is not its author but its promulgator, "God makes the Vedic propositions flash in the minds of the sages in the same linguistic form in which they are now available."[7]

The propositional view of revelation also entails a propositional view of the nature of faith. As Gustave Weigel explains it: "To a Catholic, the word 'Faith' conveys the notion of an intellectual assent to the content of revelation as true because of the witnessing authority of God the Revealer."[8] The Vatican Council of 1870 also described it as a "supernatural virtue."[9] Although there is "in some recent writings . . . a growing tendency to recognize other aspects of faith in addition to the element of intellectual assent," obviously in this context it is the most relevant aspect from which faith may be examined. In Advaita Vedānta, wherein the propositions stand by themselves rather than in relation to any author—human

6. Ibid.

7. K. Satchidananda Murty, *Revelation and Reason in Advaita Vedānta* (New York: Columbia University Press, 1959), 50.

8. Quoted in Hick, *Philosophy of Religion,* 61.

9. Ibid.

or divine—the scope of faith is now limited to faith in propositions and not in God as such.

Advaita Vedānta places its faith in the intrinsic reliability of the *text* itself, rather than the author. But although it thus severs the text from the author with an almost Derridean dispensation, it proceeds to establish the reliability of the text and the validity of its propositions on epistemological grounds. In the words of K. Satchidananda Murty,

> The Veda is a reliable authority, because it teaches us about things which are highly useful (*phalavat*) and are not known otherwise (*anadhigata*); and this knowledge is uncontradicted (*abādhita*). To the criticism of the Nyāya school that the concept of an authorless intrinsically reliable book is absurd, the Vedānta school replies that such a concept is not more absurd than the Nyāya concept of "eternal, self-conscious cognition, simultaneously apprehending all things at all places and times," which is alleged to belong to God.[10]

In modern parlance it amounts to saying that "the source of knowledge is knowledge itself. 'The origin of a body of scripture possessing the quality of omniscience cannot be sought elsewhere but in the omniscience itself,' "[11] where "omniscience" only means such knowledge in relation to the transcendental realm.

Just as the proper Christian response to the Christian propositional view of revelation is faith; the proper Advaitin response to the Advaitin propositional view of revelation is *jñāna* or knowledge. Faith is an ingredient in the overall process but the proper response is represented by knowledge of reality rather than faith in God. The role faith plays in this process is succinctly stated in the following verses of the Bhagavadgītā (4.38–42):

> There is no purifier in this world equal to wisdom. He who is perfected in *yoga* finds it in the self in the course of time.
>
> He who has faith, who is intent on it (knowledge) and who has controlled his senses, obtains knowledge and having obtained it, goes quickly to the highest peace.

10. Murty, *Revelation and Reason*, 30.

11. S. Radhakrishnan, trans., *The Brahma Sūtra: The Philosophy of a Spiritual Life* (London: George Allen & Unwin, 1960), 242.

> But the ignorant man who is without faith and of a doubting nature perishes. For the doubting self, there is not this world, nor the next, nor happiness.
>
> Actions do not bind him who has renounced actions in *yoga,* who has cast away doubt by knowledge, who possesses himself, O Arjuna.
>
> Therefore having cut away, with the sword of knowledge, this doubt in thy heart that is born of ignorance, resort to *yoga* and arise, O Arjuna.[12]

One may go even further and say that whereas in the propositional doctrine of revelation faith is a response to revelation, in Vedānta in general, and in Advaita Vedānta specifically, faith is an *advance* toward realizing the revealed propositional truths. In holding to this position Vedānta is in line with such thinkers as Rudolf Hermann Lotze, who "makes it clear that unless we start with some faith in God, the rational proofs that God exists are pleas put forward in justification of our faith." This faith according to Lotze springs from "the obscure impulse which drives us to pass in our thought—as we cannot help passing—from the world given in sense to a world not given in sense, but above and behind sense." According to Vedānta also "an initial faith is necessary for religious life and thought. This faith, though starting from a personal feeling of inadequacy and disquiet and a longing for something higher, remains a mere blind groping in the dark till it is enlightened by the teachings of the scriptures that show the way to the realization of God."[13]

The Propositional View of Revelation and Faith Revisited

Once the radical differences between the Christian propositional and nonpropositional views of revelation and faith have been recognized, it will be possible to discuss the convergences between the Christian and Advaitin

12. Deutsch and van Buitenen, *Source Book,* 40.

13. Satischandra Chatterjee and Dhirendramohan Datta, *An Introduction to Indian Philosophy* (1950; reprint, Calcutta: University of Calcutta, 1968), 367, 373–74.

views. It would be helpful to recapitulate the four points involved in the Christian propositional view of revelation and faith:

1. The "content of revelation is a body of truths expressed in statements or propositions."
2. This content is communicated by God to a rational creature.
3. This communication is done through means beyond the ordinary course of nature.
4. The content of the communication receives the "intellectual assent" of the recipient "because of the witnessing authority of God the Revealer."

God is involved in the communication of revelation in both cases, though in the Christian case as author and in the Advaitin case as transmitter. One might even say that on the propositional view of revelation in Christianity, revelation is *from* God, whereas in the case of Advaita, it is *with* God, for although it comes from God, it is not composed by God.

The conception of God as promulgator of the Vedas rather than author has led to interesting, even curious, discussions in Advaita Vedānta. Murty describes several of these.

1. "Does God repeat the Veda at the beginning of creation like an automaton, or does he repeat it after understanding the meaning of it? The Advaita replies that God, being omniscient, knows the meaning before repeating it; yet it is not to express his opinion that he does so."[14]

2. If God composes the Vedas, even if it is in accordance with the text of an earlier aeon, "though Veda's authority does not depend on God's 'opinion,' it at least depends on his composition."[15] One subschool of Advaita denies this. It claims that "even God never caused a new sequence of Vedic words and sentences," because the Vedas "are *only* manifested (*āvirbhāva*) and concealed (*tirobhāva*) respectively at the beginning and end of the aeon."[16] Another subschool concedes that God composes the Veda but as it is "only composed as it was in the previous aeon," the Veda has no independent author.[17]

3. Some Hindu scriptures describe Brahman as the cause of the Vedas. This is countered by saying that "Brahman is *only* the material cause of the

14. Murty, *Revelation and Reason*, 47.
15. Ibid.
16. Ibid., 47, 41.
17. Ibid., 46.

Veda, not its author." To the question, If Brahman is the material cause of the whole world as well as the Veda, what then is special about the Veda? the following reply is given: Although Brahman is in contact with everything the Veda is still necessary to make reality known just as "the rays of the sun are in contact with everything, including air and ether; nevertheless even in sunlight they are not seen."[18]

4. The eternality of the Veda in relation to Brahman, as distinguished from God, has also led to the adoption of different positions depending on how eternality is understood. The following distinction is helpful here:

> In Indian philosophy two kinds of eternity are distinguished, (a) *kūṭastha nityatā* and (b) *pravāharūpa nityatā.* A thing is *kūṭastha nitya* if it is unchanged for ever, while a thing has *pravāharūpa nitayatā* if though incessantly changing it does not alter its pattern (*niyati*). Roughly speaking, a rock, for example, has the former kind of reality, and a river the latter kind. The nature of a river is to flow incessantly, and so long as it does not swerve from this nature of its, it may be said to be "mutably real"; though not "enduringly real" as a rock.[19]

Śaṅkara, for one, "seems to conceive the eternity of the Veda as *pravāha nityatā,* because he distinctly uses the word *pravāha* and says that all the three worlds and creatures are a flux [*sic*], but have a pattern." Others, however, contend that the Vedas "are *only* manifested (*āvirbhāva*) and concealed (*tirobhāva*) respectively, at the beginning and the end of the aeon, and so their *kūṭastha nityatā* may be accepted."[20]

In general, transcendental eternality is reserved for Brahman; fluent eternality is accepted for the Veda, and as there "never was a first occasion" the Veda was not "*independently*" composed even by God. This is the standard position, but more and less has also been claimed for the Veda. It has been claimed, for instance, that it too is "beginningless and immutably real" like Brahman, the difference being that Brahman is *independently* and the Veda dependently so. It has also been said that the "Veda is *not* eternal, since it is produced by Brahman."[21]

But back to God. And to this question: Whether God is the author of the

18. Ibid., 48, 49.
19. Ibid., 40.
20. Ibid., 40, 41.
21. Ibid., 47, 41, 49; emphasis added.

Bible, or the promulgator of the Veda, can we still maintain that there is God because scripture says so when the scriptures contain what God says? Here Christianity and Advaita diverge. The Advaitin would say that God does not say anything as such; he only reiterates the Vedas and as such the Vedic authority on his existence is independent of his statement of it.

If the point is pressed, the Advaitin and Christian defenses of the viability of revelation diverge further. The Advaitin maintains that although God is *prior* to the Vedic revelation in terms of its present communication, the revelation is *prior* both to God and to the human knowledge of God. As God is known in Advaita Vedānta only through revelation, human beings come to know of his existence *post facto.* This is not *necessarily* the case in the propositional view of revelation in Christianity, even though in that context it could be maintained that God is prior to scripture and scripture prior to the human knowledge of God. It is not necessarily so because of the distinction that exists in traditional Christian theology between *natural theology* and *revealed theology.* As the distinction is traditionally explained, *natural theology* consists of the body of theological insights human beings can arrive at unaided by revelation, whereas *revealed theology* consists of those insights which were made accessible through revelation, whether or not human beings could have attained them unaided. It is thus held that the existence of God is an insight that the human mind could attain unaided, but the doctrine of the trinity is one that it could not.[22]

Some modern scholars, on a fresh reading of Śaṅkara, have arrived at a startlingly similar conclusion that although one could know reality (Brahman) without the aid of scripture, one could not know that Brahman is the ground of the universe without recourse to scripture.[23]

That the communication of revelation from God to the human mind is done by means beyond the ordinary course of nature is accepted by both "propositional" Christianity and Advaita Vedānta, but with a difference. Christianity asserts that God acts voluntarily; Advaita asserts that God is bound by a cosmic scheme. Moreover, for Advaita the "intellectual assent" comes from the witnessing authority of the revelation itself, rather than the Revealer.

Here one must take into account the category of testimony as a means of knowledge in Advaita Vedānta. Like several Hindu schools of thought,

22. Hick, *Philosophy of Religion,* 61–62.

23. See Arvind Sharma, "Śaṅkara's attitude to scriptural authority as revealed by his gloss on Brahmasūtra 1.1.3," *Journal of Indian Philosophy* 10 (1982): 179–86.

"western logicians, almost without exception, hold that authority [verbal testimony] cannot stand as an independent source of knowledge and is really a case of inference."[24] But Advaita Vedānta holds that verbal testimony is a valid means of knowledge and that within this category, the Vedic revelation, per se, is a valid means of knowledge about propositional truths.

According to Advaita Vedānta, although it is true that the reliability of the source that communicates a piece of knowledge is a matter of inference, the *content* of the communication cannot be placed in that category. If, for instance, a friend tells me that at this moment it is raining in another part of the city from which he has come, his experience of the rain represents his *perception,* and whether I believe him or not will be my *inference,* but the knowledge that it is or may be raining elsewhere has not been gained by me either through perception or inference. It was acquired by me *only* through testimony. Its reliability, not its content, is the subject of inference. Hence verbal testimony is a valid and independent means of knowledge.

To consider Vedic revelation a means of knowledge about propositional truths *by itself,* without the intervention of an author, may seem like a perfect example of the genetic fallacy. One should also note that *śabda* in Sanskrit denotes both *word* and *idea,* so that the ideas or laws inherently testified to by the existence of the universe could also on this view qualify as *śabda-pramāṇa.* Another traditional interpretation, however, and probably the one most acceptable to a modern mind in this context is that of Vācaspati Miśra (c. 900), who rejects a literal interpretation of Vedic revelation. As Murty explains, Vācaspati Miśra "does not believe in the eternity of words and sentences, and the various examples he gives ('fire does not wet,' 'water does not burn') shows that in his opinion moral laws are invariable like physical laws. Unswervable laws could be stated only in a uniform (*niyata*) way. That seems to be his proof of the *sameness* of the Vedas in every aeon,"[25] and the testimony of the Vedas constitutes the source of this knowledge.

The Nonpropositional View of Revelation and Faith

The nonpropositional view of revelation and faith represents in Christianity a different way to look at revelation, faith, the Bible, and theology. Another

24. D. M. Datta, *The Six Ways of Knowing* (Calcutta: University of Calcutta, 1972), 336.
25. Murty, *Revelation and Reason,* 42.

word by which the nonpropositional view of revelation and faith is referred to is *Heilsgeschichte* (salvation history). This is indicative of an altered concept of revelation: God discloses Himself through his deeds rather than through words. Revelation consists of God's action in history.

Faith in this connection then is conceived "as a voluntary recognition of God's activity in human history" and "consists of seeing, apperceiving, or interpreting events in a special way."[26] The term voluntary is important here. If God's presence were too compelling, then there would be proof of his intervention and faith would have no place; and if God were absent, there would be no occasion for the faith to arise. This situation, which preserves a human being's freedom to react of his or her own accord, makes faith a voluntary act. "Faith is thus the correlate of freedom: faith is related to cognition as free will to conation," and, Advaita Vedānta would add, as doubt to knowledge. There has to be the provision of a liminal zone for either action or faith or knowledge to proceed. Typically this liminality is expressed in terms of faith in Christian thought and in terms of knowledge in Advaita. Let the case of Advaita be examined first. In the discussion of the very first aphorism of the Brahmasūtra, "The objection is raised that an inquiry is unnecessary if *Brahman* is known (*a-sandighdha*) and futile (*a-prayojana*) if it is known. If Brahman is pure and absolute intelligence, it is open only to direct intuition and is not a proper object for inquiry and discussion. Desire to know can only be with reference to an object which is not definitely known."[27] This is the "knowledge" version of liminality. The "faith" version of this liminality is brilliantly articulated by Pascal:

> It was not then right that He should appear in a manner manifestly divine, and completely capable of convincing all men; but it was also not right that He should come in so Hidden a manner that He could not be known by those who should sincerely seek Him. He has willed to make Himself quite recognizable by those; and thus, willing to appear openly to those who seek Him with all their heart, and to be hidden from those who flee from Him with all their heart, He so regulates the knowledge of Himself that He has given signs of Himself, visible to those who seek Him, and not to those who seek Him not. There is enough light for those who only desire to see, and enough obscurity for those who have a contrary disposition.[28]

26. Hick, *Philosophy of Religion*, 69.
27. Radhakrishnan, trans., *Brahma Sūtra*, 230–31.
28. Quoted in Hick, *Philosophy of Religion*, 71.

On such a view the Bible then becomes a record not of propositional truths, but of events in which God is a participant. For instance, when the prophets speak of God's actions in the Old Testament, as John Hick explains:

> It is important to realize that the prophets were not formulating a philosophy of history in the sense of a hypothesis applied retrospectively to the facts; instead, they were reporting their actual experience of the events as they happened. They were conscious of living in the midst of *Heilsgeschichte,* salvation-history. They saw God actively at work in the world around them. For example, a well-known commentary says of the time when the Chaldean army was attacking Jerusalem, 'Behind the serried ranks of the Chaldean army [Jeremiah] beheld the form of Jahweh fighting for them and through them against His own people.' The prophets experienced their contemporary situations as moments in which God was actively present."[29]

The same is true of the New Testament, for the

> same epistemological pattern—the interpreting in a distinctive way of events that are in themselves capable of being construed either naturalistically or religiously—runs through the New Testament. Here again, in the story of a man, Jesus of Nazareth, and a movement which arose in connection with him, there are ambiguous data. It is possible to see him solely as a self-appointed prophet who got mixed up in politics, clashed with the Jerusalem priesthood, and had to be eliminated. It is also possible, with the New Testament writers, to see him as the Messiah of God giving himself for the renewing of humankind. To see him in this way is to share the faith or the distinctive way of "experiencing as" which gave rise to the New Testament documents.[30]

The parallel here from Advaita Vedānta is intriguing. According to Advaita, *such a view of the Vedas is not possible because in the Vedas the significance of the words is universal and not particular.*[31]

However, a similar view is identifiable in another body of sacred litera-

29. Ibid., 70–71.
30. Ibid.
31. Murty, *Revelation and Reason,* 17–18.

ture, acceptable to Advaita Vedānta not as revelation but as tradition. Thus in the Bhagavadgītā (11.33–34) there is the claim by God of actually intervening in battle as in the account of Yahweh, fighting against the Jews, cited earlier. In the Bhagavadgītā, God says to a wavering Arjuna:

> Therefore
> Rise up!
> Win glory!
> When you conquer your enemies,
> Your kingship will be fulfilled.
> Enjoy it.
> Be just an instrument,
> You, who can draw the bow
> With the left as well as the right hand!
> *I myself have slain*
> *Your enemies*
> *Long ago.*
>
> Do not waver
> Conquer the enemies
> *Whom I have already slain—*
> Droṇa and Bhīṣma and Jayadratha,
> And Karṇa also, and the other heroes at arms.
> Fight!
> You are about to defeat
> Your rivals in war.[32]

There is, however, one aspect of this nonpropositional conception of the Bible which can be related to the Vedas proper or revelation itself. Paul Tillich sums up this understanding of the Bible thus:

> The documentary character of the Bible is identical with the fact that it contains the original witness of those who participated in the revealing events. Their participation was their response to the happenings which became revealing events through their response. The inspiration of the biblical writers is their receptive and creative response to

32. Kees W. Bolle, *The Bhagavadgītā: A New Translation* (Berkeley and Los Angeles: University of California Press, 1979), 135, 136; emphasis added.

> potentially revelatory facts. The inspiration of the writers of the New Testament is their acceptance of Jesus as the Christ, and with him, of the New Being, of which they became witnesses. *Since there is no revelation unless there is someone who receives it as a revelation, the act of reception is a part of the event itself.* The Bible is both original event and original document; it witnesses to that of which it is a part.[33]

The contrast between the Western and Advaitin conceptions of revelation; that is, between *a revelation with a Revealer and a revelation without a Revealer* was noticed earlier, but on the point that there is *no revelation without someone who receives a revelation* the two agree. However, although they agree that revelation must have a receiver, each construes the role of the receiver in relation to the reception differently.

On the Christian side the principle operated as follows. The Old Testament did not pose a problem as it was already canonical in Judaism. The New Testament, however, was *accepted* as canonical through *due process.* The term *due process* is used here in the twofold sense of a formal process underlying the formation of the canon and a formal principle underlying the determination of what was thus included in the canon. This principle is known as that of "apostolic authority." The term *apostle* here also operates in a twofold sense: first, it refers to the apostles who were the immediate disciples of Jesus and knew him in person, specifically the twelve disciples homologous to the twelve tribes of the Israelites, and second, it refers to those who did not know him directly but knew those who knew him and constituted another circle of "apostles." The memoirs, the letters, and the accounts of the acts of the apostles all possess apostolic authority. Through due process in the first sense specified above they crystallized into the Christian canon, through which the redemption of the world was deemed to have been and was to be achieved.[34]

On the Advaitin side, the recipients of the Vedas are called *ṛṣis.* The traditional account of how they received this revelation can be pieced together from accounts cited by Śaṅkara. He relies on a *śruti* passage that states that the performance of sacrifice qualified the performers to receive the Word from those who possessed it, namely, the gods and the sages. How did they come to possess it? He relies on a *smṛti* text that states that the sages

33. Quoted in Hick, *Philosophy of Religion,* 73; emphasis added.
34. Ibid.

"saw" the Vedas, a suggestion abetted by the etymological connection, through the shared ancient Indo-European heritage, between the words "Veda" and "video." And they were able to see it now as it was in the past ages "just as a man waking from sleep is able to recollect and continue his previous waking experience." And how faithful was their recall? Very. According to Murty the passages from Śaṅkara "would imply that according to him, God makes the Vedic propositions flash in the minds of the sages in the same linguistic forms in which they are now available," and were available earlier, for the text is not supposed to vary. "Hence the sacredness of the Veda, its verbal inerrancy and the caution that change or mispronunciation of even a single letter will break one's head"[35]—however bizarre such a penalty for mispronunciation might sound to our modern ears.

From the nonpropositional view of revelation in Christianity it follows that the text is fixed. It is true that the canon was not fixed until a few centuries after the age in which Jesus lived but the canon codifies the impact of his life and the activities of his apostles. The canon had its own impact, which generated not further revelation but tradition. Hence the writings of the New Testament "together with the Hebrew Scriptures, constitute the given basis of Christian thought. Accordingly, it is not possible for Christian theology to go behind the scriptural data, taken in their totality." Not only is it not possible to go behind them, it is also not possible to go beyond them.

> It is clear, on this principle, why no later Christian writings, however profound, impressive, or uplifting, can ever rightly become included in the New Testament. For in the nature of the case, no later writings can be of apostolic origin. The only circumstance that could ever justify an enlargement of the canon to include books not now in it would be a discovery out of the sands and caves of the Middle East of ancient documents which, after the most careful scientific scrutiny, came to be accepted by the Church as authentic writings of the same category as the present contents of the New Testament—conceivably, for example, further letters by Saint Paul or the "lost ending" of Mark's Gospel.[36]

35. Murty, *Revelation and Reason,* 50.

36. The propositional view of revelation also holds that the text is fixed, but provides a greater role for tradition along with revelation (see Hick, *Philosophy of Religion,* 61, 72–73).

The Advaitin position would be similar but with some teasing exceptions. If a new branch (*śākhā*) of the Vedas were discovered—and *some are known to have been lost*[37]—then obviously it would have to be admitted into the existing corpus on the same argument that could enlarge the New Testament. But unlike the Christian the Vedic canon was never formally closed; the Vedas call themselves endless; and many believe that what we possess as Vedas is but a fraction of the original,[38] although the possibility of discovering a new branch of the Vedas is not entertained seriously enough to have affected the thinking on revelation in Vedānta (but it does seem to have had some effect on Mīmāṁsā).[39]

For all practical purposes the texts of Vedānta as we have them are final, though the triple division of Vedānta includes one class of texts which are revelation proper, the Upaniṣads, and two which properly belong to tradition, the Brahmasūtra and Bhagavadgītā; and "*all Vedānta,*" *not just Advaita,* "*true to its name accepts the authority of the three texts.*"[40] In this respect the Advaita Vedānta view of canon is perhaps closer to the propositional view of revelation and faith in Christianity. However, just as, in a sense, one cannot exceed apostolic authority, the tradition was beginning to feel already by the fifth century B.C.E. that it could not exceed the authority of the *ṛṣis.* For an early writer on the Vedas, Yāska, remarks (Nirukta 13.12.13):

> Concerning the *mantras,* none can claim to have perceived their truths if one is not a seer and a spiritual energizer. . . . When seers passed beyond, men asked the gods, "Who are going to be seers for us?" To them the gods gave reason as the seer. And hence, whatever one speaks with reason, *following the track of the Word,* becomes as good as the utterance of a seer. . . . This knowledge is a form of revealed and reasoned illumination; its farthest end is to be realized by spiritual energizing.[41]

37. P. V. Kane, *History of Dharmaśāstra* (Poona: Bhandarkar Oriental Research Institute, 1977), vol. 5, part 2, p. 1259.

38. Troy Wilson Organ, *Hinduism: Its Historical Development* (Woodbury, N.Y.: Barron's Educational Series, 1974), 180; T.M.P. Mahadevan, *Outlines of Hinduism* (1960; reprint, Bombay: Chetana, 1971), 39; Haridas Bhattacharyya, ed. *The Cultural Heritage of India* (Calcutta: The Ramakrishna Mission Institute of Culture, 1969), 1:182–83.

39. Kane, *History,* vol. 5, part 2, p. 1257.

40. Deutsch and van Buitenen, *Source Book,* 4.

41. Bhattacharyya, ed. *Cultural Heritage,* 1:323.

The Nonpropositional View of Revelation and Faith Revisited

The nonpropositional view of revelation and faith centers on *events*. As John H. Hick explains:

> The conception of revelation as occurring in the events of history—both world history and individual history—and the conception of faith as the experience of these events as God's dealings with human creatures, also suggest a different conception of the Bible from that which accompanies the propositional theory. Within the propositional circle of ideas, the Bible is customarily referred to as "the Word of God." This phrase is understood in practice as meaning "the words of God." However, within the contrasting set of ideas associated with the non-propositional view of revelation there is a tendency to return to the New Testament usage in which Christ, and only Christ, is called the divine Word (*Logos*). According to this view the Bible is not itself the Word of God but is rather the primary and indispensable witness to the Word. The New Testament is seen as the human record of the Incarnation, that is, of the "fact of faith" which is expressed in such statements as "the Word became flesh and dwelt among us, full of grace and truth; we have beheld his glory, glory as of the only Son from the Father."[42]

This twofold view of revelation may be contrasted with the fourfold view of revelation which K. Satchidananda Murty identifies as characteristic of Advaita Vedānta,[43] and which Troy Wilson Organ attributes to Śaṅkara: "Truths are revealed to man in four sorts of revelation: (1) a general revelation open to all mankind in the human experience of living in a world of name and form; (2) the Vedic revelation which is given in all the Vedic literature, but primarily in the Upanishads; (3) the revelation given through incarnations of the Gods; (4) *anubhūti* revelation, which is direct experience of truth arising from meditation on Upanishadic texts."[44]

It is clear that the propositional view of revelation and faith corresponds to item (2) above and the nonpropositional view to item (3). This becomes

42. Hick, *Philosophy of Religion*, 72.
43. Murty, *Revelation and Reason*, 6–10.
44. Organ, *Hinduism*, 248.

even more explicit when Murty points out that Vedic revelation "*is the main type of revelation accepted by Śaṅkara.*"[45] It is clear that in general the propositional view of revelation in Christianity is more congruent with the Advaita Vedānta concept of revelation than the nonpropositional view.

This is not to say that there is no correspondence between the nonpropositional view of revelation in Christianity and the Advaitin view of revelation through an *avatāra* or Incarnation. Śaṅkara's introduction to his commentary on the Bhagavadgītā leaves little room for doubt that he accepts the doctrine of *avatāra:*

> The Lord created the universe, and wishing to secure order therein He first created the Prajāpatis (Lords of creatures) such as Marichi and caused them to adopt the Pravṛitti-Dharma, the Religion of Works. He then created others such as Sanaka and Sanandana and caused them to adopt the Nivṛitti-Dharma, the Religion of Renunciation, characterised by knowledge and indifference to worldly objects. It is the twofold Vedic Religion of Works and Renunciation that maintains order in the universe. This Religion which directly leads to liberation and worldly prosperity has long been practised by all castes and religious orders (varṇa-āśrama)—from the brāhmanas downwards,—who sought welfare.
>
> *The Purpose of the Divine Incarnation*
>
> When, owing to the ascendancy of lust in its votaries, religion was overpowered by irreligion caused by the vanishing faculty of discrimination, and irreligion was advancing. . . . Without any interest of His own, but with the sole intention of helping His creatures, He taught to Arjuna, who was deeply plunged in the ocean of grief and delusion, the twofold Vedic Religion, evidently thinking that the Religion would widely spread when accepted and practised by men of high character.[46]

The doctrine of incarnation in Śaṅkara, however, diverges from the Christian in three significant ways, which has the effect of reducing the significance of the nonpropositional view of revelation for Advaita Vedānta.

45. Murty, *Revelation and Reason,* 7; emphasis added.

46. Alladi Mahadeva Sastry, trans., *The Bhagavad Gita with the Commentary of Sri Sankaracharya* (1979; reprint, Madras: Samata Books, 1985), 2–4.

1. Christianity admits of only one incarnation, that of Jesus Christ. Hinduism, however, accepts the idea of manifold incarnations of God, and Śaṅkara seems to accept the doctrine of multiple incarnations. He is credited with a hymn in praise of the ten incarnations[47]—a standard listing in the tradition. In any case his acceptance of the doctrine of multiple incarnations is clear from his comment on Bhagavadgītā 4.6–8 in which repeated incarnations are emphasized. In his commentary on 10.31 he identifies Rāma with Rāma the son of Daśaratha, though the word *avatāra* is not used.

With one incarnation it is easier to have a nonpropositional view of revelation, as one has to respond to the events of one definitive incarnation, whereas with multiple incarnations one is already dealing in revelations, rather than a revelation.

2. Śaṅkara's concept of incarnation differs from the Christian in that in this case God never really becomes a human being, but only appears to do so. Thus he describes Kṛṣṇa in his commentary on the Bhagavadgītā (6.6) as saying: "I *appear* to be born and embodied, through my own Māyā, but not in reality, unlike others."[48] This position resembles the Docetic heresy in Christianity.

3. It seems that according to Śaṅkara there can be no distinct genre of nonpropositional revelation that can replace or supersede the propositional one. This is at least K. Satchidananda Murty's understanding of his position. The reason, according to Murty's interpretation, why an incarnation in Advaita Vedānta cannot become a locus of nonpropositional revelation is that the focus of incarnatory revelation continues to be the Veda. Thus although the Bhagavadgītā clearly states (4.7–8) that an incarnation takes place in order to uphold *dharma* or the Norm, it is clearly understood that this *dharma* is the one laid down in the Veda. Śaṅkara is more explicit on this point in his preface to the Gītā than in his commentary on the verse cited above; but even here his gloss on the word *dharma* as *varṇāśramādidharma,* or the institutes of class and stages of life, points in the same direction. "In Śaṅkara's words, the teaching of an avatāra is '*samastavedārthasārasaṅgraha,*' i.e. 'the essence in brief of the meaning of the entire Veda.' "[49]

Thus the nonpropositional view of revelation suffers from serious limitations when extended to Advaita Vedānta. In one respect, however, an interesting insight is offered by this approach inasmuch as it emphasizes the

47. Radhakrishnan, trans., *Brahma Sūtra,* 38, in which the hymn in praise of Buddha is cited.
48. Sastry, trans., *Bhagavad Gita,* 121; emphasis added.
49. Murty, *Revelation and Reason,* 9.

element of "experience" in revelation.[50] An element of this has been detected in Śaṅkara and identified by Radhakrishnan in a passage a fragment from which has been cited earlier.

> There is another view of the *Veda* as *āpta-vacana* or sayings of the wise, those who had attained to a realisation of *Brahman, brahmaprāpti.* This view is supported by Ś(aṅkara) who makes out that the *Śruti* or Scripture is *pratyakṣa* or records of the direct experiences of the seers, which are of a self-certifying character. "How can one," Śaṅkara asks, "contest the truth of another possessing knowledge of *Brahman,* vouched for as it is by his heart's conviction?" The experience is intimate, ineffable, incommunicable. It is an act of pure apprehension when our whole being is welded into one, an act of impassioned intuition which excludes all conceptual activities. "Whereas I was blind, I now see." The self alone is witness to it.[51]

The mention of experience in this context recalls the distinction between natural and revealed theology alluded to earlier. As was pointed out, although revealed theology pertains specially to insights received through revelation alone, this does not preclude the presentation, in revealed theology, of insights that could also be arrived at by human intelligence functioning without the aid of revelation. Now although it is moot whether Śaṅkara allows for the knowledge of Brahman without the aid of revelation, if the evidence on this point is taken seriously (as found in his gloss on Brahmasūtra 1.1.2), then it becomes possible to suggest a reconciliation of the two points of view on the model of natural and revealed theology. It could be argued that although Śaṅkara concedes the possibility, more or less, of knowledge of Brahman arising through the operation of natural theology he emphasizes the role of revealed theology as being primary (instead of being absolutely exclusive) in this respect. It can then be further argued that it is the ineffability of the direct experience of Brahman, achieved naturally, which compels one to turn to the Vedas. In other words the distinction between natural and revealed theology is as blurred in Advaita Vedānta as it is in Protestant Christianity when primacy is accorded to experience, for

50. Hick, *Philosophy of Religion,* 72.
51. Radhakrishnan, trans., *Brahma Sūtra,* 243–44.

> the experience of *Brahman* cannot be adequately expressed in words. This is true even of ordinary immediate experiences of given objects. Vācaspati says: "the distinctive attributes of various things cannot, indeed, be declared, though experienced. The difference in the sweetness of the sugar-cane, milk and jaggery cannot, verily, be given expression to, even by the Goddess of Learning." The experiences which we cannot know from perception or inference are described in the *Vedas;* hence their authoritativeness. Even those who look upon *Brahman* as personal God admit that his nature is inconceivable except through the *Vedas.*[52]

The reference to the direct experience of the seers or *ṛṣis* at the beginning of the passage is also significant. As Hiriyanna explains it: "But, theological considerations apart, it should be admitted that the truths for which the Veda stands, whether or not it is now possible to ascribe them to specific thinkers, should eventually be traced to some human source; and the fact seems to be implied in the description of those truths as having been *seen* by inspired sages (*ṛṣis*) of old. If it be so, the Veda also must be reckoned as communicating to us the results intuited by ancient sages."[53]

52. Ibid., 244.

53. M. Hiriyanna, *The Essential of Indian Philosophy* (London: George Allen & Unwin, 1948), 45. The role of revelation and experience in Advaita is a subject of renewed debate that can be profitably juxtaposed with chapter 6 of the fourth edition (1990) of John H. Hick's *Philosophy of Religion.* See Anantanand Rambachan, *Accomplishing the Accomplished: The Vedas as a Source of Valid Knowledge in Śaṅkara* (Honolulu: University of Hawaii Press, 1991), and its review in *Philosophy East and West* 43 (October 1993): 737–44. For an experiential approach to Advaita in the same context, see also Arvind Sharma, *The Experiential Dimension of Advaita Vedānta* (Delhi: Motilal Banarsidass, 1993), and for a perceptual approach see Bina Gupta, *Perceiving in Advaita Vedānta: An Epistemological Analysis and Interpretation* (Lewisburg, Pa.: Bucknell University Press, 1991).

6

Faith in Advaita Vedānta

If one accepts the propositional view of revelation and concedes that the existence of a revealer, that is, God, is not demonstrable from universally accepted premises, then one is obliged to believe certain statements on insufficient evidence. This gap between belief and proof, then, has to be overcome by faith which is no more or less than "the believing of propositions upon insufficient evidence."[1] It is as if a gap is created between a proposition and the evidence proving it which generates an emotive tension, and faith is the electrical charge that leaps across this gap. This may happen spontaneously, and we would then call it the miracle of faith. This may also be induced. As John Hick puts it, "Many philosophical defenders of religion share the same assumption and propose various expedients to compensate for the lack of evidence to support their basic convictions. The most popular way of bridging the evidential gap is by an effort of the will."[2] These "various expedients" are called the voluntarist theories of faith.

It is important here to distinguish knowledge and belief from faith. If a person *knows* something to be the way it is, then the question of faith does not arise. To put it another way,

> no one can believe something to be the case, in spite of *known* evidence to the contrary; for however much one may hold fast to the absurd "in the passion of inwardness," one cannot coerce himself to believe. A man can ignore evidence, which is unsettling or dangerous

1. John H. Hick, *The Philosophy of Religion*, 3d ed. (Englewood Cliffs, N.J.: Prentice Hall, 1983), 62.
2. Ibid.

> to his settled way of life or thought; and he may come to form a habit of disregarding contrary evidence. Nevertheless this does not prove that one can believe X to be Y, when he clearly knows X is not Y. He may presume a mistake on his part, or he may bring in the plea that all human reason and perception is fallible; but he can never make himself believe that what he knows for certain (say) as a horse is a cat. Men may come to hasty conclusions, they may be credulous and believe what they are told; but it is impossible for them to ignore what they take to be established evidence (whether it is perceptual or logical). To sum up, belief is not a voluntary action.[3]

But faith is (unless it be of the spontaneous type alluded to earlier).[4] As Dorothy Emmet explains: "Faith is distinguished from the entertainment of a probable proposition by the fact that the latter can be a completely theoretic affair. Faith is a 'yes' of self-commitment, it does not turn probabilities into certainties; only a sufficient increase in the weight of evidence could do that. But it is a volitional response which takes us out of the theoretic attitude."[5]

What about the role of faith in Advaita Vedānta?

One must begin by distinguishing between the role of the Veda in Mīmāṁsā and in Advaita Vedānta. The Mīmāṁsā commitmennt to faith in the Vedas is illustrated by the following anecdote from the life of Kumārila, who was

> educated, according to various claimants, in Bihar, Assam, Kashmir, Banaras, or South India, and was converted at an early age to Buddhism. But he still had a great reverence for the Hindu scriptures and was once observed to weep bitterly when his Buddhist teacher criticized the Vedas. Suspecting him of being a heretic and also jealous of the love his teacher had for him, his fellow students pushed Kumarila off a high terrace. In falling he cried out, "If the Vedas are true they will save me from harm." He escaped with his life, but lost an eye for voicing doubt in his "If."[6]

3. K. Satchidananda Murty, *Revelation and Reason in Advaita Vedānta* (New York: Columbia University Press, 1959), 322–23.
4. I have Anselm's *credo ut intelligam* in mind here.
5. Quoted in Hick, *Philosophy of Religion*, 62.
6. Benjamin Walker, *Hindu World* (London: George Allen & Unwin, 1968), 1:571.

Advaita Vedānta is more restrained in its approach. It is helpful to remind oneself here that what holds for God in the Christian view has often to be applied to the Veda in the context of one of the two Hindu schools based on it, namely, Mīmāṁsā and Vedānta.

The various voluntarist theories of faith may now be examined in the context of Advaita Vedānta.

The Views of Blaise Pascal

One voluntarist theory of faith in the context of the propositional view of revelation was formulated by the French philosopher Blaise Pascal (1623–62).

> Pascal's "wager" treats the question of divine existence as an enigma concerning which we can take up a position only on the basis of a calculation of risks. If we wager our lives that God exists, we stand to gain eternal salvation if we are right and to lose little if we are wrong. If, on the other hand, we wager our lives that there is no God, we stand to gain little if we are right but to lose eternal happiness if we are wrong. "Let us weigh the gain and the loss in wagering that God is. Let us estimate these two chances. If you gain, you gain all; if you lose, you lose nothing. Wager, then, without hesitation that He is."[7]

Despite this parallel, Advaita Vedānta does not seem to have formulated a similar "wager argument." Rather, it seems to side with another statement of Pascal, that "man is obviously made to think. It is his whole dignity and his whole merit; and his whole duty is to think as he ought."[8] Advaita Vedānta argues for reason against risk. Thus "only a rational being can understand the meaning of Shruti. It cannot reveal itself to a beast."[9] The important difference between Pascal's position and the Advaitin position is that in Advaita God is unknown, but the text of the Veda is not, and this allows for the operation of reason in a way not possible in theistic terms. It accepts with Christianity the position that "God is an article of faith" but it

7. Hick, *Philosophy of Religion*, 63.
8. Quoted in Murty, *Revelation and Reason*, 325.
9. Chandradhar Sharma, *A Critical Survey of Indian Philosophy* (London: Rider, 1960), 288.

further maintains that the Vedas are "the only *proof* of the existence of God." This inversion of the God-Scripture position changes the context and, by allowing more scope for reason in the understanding of scripture, obviates the need for the wager. According to Chandradhar Sharma.

> Shankara, like Kant, believes that God cannot be *proved* by our finite thought. All attempts to do so end in failure. They lead to, what Kant has called, the antinomies. The cosmological proof can give only a finite creator of this finite creation and a finite creator is no creator at all. The teleological proof can only point to the fact that conscious principle is working at the root of creation. The ontological proof can give only an *idea* of God and not God as a *real object.* The Nyāya arguments to prove the existence of God are futile. God is an article of faith. Shruti is the only *proof* for the existence of God. As Kant falls back on faith, so Shankara falls back on Shruti. Shankara agrees with Gaudapāda's view of Ajāti. There is no *real* creation. God, therefore, is not a "*real*" creator. God alone is *real;* the creation is only an *appearance* of God.[10]

It can further even be claimed in Advaita Vedānta that "God is God only to the jīva who is labouring under Avidyā. God Himself never feels Himself as God; He feels Himself essentially one with Brahman, for Avidyā in its negative aspect of concealment never operates on Him. God is the Lord of Māyā, while jīva is constantly troubled by Māyā. God always enjoys the Bliss of Brahman while jīva is tortured by the pangs of Avidyā. When Brahman is viewed as saṁsāra, God, Soul and Nature arise simultaneously and when Brahman's own essence is realized, God, Soul and Nature vanish simultaneously."[11]

The Views of William James

William James (1842–1910) formulated another voluntarist theory of faith somewhat similar to Pascal's. Pascal represents the option between faith and no faith; William James begins by assuming a position initially close to his:

10. Ibid., 281.
11. Ibid.

"We cannot escape the issue by remaining skeptical and waiting for more light, because, although we do avoid error in that way *if religion be untrue,* we lose the good, *if it be true,* just as certainly as if we positively chose to disbelieve."[12] James has broadened the concern from God to religion; second, he has shown that skepticism or even "a wait and see" attitude is not as sound an option as might appear at first sight and finally suggests "*Better risk loss of truth than chance of error*"[13] with a passion exceeding Pascal's rational appeal. Although Santayana said that James "merely believed in the right of believing that you might be right if you believed," it seems that James is saying more than that: he is saying that unless you take the initiative how can the world which the key of faith unlocks ever become accessible to you—should it exist. As S. Radhakrishnan explains:

> There are those who have neither experience nor rational knowledge of God. They have neither sight nor proof. They have faith in the Scriptures. In faith we believe with our hearts while in science we believe with our minds. But the word faith has another meaning. It is not merely acceptance of authority without proof or experience. It is the response of the whole man, which includes assent of intellect and energy of will. Men of faith are men of power who have assimilated the truth and made it into a creative principle. God becomes the light and life from which they act, the strange power beside which our own power is weakness. God is the name we give to that interior principle which exceeds us while forming the very centre of our being.[14]

That James might be referring to this second kind of faith is suggested by the following analogy: "Just as a man who in a company of gentlemen made no advances, asked a warrant for every concession, and believed no one's work without proof, would cut himself off by such churlishness from all social rewards that a more trustworthy spirit would earn—so here, one who would shut himself up in snarling logicality and try to make the gods extort his recognition willy-nilly, or not get it at all, might cut himself off forever from his only opportunity of making the gods' acquaintance."[15]

12. Quoted in Hick, *Philosophy of Religion,* 63–64.

13. Ibid.

14. S. Radhakrishnan, trans., *The Brahma Sūtra: The Philosophy of a Spiritual Life* (London: George Allen & Unwin, 1960), 245–46.

15. Quoted in Hick, *Philosophy of Religion,* 64.

There is, however, one danger to such openness—how does one distinguish among competing claims? James uses the example of the Mahdi who invites James to follow him and as John Hick observes: "The only reason James could offer for not responding to this pressing invitation is that it did not rank as a 'live option' in his mind. That is to say, it did not conform to the assumptions presently controlling his thinking."[16]

It is as a safeguard against this danger that Advaita Vedānta emphasizes the collective aspect of the Vedas. A vision which has unfolded to a Mahdi or any

> one single person may after all be an illusion. This is not to impugn the good faith of the saint; it only means that the excellence of the character of a teacher is no guarantee of the truth of his teaching. To avoid this possible defect of subjectivity orthodox thinkers postulate in the place of testimony, based upon the intuition of a single sage, another, viz. *śruti* or "revelation"—otherwise known as the Veda which, it is claimed, will not mislead us since it has emanated from God or is supernatural in some other sense. As commonly explained, the *śruti* is tradition which is looked upon as immemorial (*sanātana*) in its character because its origin cannot be traced to any mortal being.[17]

This may also be the place to consider

> a condition which is sometimes laid down as essential to all "revealed" teaching, viz. that it should have proved acceptable to the best minds (*mahājana*) of the community. This may appear to be only a begging of the question at issue, for non-Vedic tradition also claims to have been accepted by the best minds of the community. What, however, is meant by this new condition seems to be that, if a doubt arises as to the validity of the views handed down from the past, adherents of the present school appeal, as those of the other do not, to a community of minds which they have satisfied. Thus the standard here becomes eventually a society of men, and not an individ-

16. Ibid.

17. M. Hiriyanna, *The Essentials of Indian Philosophy* (London: George Allen & Unwin, 1948), 44. It is interesting that even the idea of God as a *single* person who promulgates the Vedas caused uneasiness among some Advaitin scholars (see Murty, *Revelation and Reason*, 32).

> ual; and, by virtue of the objective status which it thus acquires, its deliverances are taken to possess an authority which cannot belong to those of anybody's private intuition. Herein may be said to lie the superiority of *śruti.*[18]

The Views of F. R. Tennant

A third voluntarist theory of faith is associated with the name of F. R. Tennant. He established his case for faith on the models of science: the model of scientific invention, the model of scientific discovery, and the model of scientific investigation.

Science posits facts. This provides one clue to the true nature of faith. Science discovers facts. This provides a second clue to the true nature of faith. Science postulates coherence. This provides a third clue to the true nature of faith:

> Belief is more or less constrained by fact or Actuality that already is or will be, independently of any striving of ours, and which convinces us. Faith, on the other hand, reaches beyond the Actual or the given to the ideally possible, which in the first instance it creates, as the mathematician posits his entities, and then by practical activity may realize or bring into Actuality. Every machine of human invention has thus come to be. Again, faith may similarly lead to knowledge of Actuality which it in no sense creates, but which would have continued, in absence of the faith-venture, to be unknown: as in the discovery of America by Columbus. . . . Science postulates what is requisite to make the world amenable to the kind of thought that conceives of the structure of the universe, and its orderedness according to quantitative law; theology, and sciences of valuation, postulate what is requisite to make the world amenable to the kind of thought that conceives of the why and wherefore, the meaning or purpose of the universe, and its orderedness according to teleological principles.[19]

This approach of Tennant seems more in agreement with the position of Advaita Vedānta than those previously mentioned. Advaita Vedānta

18. Hiriyanna, *Essentials,* 45.
19. Quoted in Hick, *Philosophy of Religion,* 65.

emphasizes that religion is something that is, not merely something that ought to be,[20] that it can be *realized*,[21] and that its worldview coheres.[22]

John H. Hick has criticized Tennant for "bracketing together religious faith and scientific 'faith' " because a "scientist's faith is significant only as a preliminary to experimental verification. It is often a necessary stage on the way to tested knowledge, and it has value only in relation to subsequent verification"[23] but religious faith, as articulated by Tennant, "can hope for no such objective verification. All that Tennant can offer by way of verification is the effect faith has on the lives of the believers."[24]

It must be clearly recognized at this point that an Advaitin's faith is like a scientist's. Hick's criticism may apply to Tennant, but Tennant's thesis applies to Advaita Vedānta. The point is crucial and is clearly presented by M. Hiriyanna. He points out that Advaita Vedānta may be regarded by some as

> essentially dogmatic, because its truth is primarily to be known through revelation. That such a conclusion, however, does not follow will be seen when we remember the exact function of revelation. The aim here, as in the case of other Indian doctrines, is not merely to grasp the ultimate truth intellectually but to realize it in one's own experience. The scripture as such, being a form of verbal testimony, can however convey only mediate knowledge. To attain the ideal therefore means to advance farther than merely comprehending the scriptural truth. Scriptural knowledge, accordingly, is not sufficient, though necessary; and like reason, it also therefore becomes only a subsidiary aid to the attainment of the goal. The Upanishads themselves declare that when a person has seen this truth for himself, he outgrows the need for the scriptures. "There a father becomes no father; a mother, no mother; the world, no world; the gods, no gods; the Vedas, no Vedas." Thus we finally get beyond both reason and revelation, and rest on direct experience (*anubhava*). Hence if Advaita is dogmatic, the dogma is there only to be transcended. Further we should not forget that revelation itself, . . . goes back to the intuitive experience of the great seers of the past. It is that experience which is to be personally corroborated by the disciple.[25]

20. Murty, *Revelation and Reason*, 317.
21. Mahadevan, *Outlines of Hinduism*, 15.
22. Hiriyanna, *Essentials*, 168.
23. Hick, *Philosophy of Religion*, 65.
24. Ibid., 66.
25. Hiriyanna, *Essentials*, 173.

The central fact to be borne in mind here is that Advaita Vedānta allows for salvation in this life as well as in the next. (This is not true of all systems of Hindu philosophy.) This enables it to go beyond the criticism leveled by Hick against Tennant and indeed beyond Tennant himself. Tennant says: "Successful faith . . . is illustrated by numerous examples of the gaining of material and moral advantages, the surmounting of trials and afflictions, and the attainment of heroic life, by men of old who were inspired by faith. It is thus that faith is pragmatically 'verified' and that certitude as to the unseen is established."[26] Advaitin thinkers have acknowledged this in respect to those schools of Hindu thought which do not subscribe to the doctrine of pre-mortem salvation;[27] however, as Hick points out (speaking of Christianity):

> Even purely subjective verification is only for [subjective] certitude, not a proving of [objective] certainty as to external reality. The fruitfulness of a belief or of faith for the moral and religious life is one thing, and the reality or existence of what is ideated and assumed is another. There are instances in which a belief that is not true, in the sense of corresponding with fact, may inspire one with lofty ideals and stimulate one to strive to be a more worthy person. This admission reduces religious faith, as Tennant conceives it, to an unverifiable hope, and thereby undermines his attempt to assimilate religious to scientific cognition.[28]

Two points need be considered here. In Tennant's case verification is "subjective" and expressed in terms of moral excellence. Objective verification of the nature of reality is not possible. In Advaita Vedānta morality is a necessary but not a sufficient condition for knowing the nature of reality. That Reality can be known right here while one is still alive. But in a sense this pre-mortem verification in Advaita is also subjective[29]—though only in the sense that the subject alone can make it for himself. Hence whether this form of religious "cognition" is identical with scientific cognition still remains debatable. The point to grasp, however, is this, that the doctrine of living liberation or *jīvanmukti* in Advaita Vedānta radically alters the situation. If a system allows salvation only after death, then it is possible to

26. Quoted in Hick, *Philosophy of Religion*, 66.
27. M. Hiriyanna, *Outlines of Indian Philosophy* (London: George Allen & Unwin, 1964), 19.
28. Hick, *Philosophy of Religion*, 66.
29. Murty, *Revelation and Reason*, 113.

distinguish two goals in it, the goal of religion and the goal of philosophy. The goal of religion may be said to pertain to the other world and the goal of philosophy to this world. If salvation is only possible after death, then salvation—in terms of this system—becomes the goal of religion, which involves faith, and is placed out of the reach of philosophy. If, however, salvation is possible before death (with or without the possibility of post-mortem liberation as well), then salvation also becomes the goal of philosophy, since the facts of philosophical investigation are provided by our experience of the world and in this world and the possibility of living liberation allows for the investigation of how the experience *of* the world is affected by the experience of living liberation *in* this world.[30]

The common ground in the positions of Tennant and Śaṅkara is a faith that is not merely faith, but faith-pending-realization of something, a faith that is not a leap but a bridge to the unknown.

The Views of Paul Tillich

We may now examine yet another concept of faith, associated with the name of Paul Tillich (1886–1965). Can his concept of faith be made commensurable with Advaita Vedānta?

Paul Tillich defines faith as "the state of being ultimately concerned."[31] This is reminiscent of the first aphorism of the Brahmasūtra, which contains the expression *brahmajijñāsā*[32]—a term which in this context may be ren-

30. Hiriyanna, *Outlines,* 381–82. Earlier in the same work Hiriyanna points out that "it might be thought that the idea of mokṣa, being eschatological, rests on mere speculation and that, though it may be regarded as the goal of faith, it can hardly be represented as that of philosophy. Really, however, there is no ground for thinking so, for, thanks to the constant presence in the Indian mind of a positivistic standard, the mokṣa ideal, even in those schools in which it was not so from the outset, speedily came to be conceived as realizable in this life, and described as jīvan-mukti, or emancipation while yet alive. It still remained, no doubt, a distant ideal; but what is important to note is that it ceased to be regarded as something to be reached in a life beyond. Man's aim was no longer represented as the attainment of perfection in a hypothetical hereafter, but as a continual progress towards it within the limits of the present life. Even in the case of doctrines like the Nyāya-Vaiśeṣika or the Viśiṣṭādvaita which do not formally accept the jīvan-mukti ideal, there is clearly recognized the possibility of man reaching here a state of enlightenment which may justifiably be so described because it completely transforms his outlook upon the world and fills with an altogether new significance the life he thereafter leads in it."

31. Paul Tillich, *Dynamics of Faith* (New York: Harper & Row, 1957), 1.

32. Radhakrishnan, trans., *Brahma Sūtra,* 227.

dered as a "state of being concerned with the ultimate," where Brahman denotes the ultimate reality.[33] *Jijñāsā* (literally the desire to know and hence the object of concern) creates a slight difficulty in relation to faith as when S. Radhakrishnan remarks that "the knowledge of *Brahman* is not a matter of faith but the result of inquiry. Science comes from observation, not by authority."[34] If, however, one recognizes that "concern" involves passionate commitment to inquiry, the difficulty is resolved. Tillich here is blasting the word "faith" into a new semantic orbit; Radhakrishnan is using it in the traditional sense.

Ultimacy, of course, can be posited of many things. As John Hick puts it, "People are in fact ultimately concerned about many different things—for example their nation, or their personal success and status; but these are properly only preliminary concerns, and the elevation of a preliminary concern to ultimacy is idolatry."[35]

One must therefore revert to the first aphorism of the Brahmasūtra to appreciate Tillich's position in the context of Advaita Vedānta. The full text of the aphorism runs: "*athāto brahmajijñāsā*—'now therefore the desire to know Brahman' (the ultimate reality),"[36] in which "the word *atha* indicates that the desire to know Brahman arises subsequent to the fulfillment of certain conditions, according to Ś(aṅkara)."[37] These conditions include *vairāgya* (detachment), namely, the abandonment of what are referred to as preliminary concerns above. Two points are of further interest here. First, *atha* is interpreted differently by different scholars. In this tradition Paul Tillich offers, it would appear, his own interpretation of *atha.* Second, because of the iconoclastic monotheism of Christianity these other concerns are called idols. Hinduism is "polytheistic," and Pratima Bowes has shown how polytheistic societies are less antagonistic to "other" concerns.[38] There can be little doubt, however, that once the ultimate concern is *mokṣa* (salvation) other concerns, represented by *dharma* (duty), *artha* (wealth), and *kāma* (pleasure), are considered antagonistic to it.[39]

Tillich then proceeds to describe ultimate concern as follows:

33. Ibid.
34. Ibid., 230.
35 Hick, *Philosophy of Religion,* 66.
36. Radhakrishnan, trans., *Brahma Sūtra,* 227.
37. Ibid.
38. Pratima Bowes, *The Hindu Religious Tradition: A Philosophical Approach* (London: Routledge & Kegan Paul, 1977), 282.
39. Hiriyanna, *Essentials,* 50.

> Ultimate concern is the abstract translation of the great commandment: "The Lord, our God, the Lord is one; and you shall love the Lord your God with all your heart, and with all your soul, and with all your mind, and with all your strength." The religious concern is ultimate; it excludes all other concerns from ultimate significance; it makes them preliminary. The ultimate concern is unconditional, independent of any conditions of character, desire, or circumstance. The unconditional concern is total: no part of ourselves or of our world is excluded from it; there is no "place" to flee from it. The total concern is infinite: no moment of relaxation and rest is possible in the face of a religious concern which is ultimate, unconditional, total, and infinite.[40]

This passage, to a student of Advaita Vedānta, is strongly reminiscent, in style and content, of the description of Brahman as *saccidānanda.* What the expression *saccidānanda brahman* means—with *brahman* as the object of ultimate concern—is explained by M. Hiriyanna with three successive questions pertinent to any ultimate concern: (1) Is it real? (2) If it is real, is its reality material or spiritual in nature? (3) Given that it is real, and irrespective of whether its reality is material or immaterial, is it ultimately one or many?

The description of Brahman as *saccidānanda* answers these questions. To the question, Is Brahman real? the word *sat* provides the answer. The word *sat* denotes reality. The answer therefore is that the object of our ultimate concern is real, it indeed exists. This leads to the next question, What is the nature of this reality? Is it material or is it spiritual? The word *cit* answers this second question. *Cit* means consciousness, which is nonmaterial or spiritual in nature. This leads to the third question, Granted that the object of our ultimate concern is real and possesses a reality spiritual in nature, is it one or many? The word *ānanda* answers this question—but indirectly. *Ānanda* means bliss. "Inasmuch as variety is the source of all trouble and restlessness," describing *brahman* as bliss implies oneness.[41]

It has been asked of Tillich's definition of faith as ultimate concern whether "ultimate concern" refers "to a concerned state of mind or to a supposed object of this state of mind?"[42] The answer lies in the passage

40. Paul Tillich, *Systematic Theology* (Chicago: University of Chicago Press, 1951), 11–12.
41. Hiriyanna, *Essentials,* 22.
42. Hick, *Philosophy of Religion,* 67.

itself: " 'Unconditional' suggests that it refers to an attitude of concern, 'infinite' suggests that it refers to an object of concern, and 'ultimate' and 'total' could perhaps apply to either."[43]

What results does one obtain when such an operation is carried out on the words *sat, cit,* and *ānanda?* The manner in which M. Hiriyanna analyzed these terms seems to indicate that they belong to the object of the state of mind. But there is another way of interpreting them when they become characteristic of the concerned state of mind:

> 1. Brahman is real and, in essence, is without quality of distinction.
> 2. "Brahman" stands for undifferentiated being, for pure unqualified consciousness. "Brahman" means *nirguṇa* Brahman, qualityless reality.
> 3. Brahman may, *for purposes of orienting the mind towards it* and for pointing out the basic features of one's experience of it, be represented or designated as *saccidānanda*—as the fullness of being (*sat*), awareness (*cit*), and joy of being (*ānanda*). In its status of pure being, though, no attribution can be made with respect to Brahman. It is *neti neti,* not this, not that; it is the negation of everything that is thinkable.[44]

The definition of faith as "the state of being ultimately concerned" was cited from Paul Tillich's *Dynamics of Faith;* his description of this ultimate concern, from his *Systematic Theology.* That description raised the question of whether ultimate concern pertained to the *object* concerned or the *mind* concerned. John Hick explains that Tillich eliminated the distinction between them in *Dynamics of Faith* by "identifying the attitude of ultimate concern with the object of ultimate concern."[45] Tillich's own statements in this connection are quite significant in the context of Advaita Vedānta.

> The ultimate of the act of faith and the ultimate that is meant in the act of faith are one and the same.[46]

43. Ibid.

44. Eliot Deutsch and J.A.B. van Buitenen, *A Source Book of Advaita Vedānta* (Honolulu: The University of Hawaii Press, 1971), 308; emphasis added.

45. Hick, Philosophy of Religion, 67.

46. Tillich, *Dynamics of Faith,* 11.

> . . . the disappearance of the ordinary subject-object scheme in the experience of the ultimate, the unconditional.[47]

> "God" . . . is the name for that which concerns man ultimately. This does not mean that first there is a being called God and then the demand that man should be ultimately concerned about him. It means that whatever concerns a man ultimately becomes god for him, and, conversely, it means that a man can be concerned ultimately only about that which is god for him.[48]

In the end then one is left with a situation in which "one can either define faith in terms of God, as one's concern about the Ultimate, or define God in terms of faith, as that—whatever it may be—about which one is absolutely concerned."[49]

It is quite clear that in Advaita Vedānta faith is to be defined as one's concern about the ultimate and not vice versa. In other words, faith has to be understood substantively, not functionally in the sense that *anything* that functions as an ultimate concern evokes faith. Faith does have a function in Advaita Vedānta but that function is to lead the seeker to the realization of reality. This is true both in a general way in the tradition of *jñānamārga*[50] or the path of gnosis associated with Advaita Vedānta, and as it applies specifically to the system of Śaṅkara wherein, along with *śama* (calmness), *dama* (control), *titikṣā* (indifference to objects), *uparati* (turning away from them), and *samādhi* (concentration), faith also constitutes the propaedeutic for the investigation of Brahman, and is referred to as *śraddhā*.[51] Hiriyanna's comment that *mokṣa* or actual realization "though it may be regarded as the goal of *faith* can hardly be regarded as that of philosophy" applies particularly to the philosophy of Advaita because it is "conceived as realizable in this life, and described as jivan-mukti, or emancipation while yet alive."[52] As distinguished from the position of Advaita Vedānta, however, Hindu thought elsewhere does allow for the twofold movement associated by Tillich with faith. It seems implied in some verses of the Bhagavadgītā[53] and has been

47. Ibid.

48. Tillich, *Systematic Theology,* 1:211.

49. Hick, *Philosophy of Religion,* 68.

50. See Bhagavadgītā 4.36–42; for translation, see Deutsch and van Buitenen, *Source Book,* 40. Note especially the use of the term *śraddhāvān* in verse 4.39.

51. Radhakrishnan, trans., *Brahma Sūtra,* 227.

52. Hiriyanna, *Outlines,* 19.

53. Bhagavadgītā 17.1.

clearly identified on the basis of a historical study of the concept of faith by other scholars.[54]

A few other aspects of Tillich's concept of faith may now be discussed in the light of Advaita Vedānta: (1) the disappearance of the subject-object scheme; (2) the idea that ultimate concern is a "form of the human mind's participation in the ground of its own being";[55] and (3) the contrast between the cosmological and the ontological as types of philosophy of religion—the former reaching out for God "out there" and the other representing God as the ground of our own being.

It is commonplace to assert that in Advaita, in the ultimate realization, the subject-object distinction disappears. As Yājñavalkya explains to his wife Maitreyī in the Bṛhadāraṇyaka Upaniṣad: "but where everything has become just one's own self, by what and whom should one see . . ."[56] However this annihilation of the subject-object distinction has an *ontological* character in Advaita, whereas it has a *psychological* character in Tillich. Similarly, the idea of the ultimate concern being a form of the human mind's participation in the ground of its own being has echoes again of an ontological rather than a psychological kind in Advaita. For Śaṅkara "says that *Brahman* is known for one's own self, *ayam ātmā brahma.* No one thinks that he does not exist. Each one cognises the existence of himself. Yet an enquiry into the nature of *Brahman* is essential since there are conflicting views about its nature. *Brahman* is often confused with the body, the sense-organs, mind or intelligence."[57]

This point highlights further the contrast between cosmological and ontological philosophies of religion as developed by Tillich in at least three ways. First, Advaita Vedānta, as compared to Christianity, seems to be on the whole less interested in cosmology, especially in the details of cosmogony. As Chatterjee and Datta explain it, "Śaṅkara finds it difficult to reconcile the Upaniṣadic statements about creation, taken in the literal sense, with those denying the world of multiplicity. Considered in the light of the general trend and spirit running throughout the Upaniṣads, the stories of creation seem, to him, to be out of joint."[58] This may be contrasted with the importance ac-

54. K. L. Seshagiri Rao, *The Concept of Śraddhā* (Patiala: Roy Publishers, 1971), 188–89.

55. Hick, *Philosophy of Religion,* 67.

56. S. Radhakrishnan, ed., *The Principal Upaniṣads* (London: George Allen & Unwin, 1953), 286.

57. Radhakrishnan, trans., *Brahma Sūtra,* 231.

58. Satischandra Chatterjee and Dhirendramohan Datta, *An Introduction to Indian Philosophy* (1950; reprint, Calcutta: University of Calcutta, 1968), 375.

corded to God as the creator in Christianity. Second, to quote Chatterjee and Datta further, the following statement about Śaṅkara confirms that he shares the inclination of Tillich: "Atheism believes only in the world and not at all in God, and ordinary theism believes in both, the world and God, Śaṅkara believes only in God. For him God is the only Reality."[59] There is need for caution here, however. It is possible that for Tillich Śaṅkara flies too high, for if we look at theistic belief in terms of levels "at the first level, the world alone is real; at the second, both the world and God; at the last, only God. The first is atheism. The second represents theism as we find in Rāmānuja and others. The last is the Absolute monism of Śaṅkara."[60] Perhaps Tillich tilts the coexistence of world and God more toward God, but Śaṅkara is prepared to move to another level. This brings us to the third point—the distinction in Advaita Vedānta between the definition of Brahman as it is in itself and as related to the universe. "Description of God as the Creator of the world is true only from the practical point of view, so long as the world-appearance is regarded as real. Creatorship of the world is not God's essence (svarūpa-lakṣaṇa); it is the description of what is merely accidental (taṭastha-lakṣaṇa) and does not touch His essence."[61] As this distinction seems to anticipate Tillich's contrast between an ontological and a cosmological philosophy of religion, in Chatterjee and Datta's words, "Let us try to understand with the help of an ordinary example the distinction that Śaṅkara wants to make here. A shepherd appears on the stage in the *role* of a king, wages war, conquers a country and rules it. Now, the description of the actor as a shepherd gives what he is from the *real point of view*. It is an *essential* description of him (svarūpa-lakṣaṇa). But the description of him as a king, ruler, and conqueror is applied to him only from the *point of view* of the stage and his *role* there; it is merely a description of what is accidental to the person (taṭastha-lakṣaṇa) and does not touch his essence."[62]

Again Tillich may not wish to go as far as Śaṅkara but they seem at least headed in a similar direction.

59. Ibid., 401.
60. Ibid., 399.
61. Ibid., 394.
62. Ibid.

7

Religious Language

The ultimate reality in Advaita Vedānta is described as Brahman—but Brahman cannot be described. Here, then, in a nutshell, lies the problem of language in relation to Brahman in Advaita Vedānta. To examine how Advaita Vedānta tries to solve this problem, one must begin by analyzing why Brahman can't be described.

To be describable Brahman would have to possess distinguishing attributes. Brahman, however, in Advaita Vedānta is said to be devoid of all distinctions, both external and internal. It is on account of this absence of distinctions that it is called *nirguṇa*—a term best rendered by such words as "indeterminate," "characterless," "featureless," and so on. Distinctions are said to be of three kinds in Advaita: (1) between one class of things and another (*vijātīya*), (2) between members of the same class (*sajātīya*), and (3) within a member of a class (*svagata*). Trees are distinct from cars—an instance of *vijātīya.* One tree is distinct from another—an instance of *sajātīya.* The various parts of a single tree such as the branches, leaves, and trunk are distinct from one another—which is an instance of *svagata.* Brahman is free from distinctions of all kinds.[1]

This linguistic inaccessibility of Brahman is illustrated by an anecdote cited by Śaṅkara. Radhakrishnan reports that "Śaṁkara in his commentary on the *Brahma Sūtra* refers to an Upaniṣad text which is not to be found in any of the extant Upaniṣads. Bāhva, asked by Bāṣkali to expound the nature of *Brahman,* kept silent. He prayed, 'Teach me, sir.' The teacher was silent,

1. R. Balasubramanian, *Advaita Vedānta* (Madras: University of Madras, 1976), 117.

and when addressed a second and a third time he said: 'I am teaching but you do not follow. The self is silence.' "[2]

It seems that if the matter is examined closely, there are at least four interconnected reasons why Brahman cannot be described. First, Brahman cannot be described because it has no attributes by which it may be described. Furthermore, every description imposes a limitation, for the purpose of predication is to set what is predicated apart from everything else. Thus predication implies delimitation and therefore limitation. In fact one can go a step further and assert with Spinoza that "every determination is negation." This insight led Spinoza to consider God indeterminate, and in Advaita Vedānta Brahman is described as *nirguṇa* or indeterminate.[3]

Second, Brahman cannot be described because it is the sole reality. Any description of the whole suggests a point outside the whole, which is impossible. If everything that is described is Brahman, how is Brahman to be described? Certainly not in terms of the forms it might assume, no more than gold can be described by the shapes it might assume, for it consists not of the shapes but their substance[4] and cannot be described in terms of these shapes for "gold is not an ornament but the ornament is nothing but gold."

Third, Brahman cannot be described because it is different from everything else. How does one describe what is unique?

Fourth, Brahman cannot be described because it is identical with Ātman. Can something so subtle be described? As Vācaspati explains, "No body can point to the concrete difference between sugarcane, honey and jagary as 'this,' because the difference is verbally inexpressible. If this is the case when objective things are concerned, how much more difficult it is to find words which can indicate"[5] the Ātman which is identical with Brahman.

Apart from these four metaphysical arguments, Śaṅkara produces a *linguistic* argument to establish why Brahman cannot be described by words. It is important to familiarize oneself with four terms in order to follow Śaṅkara's argument. These are (1) *jāti* (genus), (2) *guṇa* (quality), (3) *kriyā* (act), and (4) *sambandha* (relation). It is through these categories that words as signs relate to their referents.[6]

2. S. Radhakrishnan, ed., *The Principal Upaniṣads* (London: George Allen & Unwin, 1953), 67.

3. M. Hiriyanna, *Outlines of Indian Philosophy* (London: George Allen & Unwin, 1964), 373.

4. Balasubramanian, *Advaita Vedānta,* 29; K. Satchidananda Murty, *Revelation and Reason in Advaita Vedānta* (1959; reprint, New Delhi: Motilal Banarsidass, 1974), 56–57.

5. Murty, *Revelation and Reason,* 56.

6. Ibid., 58.

Śaṅkara proceeds to demonstrate that Brahman cannot be associated with any of these categories and therefore cannot be described with words. It has no class characteristic or *jāti;* it possesses no characteristic quality or *guṇa* such as size or color; it cannot be connected with action (*kriyā*) on account of its immutability; and it cannot be spoken of as in relation (*sambandha*) to anything as there is no other object outside it, because "it is the sole reality without a second. Since it is never the object but is always the self, it is but proper that no words can signify it; and the Upaniṣads also confirm this."[7]

If Brahman cannot be described, then the question naturally arises, What empirical relevance, if any, does the word "Brahman" possess? K. Satchidananda Murty writes:

> In view of the importance attained by linguistic philosophy at present, the following problem becomes important. It is now recognised that there are many levels of language; each level giving its own insight into the "situation." At the same time all language tries to clarify what Quine has called the "irreducible posit." Language at other levels refers to what is "objective," i.e. what can be seen, heard, touched, tasted and smelt. For instance, while common-sense language has direct empirical relevance, scientific language has indirect relevance. But what empirical relevance has Brahman-language? How are we to understand the word "Brahman" occurring in the Upaniṣads? And why would a man *desire* at all to know Brahman, which he has not come across in experience?[8]

The answer to the problem is existential. One may not desire to know Brahman but one desires bliss and constantly fails to attain it in the course of normal living. "In the Taittirīya Upaniṣad the pupil approaches the father and asks him to explain to him the nature of Brahman" and after successive attempts the "son finally arrives at the truth that spiritual freedom or delight (*ānanda*), the ecstasy of fulfilled experience is the ultimate principle. Here the search ends."[9] S. Radhakrishnan remarks: "There are those who affirm that *ānanda* is the nearest approximation to Absolute Reality, but is not itself the Absolute Reality. For it is a logical representation."[10] It is clear, however, that in the connection of bliss with Brahman one finds the bridge that

7. Ibid., 58–59.
8. Ibid., 53.
9. Radhakrishnan, ed., *Principal Upaniṣads*, 56, 57.
10. Ibid., 57.

imparts to the transcendental an empirical relevance. If one knows that Brahman is associated with the experience of bliss, it seems reasonable to inquire into it. Thus even if "Brahman is not known in any other way, except through the Veda"[11] there is still a good reason to desire to know Brahman. And if "Brahman is known from Vedānta (Upaniṣadic) sentences, he who studies them will know it" but "although he may have no further desire to know it,"[12] he may have the desire to *realize* it.

The paradox is that *although Brahman is not empirically knowable, it is not empirically unknown,* both at the objective and the subjective level. That the objective world is a manifestation of Brahman is the vital clue here. According to Advaita we know Brahman itself in all cognition in the world at large, but we do not come to know it in its purity, for empirical knowledge involves the triad of the knower, the (means of) knowledge, and the known (object). And whereas Brahman is pure consciousness, in ordinary perception, "the consciousness limited by the mind is the consciousness associated with the subject or knower, that limited by the mental state is the consciousness associated with the means of knowledge; and that limited by [say] a jar is consciousness associated with the object."[13]

A twofold rather than a threefold analysis of empirical knowledge points in the same direction. In this case a distinction is drawn between *sāmānya* knowledge and *viśeṣa* knowledge. *Sāmānya* knowledge of a pot, for instance, would consist of a knowledge of its form and structure. *Viśeṣa* or special knowledge about it would consist of knowing its essence. As P. M. Pattanayak puts it, "We must know what it is in itself—a mass of clay (*mṛtpiṇḍa*). This second type of knowledge (*viśeṣa jñāna*) is different from the first. Extending this inadequate analogy to Brahman also, it may be said that while we have underlying all knowledge the notion of a reality abiding amidst all change, we do not know its exact nature."[14]

Similarly, the identity of Brahman and Ātman means that at the subjective level as well one is not totally out of touch with Brahman. Hiriyanna explains: " 'A man,' it is said, 'may doubt of many things, of anything *else;* but he can never doubt of his own being,' for that very act of doubting would affirm its existence. It is thus eventually through something in ourselves

11. Murty, *Revelation and Reason,* 53.

12. Ibid.

13. P. M. Pattanayak, *A Graphic Representation of Vedanta Sara* (New Delhi: Harman Publishing House, 1987), 24.

14. Murty, *Revelation and Reason,* 7; emphasis added. Murty does not state why the analogy is inadequate.

that, according to Śaṁkara, we are able to judge of reality and unreality. Such a view does not mean that the self is known to us completely. Far from it. But, at the same time, it does not remain wholly unknown, being our own self."[15] (Recall Saint Augustine's "You would not be searching for me if you had not already found me.")

To say that Brahman at the objective or subjective level is not knowable means that it is not knowable empirically in its transcendental dimension. Hiriyanna consistently emphasizes this point. Thus speaking of *nirguṇa* Brahman he writes: "In itself, the absolute transcends being *as well as knowledge, as familiar to us.*"[16] Of the Ātman he says that the idea "is that it is unknowable in the *ordinary sense* of the term. One Upaniṣad brings out the uniqueness of the self by stating paradoxically that it is known only to those who do not *know* it, meaning that, though intuitively realizable, it cannot be made an *object* of thought."[17]

If then, the inquiry into Brahman is both desirable and possible, the question arises: "As no inquiry into its nature can be instituted without some description," and it eludes description, what linguistic resources does one possess to bring it within the field of inquiry?[18]

Advaita Vedānta adopts the view that although neither Brahman nor Ātman can be approached through description, both can be approached in other ways.

Śaṅkara's Approach

Śaṅkara employs at least three techniques to convey a sense of the nature of Brahman: (1) attribution and denial, (2) indication, and (3) negation.

Attribution and Denial

Śaṅkara uses this technique in his commentary on the Bhagavadgītā 13.12, wherein Brahman is described as other than *sat* (being) and *asat* (nonbeing). Śaṅkara points out that as Brahman cannot be described as 'being' in the

15. M. Hiriyanna, *The Essentials of Indian Philosophy* (London: George Allen & Unwin, 1948), 162–63.
16. Ibid., 168; emphasis added.
17. Ibid., 21; emphasis added.
18. This section relies heavily on Murty, *Revelation and Reason*, chap. 4.

usual sense, it might lead some to conclude that "it is not." To correct this impression the next verse describes Brahman as possessing many hands and feet, and so on. Lest this description leave the impression that Brahman is empirically knowable, the next verse describes it as devoid of qualities (*nirguṇa*). Śaṅkara explains that though the attribution of hands and feet to Brahman is illusory,

> still it is spoken of—in the words that "It has hands and feet everywhere"—as though it were an attribute of the Knowable, only with a view to indicate its existence. Accordingly there is the saying of the *sampradayavids*—of those who know the right traditional method of teaching—which runs as follows: "*That which is devoid of all duality is described by adhyāropa and apavāda,* i.e., by superimposition and negation, by attribution and denial. Hands, feet and the like, constituting the limbs of all bodies in all places, derive their activity from the Energy inherent in the Knowable, and as such they are mere marks of Its existence and are spoken of as belonging to It only by a figure of speech—All the rest should be similarly interpreted. It (Brahman) exists in the world, in the whole animal creation, pervading all.
>
> *Brahman is unconditioned.*
>
> The purpose of this verse[19] is to prevent the supposition that the Knowable is (*really*) possessed of the upādhis—the sense-organs such as hands, feet, and the like—which are merely superimposed (upon It).[20]

This approach consists of first attributing qualities to Brahman and subsequently denying them in such a way to avoid misapprehension.

Indication

Śaṅkara uses indication in his commentary on Taittirīya Upaniṣad 2.1, which contains the well-known description of Brahman as reality, knowledge, and infinity. The question is, Does this constitute a description of Brahman?

19. This refers to the succeeding verse.

20. Alladi Mahadeva Sastry, trans., *The Bhagavad Gita with the Commentary of Sri Sankaracharya* (1979; reprint, Madras: Samata Books, 1985), 348–49.

In normal discourse, yes, this would constitute a description. In the expressions "blue lotus" and "red rose," blue describes the lotus and red describes the rose. Lotus and rose are objects, and "blue" and "red" are modifiers that describe them.

But is such a procedure admissible in the case of Brahman, which is *not* an object?[21] Brahman is spoken of as *nirguṇa* or "featureless,"[22] by which is meant that Brahman "transcends the distinction between substance and attribute."[23] Śaṅkara argues that in this case modifiers applied to Brahman are not meant to qualify it, but that "each of them is related to the word Brahman independently of the other" and that each qualifies the other. Thus the passage of the Taittirīya Upaniṣad, that Brahman is reality, knowledge, and infinity, means "Reality is Brahman" and "Knowledge is Brahman" and, finally, "Infinity is Brahman." The terms "Reality" (*satyam*), "Knowledge" (*jñānam*), and "Infinity" (*anantam*) are meant to be individually and progressively applied to Brahman. It is first said, then, that Reality is Brahman. This raises the question, Is reality material? This question is clarified by saying, Knowledge is Brahman. As knowledge is immaterial, the immateriality of Brahman is established. But knowledge as we know it is limited. Is the knowledge of Brahman limited? This point is clarified by saying, Infinity is Brahman.

Śaṅkara's position may be briefly summarized here prior to its further elaboration. Modifiers—adjectives and (sometimes) nouns—are used to describe things and their characteristics. If, as Śaṅkara insists, Brahman is not a thing in the popular sense of the word and, in fact, if anything, is a no-thing and further is devoid of any characteristics, then what possibly could be the significance of any modifiers applied to it, for taken literally they are meaningless. But, if applied to Brahman individually and progressively, they define rather than describe. However, in this general process of definition, each step, denoted by each successive word, has to be undertaken with great care. And such a careful analysis shows that whereas the first two terms define Brahman, the third, "infinity," serves to extend the definition by qualifying the previous two. Thus "reality" and "knowledge" are used in their own senses, but "infinity" negates "finitude" with respect to reality and knowledge.[24]

21. Murty, *Revelation and Reason,* 56.
22. Hiriyanna, *Essentials,* 162.
23. Ibid., 163.
24. Murty, *Revelation and Reason,* 62.

The objection could be raised at this point that Brahman is indivisible, but is being described in terms of distinct attributes. This, however, is not really the case, for "reality," "knowledge," and "infinity" are actually applied to Brahman simultaneously. The appearance of a logical series—Brahman is reality, reality can be material or immaterial; Brahman is knowledge, knowledge is immaterial, hence an immaterial reality, and so on—is an artifact of language. This point is clearly made by a later scholar, Vidyāraṇya, who compares the above statement of the Upaniṣad to a sentence like "The most shining (thing) is the moon" given in response to someone asking, "What is moon?" "The two words—'shining' and 'most'—taken by themselves have different meanings but this does not mean that, in the present case they imply two different objects to which they apply, for it is clear from the context that they apply to only one object, the moon. However, it should be noted that both the words are required, 'shining' to exclude what is in the sky but does not shine and 'most' to exclude those that shine but not as brightly."[25]

Another possible objection could be that "eternal infinite knowledge," an implication of the statement of the Taittirīya Upaniṣad, is difficult to conceive of and may even be logically improper. To this Śaṅkara's response would be that though the term severely strains our everyday concept of knowledge it is precisely this cognitive dissonance which enables the mind to grasp the logical uniqueness and mystery of Brahman. The point becomes clearer when such statements are considered as analogous to the koan of Zen Buddhism. Although the koan aims at imparting an existential rather than linguistic insight by creating an intellectual impasse, it is difficult to imagine Śaṅkara not being sympathetic to the technique. In fact it can be argued that some of the *mahāvākya*s or the grand statements of the Upaniṣads seen to function in a similar way. Thus when it is said that "that thou art" or "I am Brahman" the two elements in the statement are so "mutually incompatible that the mind abandons the explicit sense of the terms, and travels beyond those attributes to that in which they are grounded (*nirviśeṣa vastu*) as constituting the true import of the proposition."[26] A similar process is at work here, whereby "the uniqueness of Brahman from all 'objects' and all empirical 'subjects' is effectively shown."[27]

25. Ibid., 66.
26. Hiriyanna, *Outlines*, 374.
27. Ibid., 64.

Negation

The third method employed by Śaṅkara to convey a sense of the nature of Brahman is the negation of every empirical attribute in relation to it, as in the famous Upaniṣadic utterance *neti neti* ("not this, not this"), quoted here in the version found in Bṛhadāraṇyaka 2.3.6.

> Now therefore there is the teaching not this, not this, not this for there is nothing higher than this.[28]

Śaṅkara's comment on Bṛhadāraṇyaka 2.3.6 is quite significant. Careful analysis of his use of negation to describe Brahman reveals that the process of negation plays both a linguistic and a soteriological role for him. The linguistic role of negation, already mentioned, consists in making clear how Brahman cannot be described by speech, for words were said to be capable of conveying meaning pertaining only to the categories of *jāti* (class), *guṇa* (quality), *kriyā* (action), and *sambandha* (relation), and Brahman cannot be brought in relation to these.[29] In this context, according to Murty, Śaṅkara considers the *via negativa* to be the best way of talking about Brahman because its logic does not involve superimposition, that is, first imposing certain features and then denying them. However, it should be obvious from a consideration of the *mahāvākyas* of the Upaniṣads that in the end negations also *negate,* that is, in the soteriological role, negation is applied to that which binds the aspirant. The technique of negation or the "making of a definite statement (*ādeśa*) about [Brahman] to say: 'not this, not this' " assumes a special potency for "this [*ādeśa*] serves to eliminate all specifications and all differences due to limiting adjuncts." Then, when "everything else is negated and when the desire to know other things is quelled," the aspirant realizes Brahman.[30]

Religious Language and the Nature of Ātman

In Advaita the question of language extends not just to Brahman but to Ātman as well.

28. Radhakrishnan, ed., *Principal Upaniṣads,* 194.
29. P. Sankaranarayanan, *What Is Advaita?* (Bombay: Bharatiya Vidya Bhavan, 1970), 55.
30. Murty, *Revelation and Reason,* 66, 63.

In order to understand this, first of all, the nature of the relationship of identity between the two must be correctly represented. Troy Wilson Organ explains the significance of the claim that Ātman *is* Brahman with great clarity; because I despair of equaling it, I quote it here in extenso:

> The question to be asked first is about the meaning of the connective "is." The word "is" has at least five logically discernible meanings: (1) predication, e.g., "This apple is green"; (2) class inclusion, e.g., "Fido is a dog"; (3) class membership, e.g., "Brown pelicans are vanishing"; (4) equality, e.g., "Two and two is four"; (5) identity, e.g., "IV is [equivalent to] 4." *Ātman* is Brahman seems to be a form of identity or equivalence. There are many classes of identity: (1) absolute physical identity, e.g., "A is identical with A"; (2) relative physical identity, e.g., identical twins; (3) same entity at various stages of development, e.g., Joe Doakes as boy and J.D. as man; (4) same species, e.g., Harry Truman as man and Herbert Hoover as man; (5) same being in different contexts, e.g., Jane as mother and Jane as wife; (6) whole and part, e.g., a cup of water dipped from the Atlantic Ocean and the Atlantic Ocean; (7) appearance and reality, e.g., a photograph and the person of whom it is a photograph; (8) the same object considered from different perspectives, e.g., the duck-rabbit example of perception. Probably the last subclass of identity is the identity of *Ātman* and Brahman: *Ātman* is Totality viewed internally; Brahman is Totality viewed externally.[31]

This helps explain what is meant by identity. It is equally important to realize what is *not* meant by identity. First, when it is claimed in Advaita Vedānta that Ātman is Brahman, it is not claimed that Ātman *becomes* Brahman, as, for example, in a moment of realization. If anything, the realization consists of the fact that Ātman is Brahman, was Brahman, and will ever be Brahman. The point may be explained with the help of the parable "Like the King's Son," in which "a prince, brought up as a hunter from infancy, discover[s] afterward that he is of royal blood. It involves no becoming, for he has always been a prince and all that he has to do is to feel or realize that he is one."[32] The metaphysical moral of the whole story is that there was never a time when the mountaineer was not the Prince. He did not become

31. Troy Wilson Organ, *Hinduism: Its Historical Development* (Woodbury, N.Y.: Barron's Educational Series, 1974), 114.

32. Hiriyanna, *Outlines*, 378.

a Prince when told he was one. He already was. He only recognized as a fact something already true.

Second, when it is claimed in Advaita Vedānta that Ātman is Brahman it is *not* meant that Ātman merges into Brahman. An example from astronomy will be helpful here. For a long time astronomers identified two distinct stars—a "morning star" and an "evening star," till it was discovered that both were Venus. Did it then mean that the morning star merged into the evening star, or the evening star merged into the morning star? As both were already and always Venus, nothing of this sort can be said to have happened.

Third, it is sometimes suggested that " 'Ātman is Brahman' is not a metaphysical statement but a soteriological statement."[33] Consider the following interpretation offered by Rudolf Otto: "The word 'is' in the mystical formula of identification [*Ātman* is Brahman] has a significance which it does not contain in logic. It is no copula as in the sentence: *S* is *P;* it is no sign of equality in a reversible equation. It is not the 'is' of a normal assertion of identity." In order to suggest what the statement is attempting to express, Otto adds, "For instance one might say instead of 'I am Brahman,' 'I am "existed" by Brahman' or 'essenced' by Brahman, or 'Brahman exists me.' "[34] The suggestion is intriguing but not acceptable as such within Advaita Vedānta.

Fourth, Ātman is Brahman does not mean that Ātman is a portion of Brahman. The *jīva*s or the embodied Ātmans may in an extended sense be said to be comprised in Brahman as parts of the universe of which it is the substratum but that is as much as one can say, for the truth of the matter is that "just as a pure transparent white crystal is wrongly imagined to be red on account of a red flower placed near it, or just as the colourless sky is wrongly imagined to be sullied with dirt by the ignorant, or just as a rope is wrongly taken to be a snake in the twilight, or just as a shell is mistaken for silver, similarly the non-dual Ātman or Brahman is wrongly imagined to be the empirical self."[35] Śaṅkara's comment on Brahmasūtra 2.3.50 must be employed here to point out that "the individual soul is not directly the highest Ātman . . . nor is it different from Ātman." It is not the former because it is subject to limiting adjuncts listed above metaphorically but it is not different for it is also bereft of the limiting adjuncts. Hence also the

33. Organ, *Hinduism,* 114.
34. Ibid., 114–15.
35. Chandradhar Sharma, *A Critical Survey of Indian Philosophy* (London: Rider, 1960), 282–83.

empirical selves are comprised in Brahman, but the exact nature of their relationship is a matter of debate.

What, then, is the problem in using language in relation to Ātman?

The problem in using language to describe Ātman is that Ātman is the "true subject which knows but can never be known—'the unseen seer, the unheard hearer and the unthought thinker.' "[36] In fact the existence of the Ātman's presence, called *sākṣī* (witness), in the empirical situation is "deduced from the principle that what knows must be other than what is known."[37] In a word, it is the nonrelational character of Ātman that places it beyond the pale of language. This is said to be the philosophical significance of Bṛhadāraṇyaka 4.4.22: "Ātman is unattained, for it does not attach itself."[38] If the knower must be different from the known, the moment I think of myself as the knower, "It becomes an object of thought and the knower recedes further ad infinitum. Thus the Ātman cannot be made the object of language. According to the Bṛhadāraṇyaka Upaniṣad, once the pure self is experienced duality disappears and if duality has disappeared: 'Then by what and to whom should one speak?' "[39]

There are five ways, however, in which something can be conveyed about the Ātman. Three of these have been elaborated by Śaṅkara's disciple Sureśvara.

Ātman Known as Unknowable

How does one know Ātman? One knows Ātman but one does not know how. Ātman "cannot be denied; for it is the self of even the one who denies. We know *that* the self *is;* we do not know *what* it is."[40] Śaṅkara says: "Everyone believes that he exists, and never thinks 'I am not.' "[41] Suppose we question or doubt this statement of Śaṅkara—thus one can doubt but one cannot doubt that one is doubting. In other words, the self is given in all situations and this fact enables it to be indicated. Just as one cannot hold fire *as such* in one's hands, but can hold a red-hot ball *of* fire; one cannot describe the self

36. Hiriyanna, *Essentials,* 20–21.

37. Ibid., 166.

38. See William M. Indich, *Consciousness in Advaita Vedānta* (Delhi: Motilal Banarsidass, 1980), 106–7; see also 37.

39. Radhakrishnan, ed., *Principal Upaniṣads,* p. 201.

40. T.M.P. Mahadevan, *Outlines of Hinduism* (1960; reprint, Bombay: Chetana, 1971), 146.

41. In his commentary on Brahmasutra 1.1.1; cited in Satischandra Chatterjee and Dhirendramohan Datta, *An Introduction to Indian Philosophy* (1950; reprint, Calcutta: University of Calcutta, 1968), 146.

but one can see it implicit in the words "I" or "I-consciousness" we use. "These words directly signify the *ahaṃkāra* (the sense of 'I'-ness or 'I'-awareness, which is not really 'I'; for 'I', the eternal subject, can never become an object of an awareness); but since *ahaṃkāra* is very much *contiguous* to Ātman and is confused with Ātman, words denoting it inadequately imply Ātman; just as when we say 'the red-hot iron-piece burns,' it is not exactly the iron-piece that is capable of burning, but the fire that is in association with it."[42]

Ātman Known Somehow

It was pointed out earlier that the Ātman cannot be linguistically articulated. Now there are forms of linguistic discourse in which something is indicated without it having any connection between the sign and the signified. Similarly, the Ātman, without being linguistically articulated, can be implied. As Murty puts it: "In the sentence, 'The hamlet is on the Ganges,' what is meant to be conveyed is that there is a hamlet on the *bank* of the Ganges; and this is conveyed by implication, though the word Ganges does not directly signify (and so is not related to) the bank, but the river."[43] In ordinary parlance we say, "The house is on the road" when what we imply is that the house is *on the side* of the road. Despite this, *somehow* we grasp the sense.

Ātman Known Anyhow

Sureśvara gives the example of a sleeping person who is awakened by his name being called. Now if a person is asleep, he can't hear. If a person is awake, he can hear the words but as he is already awake there is no need to awaken him. How, then, does calling the name of a person awaken him? It seems logically problematical but *anyhow* he wakes up in real life. Similarly, Sureśvara argues that "though there is no connection of Ātman with the express sense of 'I' or 'Thou,' and though there is no knowledge of any such connection, Ātman is understood as the meaning of 'I' and this is done by implication."[44]

It is clear from the above examples, however, that the Ātman, on account

42. Murty, *Revelation and Reason,* 66–67.
43. Ibid., 67.
44. Ibid.

of it being the "witness" and therefore "the implication of empirical thought," can by implication be indicated in all of these linguistic modalities. The three examples given by Sureśvara pertain to class (bank), quality (burning), and action (awakening)—and now a fourth example may be cited which relates to possession.

Ātman Known as Knower

In the context of empirical knowledge the Ātman is known as the knower when it becomes the subject of knowledge. When the world reality is understood in its broadest sense and it is claimed that according to "Advaita there is no Reality outside what either knows or is known," then Ātman is the one who knows, as the empirical self, the complex of the *sākṣī* and the *antaḥkaraṇa,* that is, the spirit connected with the mind. This represents the empirical self. The consciousness of the self is "a constant feature of all experience. It is this sense of self that explains how one person is able to distinguish his experience from that of others." However, since the *jīva* = *śākṣī* + *antaḥkaraṇa,* that is to say, the empirical self is a complex of spirit and matter, the *jīva* and *sākṣī* are not identical. Ātman as *sākṣī* "is the pure element of awareness in all knowing."[45] This leads us to the next topic.

Ātman as Know-How

The clue to the situation is provided by the distinction between the subject-object dichotomy of Western philosophy and the *dṛk-dṛśya* distinction of Advaita. M. Hiriyanna explains that "the cognitive situation is usually taken to involve a subject and an object. The Advaitin substitutes for them *dṛk* and *dṛśya,* the former meaning the self or what reveals and the latter, what is revealed. The reason for this substitution is that the other division is not logically quite satisfactory. The subject includes not only *dṛk* but also *dṛśya.* This is clear from statements like 'I know myself.' "[46]

How does one know the Ātman? One knows it from the fact that one does not know it. And how does the Ātman know? It knows through the mind or the internal organ. And all this know-how about the Ātman is deduced in Advaita from the simple fact of language—the fact that I can say: "I know myself"![47]

45. Hiriyanna, *Outlines,* 343, 347.
46. M. Hiriyanna, *Indian Philosophical Studies* (Mysore: Kavyalaya Publishers, 1957), 135.
47. Hiriyanna, *Outlines,* 343, 354.

8

Advaita Vedānta and Religious Language

Religious language is peculiar. The religious context is so taxing that words used in it undergo a semantic shift. As Hick puts it: "For example, when it is said that 'Great is the Lord,' it is not meant that God occupies a large volume of space; when it is said that 'The Lord spoke unto Joshua' it is not meant that God had a physical body with speech organs which set in motion sound waves which impinged upon Joshua's eardrums."[1] In fact both Christianity and Advaita Vedānta firmly maintain that the words used in religious discourse possess the same denotations as they do in normal usage. It is their connotations which change, as in these examples, which illustrate "a long shift of meaning between the familiar secular use of these words and their theological employment." For instance, a famous verse from the ṚgVeda describes the cosmic person as possessing a thousand heads and a thousand eyes. Taken too literally the point would arise whether if the cosmic being had a thousand heads should it not possess two thousand eyes, unless each head happened to be one-eyed. The semantic transition from secular to sacred usage could be so peculiar that the semantic shift involved might well invite the charge of being absurd. Thus Arthur C. Danto is led to remark:

> Suppose I am told of a new theological discovery, namely that Brahma wears a hat. And then I am told that it is a divine hat and worn infinitely, since Brahma has neither head nor shape. In what sense then is a hat being worn? Why use these words? I am told that

1. John H. Hick, *The Philosophy of Religion,* 3d ed. (Englewood Cliffs, N.J.: Prentice Hall, 1983), 76–77.

> God exists but in a "different sense" of exists. Then if he doesn't exist (in the plain sense) why use that word? Or that God loves us—but in a wholly special sense of love. Or God is a circle whose centre is everywhere and circumference nowhere. But this is then to have neither a centre nor a circumference, and hence not to be a circle. One half of the description cancels out the other half. And what is left over but just noise?[2]

Advaitins such as Śaṅkara are fully aware that religious language uses the "ordinary words of day-to-day discourse in an extraordinary way," often culminating in paradoxical statements. Thus Śaṅkara remarks:

> The scriptural passages which refer to Brahman are of a double character; some indicate that Brahman is affected by difference, so, e.g. 'He to whom belong all works, all desires, all sweet odours and tastes' [Chāndogya Upaniṣad 3.14.2]; others, that it is without difference, so, e.g. 'It is neither coarse nor fine, neither short nor long,' &c. [Bṛhadāraṇyaka Upaniṣad 3.8.8]. Have we, on the ground of these passages, to assume that Brahman has a double nature, or either nature, and, if either, that it is affected with difference, or without difference? This is the point to be discussed.[3]

Advaitins are also aware of the problem, namely, that "in all those cases in which a word occurs both in secular and in theological contexts, its secular meaning is primary."[4] Thus Śaṅkara remarks in the course of his commentary on Bṛhadāraṇyaka Upaniṣad 2.1.20: "Scripture does not speak about an unknown thing without having recourse to conventional words and their meanings."[5] But this situation creates a complication because adjectives such as "nice," "good," "honest," and "virtuous" or verbs such as "gives,"

2. Cited in John A. Grimes, "Advaita Vedānta and the Problem of Religious Language" (Ph.D. diss., University of Madras, 1984), 6.

3. Eliot Deutsch and J.A.B. van Buitenen, *A Source Book of Advaita Vedānta* (Honolulu: The University of Hawaii Press, 1971), 196–97.

4. Hick, *Philosophy of Religion,* 77.

5. Quoted in Grimes, "Advaita Vedānta," 269 n. 10. John H. Hick adds in the context of the previous citation that the "secular meaning is primary in the sense that it developed first and had accordingly determined the definition of the word" (*Philosophy of Religion,* 77). In view of the doctrine of the eternality of words *this explanation* of the primacy of the secular meaning may not be acceptable to Śaṅkara. See Deutsch and van Buitenen, *Source Book,* 165. Also see K. Satchidananda Murty, *Revelation and Reason in Advaita Vedānta* (1959; reprint, New Delhi: Motilal Banarsidass, 1974), 15–21.

"forgives," and so on, which make apparent sense when applied to human beings become problematical when applied to, say, God. To take only two examples, when God is called good "it is not meant that there are moral values independent of divine nature, in relation to which God may be judged as good; nor does it mean (as it commonly does of human beings) that God is subject to temptations but succeeds in overcoming them." Then what does it mean? The word "love" used so often in relation to God poses a similar problem. Normally the sentiment of love is shared by human beings who possess a body and express the sentiment of love toward each other in palpable ways. However, God is regarded as an entity "without body, parts or passion." One might still get over part of the difficulty that a person could love in the abstract, as in "loving" poetry or music or an ethical cause. This, however, only solves part of the problem, for God is supposed to love us too who are human beings. The concept of "disembodied love" may be salvaged so long as one pole is disembodied but if God loves our soul and both poles become "disembodied," what could that mean?[6]

The Nature of Religious Language

Efforts have been made by scholars to explain the peculiarity of religious language. The doctrines that have evolved in this field of inquiry may be classified as (1) cognitive, (2) noncognitive, or (3) quasi-cognitive. The cognitive view of religious language holds that the statements made thereby are "factual, formal and verifiable." The noncognitive view of religious language holds that the statements made hereby are "non-factual, pictorial, imaginative, emotive and non-verifiable." Very briefly, "the cognitive approach demands factual meaningfulness and verifiability (or at least probability) while a non-cognitive approach is concerned with a particular function or use of statement. And in-between these two options lies the semi-cognitive approach trying to find a happy medium."[7]

We shall commence our investigation with the "happy medium," as it constitutes "one of the oldest approaches to the problem of religious language."[8] This approach is particularly concerned with "the special sense

6. Hick, *Philosophy of Religion*, 76–77.
7. Grimes, "Advaita Vedānta," 10.
8. Ibid.

that descriptive terms bear when they are applied to God."[9] We can then move on to examine "the basic function of religious language"[10]—that is, whether it is "description" or "prescription."[11]

The Quasi-Cognitive Theory of Religious Language: Thomas Aquinas's Doctrine of Analogy

Aquinas developed the doctrine of analogy to convey "the special sense that descriptive terms bear when they are applied to God." Hick summarizes the doctrine of analogy as follows:

> [Aquinas] teaches that when a word such as "good" is applied both to a created being and to God, it is not being used *univocally* (that is, with exactly the same meaning) in the two cases. God is not good in identically the sense in which human beings may be good. Nor, on the other hand, do we apply the epithet "good" to God and man *equivocally* (that is, with completely different and unrelated meanings), as when the word "bat" is used to refer both to the flying animal and to the instrument used in baseball. There is a definite connection between divine and human goodness, reflecting the fact that God has created mankind. According to Aquinas, then, "good" is applied to creator and creature neither univocally nor equivocally but *analogically.*[12]

This doctrine can be developed downward and upward. It may be said to have been developed downward when the analogy is developed from man to dog, for instance. Dogs are known for their faithfulness. One cynic actually said, "The more I see men the more I love dogs." Despite our cynic's loss of faith let us assume that human beings also display the virtue of faithfulness. To the extent that the quality of loyalty displayed both by dogs and human beings is comparable, the word "faithful" may be used in relation to both. In what way, however, can this use be accurately described? It is clear that we

9. Hick, *Philosophy of Religion,* 76.
10. Ibid.
11. Grimes, "Advaita Vedānta," 9.
12. Hick, *Philosophy of Religion,* 77.

are not using the word "faithful" in entirely different senses, for otherwise we wouldn't be using the same word in the two contexts. In other words our use of the word "faithful" is not *equivocal.* On the other hand, it would also be difficult to argue, given the difference between dogs and human beings, that we are using the word "faithful" in exactly the same sense in the two contexts, that is to say, to convey exactly the same sense. So, our use of the word is not *univocal* either. As Hick puts it,

> We are using it analogically, to indicate that at the level of the dog's consciousness there is a quality that *corresponds* to what at the human level we call faithfulness. There is a recognizable likeness in structure of attitudes or patterns of behavior that causes us to use the same word for both animals and people. Nevertheless, human faithfulness differs from canine faithfulness to all the wide extent that a person differs from a dog. There is thus both similarity within difference and difference within similarity of the kind that led Aquinas to speak of the *analogical* use of the same term in two very different contexts.[13]

When we talk of God, however, we apply the analogy upward. Baron F. von Hügel explains, however, that the "source and object of religion, if religion be true and its object be real—*cannot* indeed, *by any possibility,* be as clear to me even as I am to my dog." We are always in an inferior position to God just as animals and plants are in an inferior position to us. But it is not only the case that the inferior cannot comprehend the superior fully; it could equally well be the case that the superior can also comprehend the life of the inferior only inadequately, just as a human being leading a human existence may not fully comprehend canine existence. This possibility is not entertained by von Hügel, who concludes rather that the "obscurity of my life to my dog, must be greatly exceeded by the obscurity of the life of God to me."[14]

Now if the Deity is as obscure to us as we are to dogs, How can we (Hick asks) know "what goodness and the other divine attributes are in God[?] How do we know what perfect goodness and wisdom are like? Aquinas's answer is that we do not know." This admission of unknowability on the part of Aquinas must be understood very carefully. We must distinguish here

13. Ibid., 78.
14. Quoted in ibid., 79.

between our knowledge of God's perfections and our understanding of the words used to describe them. The issue here pertains to how these words are to be understood, and Aquinas suggests that they are to be understood analogically, a suggestion that has the assent of numerous Christian and Jewish thinkers.[15]

In order to comprehend how analogy is employed in the context of Advaita Vedānta one must begin by formulating its doctrine of *lakṣaṇā* (analogy). According to *lakṣaṇā,* words can be understood in terms of their "literal meanings" or in terms of their "signified meanings." As *artha* means "meaning," *vācya* means "literal," and *lakṣya* means "signified"—the literal meaning is referred to as *vācyārtha* and the signified meaning as *lakṣyārtha.*

It was noted earlier that in relation to the referents of religion in Advaita, literal language does not apply. Literal language describes objects of sense perception (such as tables or chairs) in a literal way, but Brahman is *atīndriya*—not an object of sense perception. Literal language differentiates objects from one another (such as tables from chairs), but Brahman is *bhedarahitam*—without distinctions of any kind. Advaita acknowledges differences of three kinds: (1) between objects of the same class, (2) between objects belonging to different classes, and (3) within an object. They are known as *sajātīya, vijātīya,* and *svagatabheda.* The differences between one mango tree and another are *sajātīya,* between a mango tree and a fig tree *vijātīya,* and within a mango tree among its trunk, leaves, and bark are *svagata.*[16] Brahman is without such differences.

Moreover, language describes individual items of the universe, an object, a thought, a feeling, but Brahman is said to be *sarvam*—all. To describe something one must stand outside it, but there is no place to stand outside Brahman. Language describes qualities, such as colors, but Brahman is said to be *nirguṇa*—without qualities. Language describes action, "to go to another place, to attain some object, to effect a transformation, or to purify something," but Brahman is said to be *niṣkriyam*—without action. As Sankaranarayanam puts it, "Brahman cannot be described by speech. For speech can declare only what has been known by the mind. Words can convey ideas pertaining to one or more of the following, namely *class,* . . . *quality,* . . . *action,* . . . or *relation.* . . . Brahman possesses none of these. It

15. Ibid., 78–79.
16. P. Sankaranarayanan, *What Is Advaita?* (Bombay: Bharatiya Vidya Bhavan, 1970), 52.

belongs to no class, it has no quality, it does no action and enters into no relation."[17]

In short, Brahman cannot be described literally.

The question arises, Can it be described analogically? Or to use technical terms, if Brahman cannot be *vācyārtha,* can it be *lakṣyārtha;* if it cannot be described literally, can it be indicated or signified?

We know, for instance, that there are cases when *vācyārtha* (literal meaning) makes no sense, but that does not mean that the statement makes no sense. When the literal sense makes no sense, "what may be called the indicative or lakṣyārtthah will have to be taken. For example, when it is said of a man 'he is a lion,' it is not meant that he is a carnivorous wild animal, the king of beasts (which is the literal import; vācyārtthah), but that he is brave as a lion (which is the signified import; lakṣyārttha)."[18]

If this is possible in ordinary discourse, could it not be possible in religious discourse?

Advaita Vedānta believes that such usage is possible and has elaborated what has been called the theory or doctrine of *lakṣaṇā* (indicated or signified meaning). It begins by first distinguishing between three types of *lakṣaṇās,* which are called (1) *jahallakṣaṇā,* (2) *ajahallakṣaṇā,* and (3) *jahadajahallakṣaṇā* or *bhāgalakṣaṇā.* A well-known manual of Advaita Vedānta, the *Vedānta Paribhāṣā,* composed in the seventeenth century by Dharmarāja, offers an authoritative and concise exposition of these three types.

> In another way, implication is of three kinds—exclusive (*jahat*), inclusive (*ajahat*) and quasi-inclusive (*jahad-ajahat*). Of these, exclusive implication occurs where, excluding the primary meaning, some other meaning is comprehended. As, in the sentence, "Take poison," discarding the original meaning of the words, abstention from eating in an enemy's house is implied. Inclusive implication occurs where, along with the primary meaning, some other meaning is comprehended: as, "A white [jar]." Here the word "white" includes its original meaning, viz., the quality white colour, and yet refers by implication to a substance possessing it. Quasi-inclusive implication occurs where a word signifying some qualified entity discards one

17. Ibid., 55.
18. Ibid., 85.

> part of its meaning and refers to another part; as, "This is that Devadatta." Here, since the qualified entities primarily meant by the two words cannot be identical, the latter refer only to the substantive (*viśeṣya*).[19]

Advaita Vedānta maintains that some of the great sayings of the Upaniṣads that describe the relationship of an individual to Brahman are to be understood along the lines of *bhāgalakṣaṇā* (quasi-inclusive implication), of which "this is that John" would be a stock illustration.

The great saying cited in this context is: *tat tvam asi* or "That thou art," from the Chāndogya Upaniṣad, which discloses the ultimate truth to the pupil. But as surely as this saying cannot be understood literally, how do we understand it analogically?

1. It cannot be a case of *jahallakṣaṇā* because in the illustration of that instance the enemy's house is *not* explicitly mentioned, whereas the individual (*tvam*) is explicitly mentioned here.
2. It cannot be a case of *ajahallakṣaṇā* because there is no need to take usual and related meanings, as with "white [jug]," because the person is directly mentioned.
3. It can be and is taken a case of *bhāgalakṣaṇā* because in "This is that John" the time and place associated with *this* and *that* are abandoned when the recognition occurs that he is the *same* John.

The Advaitins use analogy in this way to establish identity between the *jīva*, the empirical self, and *Īśvara*, the Lord of the world, who are identical *shorn of their adjuncts*. The famous medieval Advaitin, Vidyāraṇya, explains that Pañcadaśī 7.74:

> In sentences like "That thou art" only the logical rule of partial elimination is to be applied, as in the terms of "that is this, not others." (i.e., In "This is that Devadatta" we negate the attributes of time and place, both present and past, and take into account only the person himself. Similarly, in the text "That thou art" we negate the conflicting attributes such as the omniscience and the limited knowl-

19. Swami Madhavananda, *Vedānta-Paribhāṣā of Dharmarāja Adhvarindra* (Belur Math, Howrah: The Ramakrishna Mission, Saradapitha, 1963), 98. In the case of "white jar" one may also consider a sentence like "pour juice in the white one," in which "jar" is implied.

edge which characterize Īśvara and Jīva respectively, and take into account only the immutable consciousness).[20]

The point may be elucidated as follows. In Advaita Vedānta there is really no difference between "you" and "that." For instance, let us take "you" to be the *jīva* and "that" to be *Īśvara.* And for convenience let us call the former "ego" and the latter "qualified Brahman." Now according to Advaita the difference between the two or between the egos for that matter or between any ego and qualified Brahman consists entirely of the adjuncts that qualify them. As M. Hiriyanna explains: "In themselves, the egos are not distinct from one another or from qualified Brahman. This identity of the denotation of the two terms, *jīva* and qualified Brahman, while their connotations are different, is the advaitic interpretation of 'that thou art' (*Tat tvam asi*)."[21]

I would venture to suggest that this example needs to be reviewed. M. Hiriyanna asserts that the difference between the ego and qualified Brahman are "entirely due to" "differing adjuncts." However, there is a difference between how the ego and God relate to their differing adjuncts, namely, that the ego is taken in by the veiling power of *māyā* called *āvaraṇa* (obscuration) but God, who sees through it and wields it like a magician, is not. Thus despite a venerable tradition to the contrary it seems the analogy applies between the "identity" of the *Ātman* and *nirguṇa Brahman* rather than between *jīva* and *Īśvara.*

The Cognitive Theories of Religious Language

Religious Statements as Symbolic (Tillich)

An important element in Paul Tillich's discussion of religious language is his distinction between sign and symbol. In his own words, "Both point to something else beyond themselves. But a sign signifies that to which it

20. Swami Swahananda, trans., *Pañcadaśī of Śrī Vidyāraṇya Swāmī* (Madras: Sri Ramakrishna Math, 1967), 262.

21. M. Hiriyanna, *The Essentials of Indian Philosophy* (London: George Allen & Unwin, 1948), 163–64. He adds: "This does not mean, as it is so often represented to do, that man and qualified Brahman or God (to use a term which we shall soon explain) are *as such* one. Such an attitude is as blasphemous, according to Advaita, as it is to any religion or purely theistic doctrine."

points by arbitrary convention—as for instance, when the red light on the street corner signifies that drivers are ordered to halt. In contrast to this purely external connection, a symbol 'participates in that to which it points.' "[22] The usual example given here is that of the flag, which "participates in the power and dignity of the nation which it represents."[23] A few points characteristic of symbols in the thinking of Tillich may be noted here: (1) unlike signs, which are arbitrarily determined, symbols "grow out of the individual or collective consciousness"; (2) this does not, however, mean that they are eternal for they have their own "span of life"; (3) a symbol performs a twofold function, in relation to the referent it "opens up levels of reality which otherwise are closed to us" and in relation to the subject "unlocks dimensions and elements of our soul."[24] Art is said to provide an excellent example of this "twofold function," for it creates " 'symbols for a level of reality which cannot be reached in any other way,' at the same time opening up new sensitivities and powers of appreciation in ourselves."[25]

In order to compare Tillich's views on symbolic language with the theory of language in Advaita Vedānta, one needs to distinguish clearly between the *cosmological* aspect of the Advaitin theory of language and its *ontological* aspect. The views of Tillich and those found in Advaita Vedānta may be first compared at the cosmological level.

According to the traditional doctrine of language in Advaita Vedānta very few words are fixed by convention. To use Tillich's terminology, very few words are signs. Only in the case of technical and proper names is it accepted that "they are fixed by deliberate convention to refer to particulars."[26] This would appear strange to the average reader as language would appear, by and large, to be itself the result of convention. But in the traditional Advaitin view of creation, language *precedes* creation. In the biblical account, the animals appear first and then they are named; in the Advaitin account, the names appear first as part of the Vedic text. These words denote universals, and the animals, for instance, then appear in accordance with their names. "Śaṅkara says that when anyone wants to make a thing, he first recollects the word signifying it, and then makes it. He says that this is evident to us in experience, and the creation of the world was similar. The words in the Veda (as they were in the past world-cycle) manifested them-

22. Hick, *Philosophy of Religion,* 79–80.
23. Ibid., 80.
24. Paul Tillich as quoted in ibid.
25. Ibid., 79–80.
26. Murty, *Revelation and Reason,* 18.

selves in the mind of Prajāpati, the creator, before creation, and then he created things accordingly. Thus, for instance, from the word 'bhūr' (earth) which occurred in his mind he created the terrestrial world."[27]

In this sense, then, all language is symbolic as it *participates* in creation. Thus the distinction between sign and symbol is not of much help here as illustrated by Śaṅkara when he explains that "when an eternal word stands as the *sign* (*vācaka*) eternally related to its referent (which is *always* a universal), from that issue forth (*niṣpatti*) individuals capable of being denoted by the word."[28] The word "sign" here clearly corresponds to Tillich's symbol. In a very interesting though unexpected way the unusual theory of creation in Advaita illustrates Tillich's point about the twofold function of symbolic language—that it both discloses a level of reality outside us and generates the ability to perceive it within us.

Although some Advaitin scholars accept the view that objects can precede the words used to denote them, as in the biblical account, the standard Advaitin view of creation—which is, as Murty explains, always a *re*-creation of the beginningless universe—employs the following model:

> In the world we see sculptors making idols after knowing the names and forms of gods from the *śāstras* on sculpture (in which is given the relevant information), and in a similar way Hiraṇyagarbha (the four-faced Brahmā, maker of the world according to Hindu cosmogony) after learning the names and forms from the Veda creates gods, men and all things. Quoting the Upaniṣad text, "He (God) who creates Brahmā at the beginning of the aeon and promulgates (or sends = *prahiṇoti*) the Vedas for him," Appayya Dīkṣita says that from this it is clear that the Veda is given to the created Brahmā, for enabling him to know the names and forms of all things, so that depending upon this knowledge, he may recreate the world.[29]

It is clear, however, that *both* creatures and objects are created by language—that the twofold function of symbolic language is manifested at a cosmic level in Advaita in which the "world is created according to ideas, universals or forms (*jāti* or *ākṛti*) eternally present in God."[30]

Furthermore, in a sense, words have their own span of life in Hindu

27. Ibid., 35.
28. Ibid.; emphasis added.
29. Ibid., 36.
30. Ibid.

cosmology as well, another idea which coincides with Tillich's conception of symbols. Between the phases of creation and dissolution, the "word" undergoes obscuration with the universe itself. Its exact status then is a matter of philosophical debate, although it is in some sense considered eternal.

Finally, symbols for Tillich grow out of individual or collective consciousness. In Advaita, the Vedas either represent "symbols" in the consciousness of God or the collective consciousness of creation which merges in Brahman. But here again the order is reversed. They grow out of him in the sense that they flow out of him at the time of creation, but they never "grew out" in the sense of being constituted, for there was never a time when they were not.

Apparently Tillich's views of language are related not to creation but to linguistic discourse in the created world, but the extent to which they can be contextualized in the Advaitic process of creation would perhaps be of interest to philosophers of comparative religion; however, Tillich's views on language at the metaphysical level are of greater interest to Advaita Vedānta.

In this context the following points in Tillich's thought may be used as a basis for useful comparison. First, in Hick's words, "Tillich holds that religious faith, which is the state of being 'ultimately concerned' about the ultimate, can express itself only in symbolic language."[31] As Tillich puts it, "Whatever we say about that which concerns us ultimately, whether or not we call it God, has a symbolic meaning. It points beyond itself while participating in that to which it points. In no other way can faith express itself adequately. The language of faith is the language of symbols."[32] Second, Hick continues, "There is, according to Tillich, one and only one literal, nonsymbolic statement that can be made about the ultimate reality which religion calls God—that God is being-itself. Beyond this, all theological statements—such as that God is eternal, living, good, personal, that God is the Creator and that God loves all creatures—are symbolic."[33] In Tillich's words:

> There can be no doubt that any concrete assertion about God must be symbolic, for a concrete assertion is one which uses a segment of finite experience in order to say something about him. It transcends the content of this segment, although it also includes it. The segment

31. Hick, *Philosophy of Religion,* 80.
32. Paul Tillich as quoted in ibid.
33. Ibid.

> of finite reality which becomes the vehicle of a concrete assertion about God is affirmed and negated at the same time. It becomes a symbol, for a symbolic expression is one whose proper meaning is negated by that to which it points. And yet it also is affirmed by it, and this affirmation gives the symbolic expression an adequate basis for pointing beyond itself.[34]

On the first point, there is a convergence between Tillich and Advaita as represented by Śaṅkara, for it is Śaṅkara's clear conclusion that "Brahman can never be *described*, but can only be *shown* somehow approximately,"[35] that is, symbolically. Śaṅkara clearly establishes this conclusion "at three places,"[36] in his commentary on the Bhagavad Gītā (12.12), and in his commentaries on the Taittirīya (2.1) and Bṛhadāraṇyaka (1.4.7 and 2.3.6) Upaniṣads. The general point here is that although Brahman is *nirguṇa* or indeterminate and therefore indefinable, it is not so in every way, for although on the one hand nothing in the universe is apart from Brahman, on the other hand, nothing in the universe can represent Brahman either. The situation may be compared to the sun when it is obscured by a cloud cover. That the cloud cover is itself visible is due to the presence of the light of the sun, yet the sun is invisible and nothing that is visible because of the light emanating from the invisible sun can represent the sun, although to a certain extent sunlight may provide a clue to the existence of even an invisible sun. Consider the sun when it is obscured by a single dark cloud. Now the sun can be implied more precisely. The approximation is closer. Next consider the sun covered by a white cloud. The approximation in this case is even greater. Now if at the same time the full *moon* also appears in the sky then, using it as an analogy for the *solar* orb and the sunshine around as an illustration of the sun's brightness one might be able to talk of the sun with even greater similitude. It should not be forgotten, however, that the sun is nevertheless an external object, whereas Brahman, as Ātman—the seeing light—can never come into view as an item of description but may be indicated approximately by analogy from its self-luminosity.

Tillich's assertion, that only "one literal, nonsymbolic statement can be made about the ultimate reality which religion calls God—that God is being-itself"—finds a parallel in both the revelational and rational accounts

34. Paul Tillich as quoted in ibid.
35. Murty, *Revelation and Reason,* 57.
36. Ibid., 57–58.

of Advaita Vedānta. The Vedas represent revelation in Advaita but as M. Hiriyanna points out: "The fact is that the Advaita recognizes a higher, viz. the absolute standpoint from which all pramāṇas alike, inclusive of the Veda, lose their relative validity. An exception is made only in the case of Upaniṣadic statements that teach the unity of all being. These statements are pramāṇa in the absolute sense, for the knowledge which they convey is never shown to be wrong. But it does not secure for the pramāṇa itself ultimate reality, for in mokṣa where nothing but Brahman remains, even that pramāṇa as such must disappear."[37]

Can we equate "unity of all being" with Tillich's "being-itself"? The similarity is striking.

On the second point the convergence between a modern Advaitin, M. Hiriyanna, and Tillich is uncanny. Tillich admits that concrete assertions about God can be made although they must remain symbolic. Hiriyanna points out that it cannot be true in "every sense" that Brahman is beyond the reach of words for that would deprive the Upaniṣads of all significance. Tillich maintains that the concrete assertion transcends its content; Hiriyanna makes the same claim about negation, for "negation necessarily has its own positive implication." A symbolic expression like "Brahman" affirms and negates at the same time. It is negated by the reality it points to, which is paradoxically affirmed in the process. Thus Hiriyanna asserts that even if a "negative definition" is the only possible one, in Advaita negative definition is given a "secondary place" and positive the "primary place" so that ultimately "negation is only a preliminary to affirmation."[38]

Advaita distinguishes between *Sattāvāda* (doctrine of pure being) and *Advaitavāda* (doctrine of nondualism). Advaita clarifies the point that a

37. M. Hiriyanna, *Outlines of Indian Philosophy* (London: George Allen & Unwin, 1964), 359. According to other scholars Śaṅkara would not even make that concession. "Brahman, in this absolutely transcendent aspect, says Śaṅkara, cannot be described at all and it is, therefore, called indeterminate or characterless or nirguna. The description of Brahman even as infinite, real, consciousness, though more accurate than accidental descriptions, cannot directly convey the idea of Brahman. It only serves to direct the mind towards Brahman by denying of it finiteness, unreality and unconsciousness" (Satischandra Chatterjee and Dhirendramohan Datta, *An Introduction to Indian Philosophy* [1950; reprint, Calcutta: University of Calcutta, 1968], 396). However, as in describing Brahman as pure existence its characterless character is not contradicted, "so existence, in some form or other, is as wide as thought, and we cannot conceive of the absence or denial of existence. This universal, pure existence (or consciousness) is thus the only thing whose contradiction is unthinkable. Śaṅkara calls it, therefore, supreme reality (Pāramārthika sattā). He thus logically arrives also at his conception of reality as that which persists uncontradicted through all forms of existence in all places and times" (ibid., 387).

38. Hiriyanna, *Outlines*, 375.

reality denuded of all distinctive features does not imply mere abstract being.[39] Tillich also asserts that "everything that exists participates in Being-itself."[40] This has led John H. Hick to ask, If everything that exists participates in Being-itself, "what then is the difference between the way in which symbols participate in Being-itself and the way in which everything also participates in it?"[41]

At stake here is the nature of theological statements. They exist like everything else exists and participate in Being-itself—without themselves being Being-itself or God. In the jargon of Advaita Vedānta the issue is phrased as follows: If Veda is also a part of māyā, then what distinguishes it from other aspects of māyā in relation to Brahman? The Advaitin answer is that although it is *in* māyā, it points to that which is *out* of māyā. Therein lies the value of the *symbolic* nature of religious language; it participates in Being-itself by pointing to it, whereas other types of language do not.

The Advaitic position is suggestive here. It carries Tillich's statement that "everything that exists participates in Being-itself" to the point of asserting that as we exist, we also participate in it through our own existence—and that there is a *special* sense to this participation. As M. Hiriyanna explains, the negation of all specific descriptions of being are meant to point to it "as revealing itself within us." Once this is recognized several conclusions follow in its train: (1) if it is within us and we cannot deny our being, its being cannot be denied; (2) this awareness of being presupposes consciousness, which is immaterial in nature, so its spiritual nature cannot be denied; (3) as it is experienced as conscious being, it cannot be regarded as "something wholly outside the world of experience"; (4) as it reveals the world of our experience, this world in that sense cannot be entirely denied, hence "every object of experience, whether on the subject or the object side reveals it," directly or indirectly. One may thus conclude that "irrepressibility (svayaṃprakāśatva) is its very essence and, like the sun behind the clouds, it shows itself in a sense even when hidden. We seem to miss it ordinarily on account of the bewildering mass of appearances. But that is like not seeing the ocean for the waves."[42]

Another criticism of Tillich's position is seen in a new light when placed in an Advaitic context. Before this is done, however, the aspect of the

39. Ibid., 375 n. 3. Also Hiriyanna, *Essentials*, 162.
40. Quoted in Hick, *Philosophy of Religion*, 81.
41. Ibid.
42. Hiriyanna, *Outlines*, 375–76.

criticism to which an Advaitic response can be formulated must be identified. John H. Hick remarks:

> The application to theological statements of Tillich's other "main characteristics of every symbol," . . . raises further questions. Is it really plausible to say that a complex theological statement such as "God is not dependent for his existence upon any external reality" has arisen *from the conscious, whether individual or collective?* Does it not seem more likely that it was carefully formulated by a philosophical theologian? *And in what sense does this same proposition open up both "levels of reality which are otherwise closed to us" and "hidden depths of our own being"?* These two characteristics of symbols seem more readily applicable to the arts than to theological ideas and propositions. Indeed, it is Tillich's *tendency to assimilate religious to aesthetic awareness that suggests the naturalistic development of his position.*[43]

The cognition of God's independence as arising out of the individual or collective unconscious is, of course, a concept that Advaita Vedānta is not likely to welcome. What, however, if it were rephrased a little so as to suggest that although the individual may not be conscious of it, it lies dormant in consciousness? For instance, a modern Advaitin remarks while speaking of the transcendental realm that "though the human mind may not be definitely aware of what is beyond perception and reasoning, it is not altogether unconscious of it. The very statement that common experience exhausts reality implies, by placing a limit on it, that the mind has travelled beyond that limit. Our reach exceeds our grasp."[44]

Similarly, Tillich's claim that the "same proposition" can "open up" both "levels of reality which are otherwise closed to us" and the "hidden depths of our being" appears less refractory when placed in an Advaitic context. The proposition John H. Hick has in mind is the statement "God is not dependent for his existence upon any external reality." If this statement were modified to include "because there is no existence of any reality apart from God," then the convergence of opening up a level of reality and its identification with hidden depths could be established in Advaitic terms. First of all, the level of reality must be qualified. We are speaking here of *saguṇa-brahman* or Īśvara, not of *nirguṇa*-Brahman; the former being Brahman with māyā, the latter

43. Hick, *Philosophy of Religion,* 81; emphasis added.
44. Hiriyanna, *Essentials,* 44.

without it. In order to develop this point one must eschew the tendency of viewing *saguṇa* Brahman as antithetical to the *nirguṇa.* Such a perspective obscures the point that "saguṇa Brahman includes not merely reality but also appearance, which is something less than the real. The element of reality in it is the ultimate of Advaita," so that properly speaking the "nirguṇa Brahman is not the negation or the antithesis of the saguṇa, but its very truth and is immanent in everything that goes to constitute it."[45]

The assimilation of aesthetic to religious awareness is also not without parallel in Advaita Vedānta. It has not perhaps been fully integrated into the system but it is maintained that the experience of beauty is a disclosure of reality. The triune description of reality as *saccidānanda* is matched by its optional description as *satyam, śivam, sundaram* or Truth, Beatitude, and Beauty. Tentative attempts in this direction can be detected in the concept of *contemplative feeling* developed by K. C. Bhattacharyya:

> *Contemplative feeling* is sympathy with sympathy. Three persons are involved. When I enjoy contemplating an old man watching his grandchild playing with a toy, the child's joy in the toy, the grandfather's sympathetic joy, and my contemplative joy are on different levels. I am interested in the child's feeling reflected in the grandfather's as an eternal emotion or value. I no longer feel the distinction between my feeling and the child's; I become impersonal (I:353). The expression of the object is detached from the particularity of fact as an eternal value. Beauty is such an eternal value, seen not as a quality of the object or another object beside it but as the reality to which the object itself is somehow adjectival (I:352). All feeling involves identification of subject and object, but in comtemplative feeling both identity and difference are explicit. Subject merges into object and object is dissolved in subject (I:359).[46]

45. Hiriyanna, *Outlines,* 371, 376.

46. George Bosworth Burch, ed., *Search for the Absolute in Neo-Advaita* (Honolulu: The University of Hawaii Press, 1976), 48. The parenthetical references are to K. C. Bhattacharyya, *Studies in Philosophy,* vols. 1 and 2 (Calcutta: Calcutta Progressive Publishers, 1956, 1958). See also William M. Indich, *Consciousness in Advaita Vedānta* (Delhi: Motilal Banarsidass, 1980), 101–4, regarding some limitations Advaita might face in this regard. But also see T.M.P. Mahadevan, *The Philosophy of Beauty with Special Reference to Advaita Vedānta* (Bombay: Bharatiya Vidya Bhavan, 1969). In this respect the work of such Advaitins as Pandita Jagannātha and Appaya Dīkṣita, who also wrote on aesthetics, needs to be seriously taken into account. Who knows that someday they may be given the same credit for assimilating aesthetics into Advaita that is given to Madhusūdana Sarasvatī for doing the same for *bhakti* (devotion).

Yet another criticism of Tillich's doctrine of symbolic language takes on a new dimension when viewed from the standpoint of Advaita Vedānta. Tillich seems to offer, as John Hick notes, his doctrine of "participation" as an alternative to that of analogy. However, Hick notices an ambiguity in Tillich's formulation, which he illustrates with the help of the following statement: "God is good." First, if this is treated as a symbolic statement, then what exactly is the symbol in this case: "the proposition 'God is good' or the concept 'the goodness of God' "? Next, how can this be said, either way, to participate in Being-itself? The most common example Tillich provides of such participation of the symbol in the symbolized is that of the flag in the "the power and dignity" of the nation. This, however, is a secular example, and Tillich, it is said in criticism, never shows how it might apply to the world of religious symbolism, and where any similarity between the two might lie.[47]

Troy Wilson Organ, paraphrasing K. Satchidananda Murty,[48] points out that according to Śaṅkara "truths are revealed to man in four sorts of revelation." These, cited earlier, are recapitulated here for convenience: "(1) a general revelation open to all mankind in the human experience of living in a world of name and form; (2) the Vedic revelation which is given in all the Vedic literature, but primarily in the *Upanishads;* (3) the revelation given through incarnations of the Gods; (4) *anubhūti* revelation, which is the direct experience of truth arising from meditation on Upanishadic texts."[49]

In the first sense everything is part of Being-itself *through the symbolic nature of language because Vedic verbal revelation is the source of creation.* Here everything is the sign of God. In the second sense the Vedic Upaniṣadic texts *participate* in Being-itself, being the breath of God: "As from the fire kindled with damp fuel various kinds of smoke issue forth, so, verily, from this great being has been breathed forth that which is the *ṚgVeda,* the *Yajur Veda* the *Sāma Veda,* the hymns of the Atharvans and the Aṅgirasas, legend, ancient lore, sciences, sacred teachings, verses, aphorisms, explanations, commentaries, sacrifice, oblation, food, drink, this world and the other and all beings. From it, indeed, have all these been breathed forth" (Bṛhadāraṇyaka Upaniṣad 4.5.11).[50] In the third sense God participates in his own

47. Hick, *Philosophy of Religion,* 81.

48. Murty, *Revelation and Reason,* 6–10.

49. Troy Wilson Organ, *Hinduism: Its Historical Development* (Woodbury, N.Y.: Barron's Educational Series, 1974), 248.

50. S. Radhakrishnan, ed., *The Principal Upaniṣads* (London: George Allen & Unwin, 1953), 284.

symbol, his own creation. In a sense the roles are reversed—and sometimes with curious results, as when God gets carried away: "Once God incarnated himself as a female boar, and gave birth to a number of pigs. The boar lived in a dirty place very happily with her young ones. She became so attached to the life she lived that when the time came for the Lord to return to heaven, she did not want to leave the world. The gods in heaven became perturbed at the long absence of the Lord, and going to Shiva they prayed to him that he must save the situation. He went down to the place where the boar lived and killed it with a stroke of his trident. At once, the Supreme Self left the body of the boar, smiling resplendent and went to the region of heaven."[51] Moreover, in Hindu thought, as also in Advaita, the presence of God as an incarnation is not *real* in the Christian sense. It is more symbolic. He is described by Śaṅkara in his introduction to the Bhagavadgītā "as though He is born and embodied and helping the world at large; whereas really He is unborn and indestructible."[52]

One final point. John H. Hick remarks that Tillich's doctrine may be understood, in theological and religious terms, as a warning against the idolatry of anthropomorphism. The temptation of imposing the finitude of one's own mind on the object of its reflection is so great that any amount of warning against this danger is always welcome. He compares the analogical language with the negational aspect of Tillich's doctrine of symbolic language and points to their shared concern regarding the danger of literalism. In this the Tillichian emphasis on the point that symbols partially negate what they point to is considered particularly wholesome.[53]

From the point of view of Advaita Vedānta, according to Śaṅkara, "the best way of speaking about Brahman"—that is, Brahman-in-Itself—"is the *netivāda (via negativa).*"[54] This constitutes the Advaitic safeguard against bibliolatry.

Incarnation and the Problem of Meaning

How the doctrine of incarnation can be used to solve the problem of religious language needs to be explained. Central to this explanation is the

51. Swami Sambuddhananda, *Vedānta Through Stories* (Bombay: Sri Ramakrishna Ashram, 1959), 82.

52. Alladi Mahadeva Sastry, trans., *The Bhagavad Gita with the Commentary of Sri Sankaracharya* (1979; reprint, Madras: Samata Books, 1985), 3.

53. Hick, *Philosophy of Religion,* 81.

54. Murty, *Revelation and Reason,* 64.

distinction between the metaphysical and moral attributes of God. Infinity and eternity are examples of metaphysical attributes of God, whereas love and forgiveness are examples of moral attributes. Earlier in the chapter we raised the question: What does it mean to say that God loves his creatures when God is a disembodied being and love is a sentiment associated with embodied beings? The doctrine of incarnation helps answer the question of religious language posed above in the following way. According to the doctrine of incarnation, Jesus was an incarnation of God. In other words, he represented the embodiment of God. If we believe this, then we have in this belief the answer to our question, for through Jesus God came to possess a body as it were so that in the person of Jesus we could witness the divine enactment of those moral principles which involve an interpersonal dimension. So in order to find out what is meant by "God loves human beings" all we need to do is to observe how Jesus loved his fellow beings. Thus we can say that "Jesus' compassion for the sick and the blind was God's compassion for them; his forgiving of sins, God's forgiveness; and his condemnation of the self-righteously religious, God's condemnation of them."[55]

In the above approach a distinction is drawn between the metaphysical and moral attributes of God, and it is argued that Christ's actions could illustrate the meaning of the moral attributes of God. From the point of view of Advaita Vedānta this position might be difficult to accept. If all the members of the Trinity inhere in one another, then Jesus Christ as the Word becoming flesh should incarnate *both* the metaphysical *and* the moral attributes of God. Level-splitting as such, however, is an acceptable procedure in Advaitic discourse about Brahman. In the case of Christianity, where the moral attributes of God are incarnated but not the metaphysical, the split is vertical in nature, whereas in Advaita Vedānta when Brahman is considered by itself (*nirguṇa*), and when it is considered in relation to the universe (*saguṇa*), the split is not vertical but horizontal. Moreover, whereas the metaphysical and moral attributes of God are coordinated at the level of God; the attributes of Brahman in relation to the world (*saguṇa*) are often subordinate to Brahman by itself (*nirguṇa*). For in the *saguṇa* stage "mingled as Brahman then becomes with the falsity of Māyā, it perforce descends to the phenomenal level and is consequently designated the lower (*apara*) Brahman to distinguish it from the higher (*para*)."[56]

55. Hick, *Philosophy of Religion*, 82.
56. Hiriyanna, *Essentials*, 163.

A General Advaitic Response to the Cognitive and Quasi-Cognitive Theories of Religious Language

There are a few distinctions drawn in Advaita Vedānta—both at the level of reality and at the level of revelation, and further at the level of linguistic modes and the level of incarnation—which place Western cognitive and quasi-cognitive theories of language in a new light.

Distinctions at the Level of Reality

Brahman stands for reality in Advaita Vedānta, which describes Brahman as both *nirguṇa* and *saguṇa.* If we speak of two levels of language here, an important point emerges in the context of religious language. John A. Grimes proposes a "two-level" discussion of language in relation to Brahman by referring to Śaṅkara's *bhāṣya* (commentary) on Brahmasūtra 4.3.14 along with other famous Upaniṣadic dicta as follows:

> This proposal for a "two-level" theory of language stems from an analysis of a unique declaration of Śaṅkara's in his *bhāṣya* on the *Brahma sūtra.* Ordinarily, when the Advaitin is asked if there are two Brahmans, the answer is a categorical "no." However, in the fourth chapter of the *Brahma sūtra,* the opponent asks, "Are there then two Brahmans—one superior and the other inferior?" The answer is a surprising, "Quite so." This dialogue occurs in reference to propounding the place in which texts about movement may find proper scope. When the text declares, "The knower of Brahman, becomes Brahman," the question arises whether this "becoming" or "attaining" indicates movement. Quoting the *Bṛhadāraṇyaka Upaniṣad* to show that no movement is asserted in any way, the Advaitin must then explain the scope and nature of the texts indicating movement. Śaṅkara says that their place is limited to meditating on the inferior Brahman:
>
>> Accordingly, movement is possible only in relation to the inferior Brahman. That being so, it is only through a failure to distinguish between the superior Brahman and inferior Brahman that the texts about travelling that refer to the inferior Brahman are ascribed to the superior Brahman.

Thus, the first move of the Advaitin in regards to religious language is to declare that there are two levels in it. At this juncture, their radical stance propounds that first level language does directly designate the Absolute. As a methodological device it does more than merely indicate. The purport of religious language is to deny difference caused by ignorance. Whether the unreal distinctions of duality and difference are removed by denying difference or by affirming identity, the result is that the Absolute is seen to shine in its pristine splendor.[57]

Distinctions at the Level of Revelation

One can identify in Advaita Vedānta a fourfold conception of revelation, which has already been alluded to and is summarized as follows: First, there is a partial disclosure of Brahman through the graded forms of existence, from the clod of earth to the gods in heaven (*ābrahmastamba paryantam*). This is Brahman's *abhivyakti.* But this disclosure though directly present to all, is not of much help; "Seeing we see it not." Second, the Veda revealed by God at the beginning of each aeon contains the final truth about *dharma* and Brahman. Third, when people forget the eternal truth in the Veda, then in order to put them back on the right path, and reproclaim the Law, God incarnates himself and teaches the quintessence of the Veda. And fourth, in the *anubhūti* or integral experience of Brahman, which a knower of Brahman will have, the real nature of Brahman is disclosed.[58]

Distinctions at the Level of Linguistic Modes

These distinctions are best explained through the concepts of *jahallakṣaṇā, ajahallakṣaṇā,* and *jahadajahallakṣaṇā* introduced earlier. One may begin by clarifying the meaning of *lakṣaṇā* first, this time from another perspective:

> According to Hindu rhetoricians, the meaning of every word or sentence comes under one of three heads, that is, it is either literal (*vāchya*), indicative (*lakṣhya*), or suggestive (*vyaṅgya*). Their three functions or powers are termed Denotation (*abhidhā*), Indication (*lakshaṇā*), and Suggestion (*vyañjanā*). We are here concerned with

57. Grimes, "Advaita Vedānta," 214–15.
58. Murty, *Revelation and Reason,* 10.

> the middle one only, which is thus defined in the *Kāvyaprakāśa* (ii.9): "When the literal meaning is incompatible [with the rest of the sentence], and, either from usage or from some motive, another meaning is indicated, in connection with the primary one, that imposed function is called "Indication."[59]

Of the varieties of *lakṣaṇā* only three need detain us here. The first is *ajahallakṣaṇā,* as in the example, "The white is galloping," in which case the literal sense is impossible, "What is indicated is that 'the white *horse* is galloping.' Thus the word 'horse' is introduced without the abandonment of the term 'white.' "[60] This thus is an "indication in which there is the use of a word without the abandonment of the sense."[61] The second is *jahallakṣaṇā,* as in the example " 'A herd-station on the Ganges," where the word 'Ganges' abandons its own meaning in order to introduce that of the 'bank.' "[62] This thus is an "indication in which there is the use of the word *with* the abandonment of its meaning."[63] The last is *jahadajahallakṣaṇā.* It is so called because it combines these two varieties and has been defined as "indication abiding in one part of the expressed meaning, whilst another part is abandoned. As for example in the sentence 'This is that Devadatta,' whilst the meanings expressive of past and present time are abandoned, another portion of the expressed meaning remains and conveys the idea of one Devadatta."[64]

Distinctions at the Level of Incarnation

This distinction is not explicit in Śaṅkara to the best of my knowledge but can be inferred. It seems that God incarnates in order to establish *Dharma* or moral order in the world, according to Śaṅkara's commentary on the Bhagavadgītā. As Murty puts it:

> Śaṅkara explains that in himself God is eternally endowed with knowledge, power, etc., and is ever free from all limitations and

59. Colonel G. A. Jacob, *A Manual of Hindu Pantheism: The Vedāntasāra* (1881; reprint, Varanasi: Bharat-Bharati, 1972), 92.
60. Ibid., 93.
61. Ibid.
62. Ibid.
63. Ibid.
64. Ibid.

> impurities and is immutable. But through his power, i.e., by having the primal matter under his control, he is able to appear as if embodied; as if born and as if showing compassion to the world. Though he has no end to serve, out of a desire to show his grace (*bhūtānugraha jigṛkṣayā*), he taught the twofold dharma contained in the Veda once again to Arjuna, and through him to the whole world. Śaṅkara says that God chose Arjuna to impart his teaching, because Arjuna was in need of it, being immersed in sorrow and delusion, and because he was a good man; and the dharma accepted and practised by good men will eventually be accepted by all.[65]

This may be contrasted with the example Śaṅkara gives in explaining how the universe could be manifested from Brahman with no apparent motive. Śaṅkara writes:

> We see in every-day life that certain doings of princes or other men of high position who have no unfulfilled desires left have no reference to any extraneous purpose, but proceed from mere sportfulness, as, for instance, their recreations in places of amusement. We further see that the process of inhalation and exhalation is going on without reference to any extraneous purpose, merely following the law of its own nature. Analogously, the activity of the Lord also may be supposed to be mere sport, proceeding from his own nature, without reference to any purpose. For on the ground neither of reason nor of Scripture can we construe any other purpose of the Lord. Nor can his nature be questioned. —Although the creation of this world appears to us a weighty and difficult undertaking, it is mere play to the Lord, whose power is unlimited. And if in ordinary life we might possibly, by close scrutiny, detect some subtle motive, even for sportful action, we cannot do so with regard to the actions of the Lord, all whose wishes are fulfilled, as Scripture says. —Nor can it be said that he either does not act or acts like a senseless person; for Scripture affirms the fact of the creation on the one hand, and the Lord's omniscience on the other hand. And, finally, we must remember that the scriptural doctrine of creation does not refer to the highest reality; it refers to the apparent world only, which is characterised by name and form, the figments of Nescience, and it,

65. Murty, *Revelation and Reason*, 8.

> moreover, aims at intimating that Brahman is the Self of everything (II, 1,33).[66]

If creation can be for *līlā,* why not also an incarnation for a similar purpose? Indeed sometimes a distinction is drawn between two kinds of incarnations: one out of playfulness (*līlāvatāra*) and one out of compassion (*karuṇāvatāra*).

The relevance of this excursion into Advaitic material may now be established. Clearly, Aquinas and particularly Tillich are speaking of God in terms to which the two levels may be applied. Moreover, Tillich's "red light" is an illustration, it seems, of *jahallakṣaṇā* and "flag" of *ajahallakṣaṇā.* The doctrine of analogy seems to represent a case of *jahadajahallakṣaṇā.* Finally, according to an extension of Advaitic doctrine, God need not incarnate *only* to actualize moral attributes. This case could be referred to as *dharmāvatāra,* which is what a *karuṇāvatāra* often is.

Religious Language as Noncognitive

John H. Hick summarizes the distinction between the cognitive and noncognitive functions of religious language by providing illustrations of the cognitive and noncognitive uses of language. The following is an illustration of cognitive usage. "When we assert what we take to be a fact (or deny what is alleged to be a fact), we are using language cognitively. 'The population of China is 800,000,000,' 'This is a hot summer,' 'Two plus two equal four,' 'He is not here' are cognitive utterances. Indeed, we can define a cognitive (or informative or indicative) sentence as one that is either true or false." This may be contrasted with the examples of noncognitive language in the following passage: "There are other types of utterance, which are neither true nor false because they fulfil a different function from that of endeavouring to describe facts. We do not ask of a swearword, or a command, or the baptismal formula whether it is true. The function of the swearword is to vent one's feelings; of the command, to direct someone's actions; of 'I baptize thee . . . ,' to perform a baptism."[67] Hick follows up the comparison with the following observation: "There is no doubt that as a matter of historical fact religious

66. Deutsch and van Buitenen, *Source Book,* 191.
67. Hick, *Philosophy of Religion,* 83.

people have normally believed such statements as 'God loves mankind' to be not only cognitive but also true. Without necessarily pausing to consider the difference between religious facts and the facts disclosed through sense perception and the sciences, ordinary believers within the Judaic-Christian tradition have assumed that there are religious realities and facts and that their own religious convictions are concerned with such."[68]

It is important to emphasize at this juncture that the Vedic tradition within Hinduism does *not* share the Judeo-Christian tradition's assumption that religious language is cognitive. In fact whether Vedic, that is, religious language, is cognitive or noncognitive was an issue which was hotly debated within the tradition. The Mīmāṁsā school believed, no less than the Vedānta, in the Vedas as revelation, and further believed that revelation

> is authoritative *only* about matters to which neither perception nor inference gives us access; but then it is fully authoritative. This authority, as pointed out, is primarily concerned with one's duties. To give a contrastive example, the orthodox Exegetes would reject most of the Bible as Revelation: most of it they would classify as *itihāsa* or *purāṇa*, "stories about things past," describing events which were accessible to perception and hence require only the authority of perception; but, for example, the chapters dealing with the Law in Deuteronomy would be considered Revelation in the true sense, since here rules are laid down and results are set forth which escape human perception and inference.[69]

On the Mīmāṁsā view, therefore, the statement "God loves mankind" was really an *arthavāda* or a laudatory statement secondary to the main goal of encouraging human beings to show love to other beings. If we take the two statements "pray" and "God exists," the Mīmāṁsā school would argue that the injunction to pray is the essence of the biblical teaching, and the cognitive statement "God exists" is only to be understood in that context, as providing an object of worship. The Mīmāṁsā school would be noncognitive to the point of saying that in the expression "Pray to God," God is only a "grammatical dative" and the "worshipper is in no need to worry himself over the question whether there was such a being."[70]

68. Ibid.
69. Deutsch and van Buitenen, *Source Book,* 6.
70. Mahadevan, *Outlines,* 138.

The position of Advaita Vedānta, indeed of all Vedānta, differs from that of Mīmāṁsā. The difference between the position of Mīmāṁsā and Vedānta on this point reflects,[71] in the Hindu philosophical idiom, the issue of the cognitive or noncognitive nature of religious language. It is an interesting point for the philosopher of comparative religion to consider: in the Hindu tradition, traditional assumptions that religious language was noncognitive were countered by the innovation of a cognitive theory of religious language propounded by Vedānta, especially Advaita Vedānta. In the West, on the other hand, the intellectual movement has been in the opposite direction.

It might also be of interest to consider the important role intention plays in Hindu hermeneutics. The role of intention has been highlighted by the controversy regarding the cognitive or noncognitive nature of language which has arisen in the West. Thus John H. Hick writes: "The question arises whether theological sentences such as 'God loves mankind' are cognitive or noncognitive. This query at once divides into two: (1) are such sentences *intended* by their uses to be construed cognitively? (2) is their logical character such that they can, in fact, regardless of intention, be either true or false?"[72] It might be worth remarking here that in the context of the philosophy of comparative religion, regarding the first question, the modern philosophy of religion may stand to gain by what Advaita Vedānta has to offer as response. On the second, the roles are reversed and Advaita Vedānta may stand to benefit from the points raised in the modern philosophy of religion.

Intention is generally referred to in Hindu thought as *tātparya,* and it is relevant not only to the context of Indian and Western thought in isolation but also to their interface, if it is recognized that the notion of *tātparya* itself is dictated by one's notion of importance.[73] A further exploration of this point must be postponed, and one must revert to the discussion of intention or *tātparya.* The importance of *tātparya* has been emphasized in Advaita Vedānta at the level of understanding the meaning of *both* a sentence *and* a text. For

> a sentence is not really an isolated, abstract entity. It is organically related to a speaker, a context or a universe of discourse which

71. Deutsch and van Buitenen, *Source Book,* 7.
72. Hick, *Philosophy of Religion,* 83; emphasis added.
73. Murty, *Revelation and Reason,* 310.

> determine, out of the many possible meanings of a sentence, the particular meaning relevant to a particular case. It is also necessary therefore to know the intention of the speaker or the drift of the context (where the speaker is not known). So, a fourth condition,[74] namely tātparya-jñāna, or the knowledge of what is intended or relevant, must be taken into consideration. The actual meaning can be gathered from the universe of discourse, the introduction, the conclusion, etc. This condition is especially active when there is some ambiguity or when the ordinary or primary meaning does not suit and a secondary figurative meaning has to be found, e.g. in 'The crane is moving,' 'The die is cast' etc. Similarly when we are told in the Bible, that a camel can pass through the eye of a needle, but a rich man cannot enter heaven, we must understand the first sentence just in the opposite sense, only in deference to the intention of the speaker, or it would have been altogether unintelligible.[75]

But it is the role of intention in understanding the meaning of scripture that is really the point under discussion and which must now be considered. On this issue in general K. Satchidananda Murty remarks:

> For the truly religious man, the seeker of liberation (*mumukṣu*), scripture is valuable only in so far as it is able to provide him with a soteriology; and so when he takes up the study of a scripture, he does not aim to find therein history or science. For him only those passages are important which are in some way creative of spiritual reality. In eliminating irrelevancies and evolving a coherent pattern, the concept of *tātparya* developed by the Mīmāṁsā-Vedānta schools is of great value; and in determining the *tātparya* the six-fold criteria seem to be indispensable. Without the guidance of this concept of *tātparya,* a centuries old religious scripture is bound to be a morass of empty words.[76]

The contribution Advaita Vedānta can make here becomes apparent from the following consideration. Scripture "is made up of a vast array of sen-

74. The other three conditions are *ākāṁṣā* ("that quality of the words of a sentence by which they expect or imply one another"), *yogyatā* ("mutual fitness of the words" or absence of contradiction), and *sannidhi* (proximity between the words of a sentence in the sense of being continuous with one another in time and space).

75. D. M. Datta, *The Six Ways of Knowing* (Calcutta: University of Calcutta, 1972), 313–14.

76. Murty, *Revelation and Reason,* 310.

tences, and unless a coherent coordination (*samanvaya*) is achieved, one cannot develop a perspective regarding its teaching." And this can be done "only if the recurrent dominant theme, in other words *purport,* is discovered, for once it is discovered in terms of it all scriptural statements can be interpreted (*samanvaya*) and a consistent doctrine developed out of them. *Purport,* therefore, provides the clue, the aperçu, of scripture."[77] Murty then goes on to explain how the purport is known through context in Advaita Vedānta:

> The Advaita Vedānta says that the *purport* of scripture should not be determined on the basis of our presuppositions and empirical experience. Conformity with perceptual experience cannot be a guide to the interpretation of any scriptural text. Since scripture is ascertained to be having its own unique language structure; and since it deals with things which are unseen, and even of a nature which go against perceptible experience (*dṛṣṭaviparīta*), the *purport* of scripture should not be taken as that only which is in agreement with perception. The Advaita school maintains that in certain cases it is possible for scriptural *purport* to be determined even in opposition to other *pramāṇas;* for the *pramāṇas* which apprehend *purport* are the ṣadliṅga and not "non-opposition to other *pramāṇas.*"[78]

The *ṣaḍliṅga* (six-fold criteria) are "(1) unity of the initial and concluding passages (*upakramopasaṁhāraikya*); (2) the recurrence of theme (*abhyāsa*); (3) the new conclusion sought to be brought out (*apūrva*); (4) the fruitfulness of such a conclusion (*phala*); (5) the commendation or criticism of it throughout (*arthavāda*); (6) the argument throughout (*upapatti*). The Advaita Vedānta also accepts these criteria as the *pramāṇas* for finding *purport.*"[79]

We now turn to a discussion of the actual theories that maintain that religious language is noncognitive by intention.

Randall's Noncognitive Theory

According to J. H. Randall, "What is important to recognize is that religious symbols belong with social and artistic symbols, in the group of symbols that

77. Ibid., 80.
78. Ibid., 80–81.
79. Ibid.

are both *nonrepresentative* and *noncognitive*. Such noncognitive symbols can be said to symbolize not some external thing that can be indicated apart from their operation, but rather what they themselves *do*, their peculiar functions."[80]

These religious symbols perform the following four functions: (1) they arouse emotion and stimulate action; (2) they stimulate not just individual but cooperative action; (3) they communicate experience otherwise incommunicable; and (4) they "clarify the human experience of an aspect of the world that can be called the 'order of splendor' or the Divine."

> The work of the painter, the musician, the poet, teaches us how to use our eyes, our ears, our minds, and our feelings with greater power and skill. . . . It shows us how to discern unsuspected qualities in the world encountered, latent powers and possibilities there resident. Still more, it makes us see the new qualities with which the world, in cooperation with the spirit of man, can clothe itself. . . . Is it otherwise with the prophet and the saint? They too can do something to us, they too can effect changes in us and in our world. . . . They teach us how to see what man's life in the world is, and what it might be. They teach us how to discern what human nature can make out of its natural conditions and materials. . . . They make us receptive to qualities of the world encountered; and they open our hearts to the new qualities with which that world, in cooperation with the spirit of man, can clothe itself. They enable us to see and feel the religious dimension of our world better, the "order of splendor," and of man's experience in and with it. They teach us how to find the Divine; they show us visions of God.[81]

This vision of God, however, as Hick points out is not of an eternal cosmic God. It is not like an epiphany of Kṛṣṇa in the Bhagavadgītā. Hick goes on to say:

> This last statement, however, is enlivened by a philosophic rhetoric which may unintentionally obscure underlying issues. The products of the human imagination are not eternal; they did not exist before

80. J. H. Randall, *The Role of Knowledge in Western Religion* (Boston: Beacon Press, 1958), 114; cited by John Hick in *Philosophy of Religion*.

81. Quoted in Hick, *Philosophy of Religion*, 84.

> men and women themselves existed, and they can persist, even as imagined entities, only as long as men and women exist. The Divine, as defined by Randall, is the temporary mental construction or projection of a recently emerged animal inhabiting one of the satellites of a minor star. God is not, according to this view, the creator and the ultimate ruler of the universe; God is a fleeting ripple of imagination in a tiny corner of space-time.[82]

It is clear that according to Randall, "a symbol gains its meaning not from an external thing—like God—but from its peculiar function to evoke that vision—not dis-cover it."[83]

In this context it is not without interest to note that Randall is thought of as developing Tillich's views in a naturalistic direction. For ritualism is basically viewed as a symbol-system and it is acknowledged that ritual constitutes the core of Mīmāṁsā—and that the system of Mīmāṁsā is remarkably naturalistic. It is true that "the commands of the Veda should not be mistaken for those of ordinary morality." It is also true that "ordinary morality is required of a man before he gains competence to perform the rituals enjoined in the Vedas. But the rituals themselves belong to the supernatural order."[84] However, this supernatural order does not include God. The system of sacrifice is set up by the Vedas. In modern parlance we might say that the symbol-system is generated by the Veda but "in his anxiety to preserve the independence and integrity of the Veda, the Mīmāṁsaka assigns no place to God in his system. It is rather strange that the most orthodox of systems should turn out to be atheistic."[85] Mīmāṁsā seems to conform to Randall's vision of religion based on the noncognitive view of religious language.[86]

From the point of view of Advaita Vedānta, Randall's theory can be criticized at two levels: at its most general level and at the level at which it has been connected with the ritualism of Mīmāṁsā. At the most general level it could be argued that Randall dispenses with an *objective referent* in the noncognitive use of language altogether. However, in Advaita, although the

82. Ibid., 85. Hick is reacting here to Randall's remark about religious dimension being "a quality to be discriminated in human experience of the world, the splendour of the vision that sees beyond the actual into the perfected and eternal realm of the imagination." But his comments apply to the passage cited earlier as well.

83. Grimes, "Advaita Vedānta," 66.

84. Mahadevan, *Philosophy,* 135.

85. Ibid., 138.

86. Murty, *Revelation and Reason,* 70–71.

symbol may evoke the vision, this does not in itself negate the objective existence of the referent. That the function of language is noncognitive in a context does not mean that the *intention* of the language is noncognitive. As M. Hiriyanna remarks in one context: "The Advaitin's criticism of the saguṇa Brahman should accordingly be understood as showing only the inadequacy of that conception to serve as the goal of philosophy and not as signifying that it is valueless. But its value is restricted to the empirical sphere—a view which is entirely in consonance with the general Advaitic position that practical utility need not rest on metaphysical validity. It is this distinction that has given rise to what are familiarly known as the 'two grades' of teaching in the Advaita—the higher one of the nirguṇa Brahman (parā-vidyā) and the lower one of the saguṇa (aparā-vidyā)."[87]

The applicability of Randall's view of language to Mīmāṁsā may now be examined. The world of ritual generating its own world of experience would constitute, according to Advaita, a truth-system of its own. "The world of science, for instance, forms one truth-system; and the world of art, say, that of Shakespeare's *Othello* or of Scott's *Ivanhoe,* is another."[88] The treatment of religious language as noncognitive has only created yet another truth-system; it has not depicted the truth itself.

Braithwaite's Noncognitive Theory

If for Randall the function of noncognitive religious language is "mythical," for R. B. Braithwaite it is ethical. Braithwaite writes: "A religious assertion, for me, is the assertion of an intention to carry out a certain behavior policy, subsumable under a sufficiently general principle to be a moral one, together with the implicit or explicit statement, but not the assertion, of certain stories."[89]

The connection between "morality" and "story" is, according to Braithwaite, "a psychological and causal one. It is an empirical psychological fact that many people find it easier to resolve upon and to carry through a course of action which is contrary to their natural inclinations if this policy is associated in their minds with certain stories. And in many people the psychological link is not appreciably weakened by the fact that the story associated with the behavior policy is not believed. Next to the Bible and the

87. Hiriyanna, *Outlines*, 377.
88. Hiriyanna, *Essentials*, 167–68.
89. R. B. Braithwaite, *An Empiricist's View of the Nature of Religious Belief* (Cambridge: Cambridge University Press, 1955), 32.

Prayer Book the most influential work in English Christian religious life has been a book whose stories are frankly recognized as fictitious—Bunyan's *Pilgrim's Progress.*"[90] Even if religions may preach the same ethics, where they differ is in the stories with which the ethics are connected.

In brief, when it is said that God is love, what is being said is that the person wishes to lead a lifestyle based on love; that although other religions may preach the same thing, the person in question arrived at such a determination through the Bible rather than any other scripture; and his conviction to lead that life is reinforced by it. Thus Braithwaite maintains that "religious statements are noncognitive, and that they are only: (i) 'expression of feeling'; (ii) 'proclamations of some policy of behaviour'; and (iii) 'propositions which are considered without being believed' (myths) to 'psychologically assist one in carrying through his policy of living.' "[91] Further, on his view, the various religions retain their distinctions in such a theory of religious language. Murty remarks that "if these contentions are justified, there will be no problem of revelation and reason. But on the contrary, if religion does give us knowledge, and knowledge of a distinctive kind, it will raise an important problem. *In India no thinker seems to have maintained a view similar to that which has been put forward by Prof. Braithwaite.*"[92]

John H. Hick raises four problems in relation to this theory: First, the believers treat the stories as true rather than as fictitious. Second, Braithwaite's "account of Religious Language holds that moral assertions are expressions of the asserter's intention to act in the way specified in the assertion. For example, 'lying is wrong' means 'I intend never to lie.' If this were so, it would follow that it would be logically impossible to *intend* to act wrongly." Third, the Christian stories Braithwaite cites are a mixed bag. Some of them are "historical"—as with details of Jesus' life—and others parabolic or mythical. And fourth, ethical endeavour based on psychological reinforcement may not provide as strong a moral motivation as rational belief. To these the following points may also be added: (1) believers have held the stories to be true *and* have acted ethically at the same time, and (2) believers may not have held the details of the stories as distinguished from belief in God to be true *and* have acted morally at the same time.

Advaita Vedānta would tend to be critical of any view that equates moral-

90. Ibid., 27.
91. Murty, *Revelation and Reason,* 314.
92. Ibid., 314–15; emphasis added.

ity with religion either directly or indirectly, as Braithwaite's noncognitive theory of religious language seems to do. K. Satchidananda Murty writes: "There are some thinkers such as Bradley who maintain that religion is essentially practical. Prof. Braithwaite's view that religion is meant to sustain a 'policy for living' amounts to the same. This confusion of religion with morality is based upon the notion generally prevalent in the West that to be highly religious and to be highly moral are one and the same thing."[93] He goes on to say:

> Śaṅkara very rightly insisted (and in this Rāmānuja and Madhva would support him) that the supreme aim of religion is to obtain *samyakdarśana* (right vision) of Brahman, and not to discharge one's moral obligations properly; moral behaviour can at best be only a means of preparing us for the *samyakdarśana.* An important difference between dharma (moral duty) and Brahman is that, while the former is ideal, the latter is real. The moral ideal belongs to the realm of what yet is not, while Brahman is already (in Śaṅkara's words) an "accomplished reality," *siddha vastu.* "No amount of Ought-ness can be made to take the place of Is-ness," said von Hügel.[94]

Phillips's Noncognitive Theory

Z. D. Phillips, taking his cue from Ludwig Wittgenstein (1889–1951), has developed a version of language-game theory in terms of religious language. It is well known that according to Wittgenstein each realm of discourse such as science, art, or religion has its own "language-game" in terms of which the discourse is carried on. The noncognitive theory of religious language is presented by Phillips especially in the context of prayer and immortality. But it is also capable of being generalized. In the context of immortality he disregards the idea of the actual survival of the soul after death in favor of the view that it represents, rather, the present situation in a different light. The following three excerpts from his writings are self-explanatory.

> To say of someone "He'd sell his soul for money" is a perfectly natural remark. It in no way entails any philosophical theory about a duality in

93. Ibid., 317.
94. Ibid., 317–18.

> human nature. The remark is a moral observation about a person, one which expresses the degraded state that person is in. A man's soul, in this context, refers to his integrity, to the complex set of practices and beliefs which acting with integrity would cover for that person. Might not talk about immortality of the soul play a similar role?
>
> Eternal life is the reality of goodness, that in terms of which human life is to be assessed. . . . Eternity is not an extension of this present life, but a mode of judging it. Eternity is not *more* life, but this life seen under certain moral and religious modes of thought. . . . Questions about the immortality of the soul are seen not to be questions concerning the extent of a man's life, and in particular concerning whether that life can extend beyond the grave, but questions concerning the kind of life a man is living.
>
> This renunciation [of the idea of a life to come] is what the believer means by dying to the self. He ceases to see himself as the centre of his world. Death's lesson for the believer is to force him to recognise what all his natural instincts want to resist, namely, that he has no claims on the way things go. Most of all, he is forced to realise that his own life is not a necessity.[95]

The more general position Z. D. Phillips implies about the noncognitive use of religious language is thus explained by John H. Hick: "To participate wholeheartedly in, say, the Christian 'form of life' is, among other things, to use distinctively Christian language, which has its own internal criteria determining what is true and false within this universe of discourse. The internal transactions constituting a given language-game are thus invulnerable to criticism from outside that particular complex of life and language—from which it follows that religious utterances are immune to scientific and other nonreligious comment."[96] He goes on to say: "It would, for example, be an authentic piece of traditional Christian discourse to refer to the first man and woman, Adam and Eve, and to their fall from grace in the Garden of Eden, a fall that has made us, along with all their other descendants, guilty before God. According to this Neo-Wittgensteinian theory of religious language, such a way of talking does not clash with the scientific theory that the human race is not descended from a single primal pair, or

95. Cited in Hick, *Philosophy of Religion*, 92.
96. Ibid., 91.

that the earliest humans did not live a paradisal state, for science is a different language-game, with its own quite different criteria."[97]

It is of course true that the language of a religion constitutes a game of its own because each religion works within its own set of ideas and beliefs. An extreme way of formulating this idea would be to say that a scripture is valid within a tradition only, constituting the basis of the language-game of that textual community.[98] However, such a view is open to criticism. John H. Hick points out that according to a language-game view of religious language the "idea that religion tells us about the actual structure of reality, revealing a larger context of existence than our present earthly life, is on this view a basic mistake," but, as he adds parenthetically, "If it is a mistake, it is one that virtually all the great religious teachers and founders seem to have made!" (So the question arises, Who is really making the mistake?) Hick also presents the fundamental criticism that Phillips's view invites from a Christian perspective:

> Indeed, the basic criticism that has been made of the Neo-Wittgensteinian theory of religious language is that it is not (as it professes to be) an account of normal or ordinary religious language use but rather is a proposal for a radical new interpretation of religious utterances. In this new interpretation, religious expressions are systematically deprived of the cosmic implications that they have always been assumed to have. Not only is human immortality reinterpreted as a quality of this present mortal life but, more fundamentally, God is no longer thought of as a reality existing independently of human belief and disbelief. Rather, as Phillips says, "What [the believer] learns is religious language; a language which he participates in along with other believers. What I am suggesting is that to know how to use this language is to know God." Again, "To have the idea of God is to know God." The skeptical possibility for which such a position does not allow is that people have the idea of God, and participate in theistic language, and yet there is no God.[99]

This last statement reflects a curious inversion of the ontological argument that it is enough to have the idea of God to know God.

97. Ibid.
98. Thus Murty, *Revelation and Reason*, 309.
99. Hick, *Philosophy of Religion*, 92–93.

The existence of God gets somewhat compromised in the noncognitive approach to religious language, as exemplified by Phillips. Advaita Vedānta, however, as it allows for a Reality beyond God, is less likely to be offended by such an implication than Christian theism. Saguṇa Brahman or God is criticized in Advaita Vedānta as a penultimate level of reality but is also utilized, as without it

> . . . we would land ourselves in subjectivism reducing the world to a mere private show, for there would then be no reason for postulating anything beyond what is present to individual consciousness. The Advaitin's criticism of the saguṇa Brahman should accordingly be understood as showing only the inadequacy of that conception to serve as the goal of philosophy and not as signifying that it is valueless. But its value is restricted to the empirical sphere—*a view which is entirely in consonance with the general Advaitic position that practical utility need not rest on metaphysical validity.*[100]

It is clear that this "general Advaitic position" is not at odds as such with the noncognitive theories of language as developed by Randall and Braithwaite.

There is a doctrine of Advaita Vedānta comparable to the language-game theory of religious language. The difference is that Advaita Vedānta does not abandon its claim to being cognitive *even though it accepts that its entire linguistic and semantic apparatus is nothing but a language-game.* The doctrine of Advaita Vedānta alluded to here is that of *mithyātva* of the Vedas. In order to grasp the doctrine and its radical significance one may say that according to Advaita all of creation is a language-game.

It is a cosmological language game in the sense that this entire universe is a universe of discourse brought into material existence by the language of the Vedas. Recall that according to Advaitic etiology the universe is fashioned in accordance with the Vedas as they are revealed at the beginning of each aeon. It is a metaphysical language-game because according to it the universe is an appearance superimposed on Brahman. This universe, with its diversity, is often referred to as "name and form" (*nāma rūpa*). Now, as M. Hiriyanna points out, "All admit that the name (*nāma*) with which we label a thing is conventional; the 'what' (*rūpa*) of it also is the same according to Śaṁkara. The only true reality is that which underlies this conventional

100. Hiriyanna, *Outlines,* 377; emphasis added.

peculiarity of common things."[101] A few points may be clarified here. Hiriyanna has described the name (*nāma*) of a thing as conventional; it should not be forgotten that an eternal convention is involved here, a permanent linguistic covenant.[102] Second, the "world and the Veda have the *same* status; i.e. they are capable of being experienced, but they are not real."[103]

Thus, Advaita Vedānta as *a system of philosophy* is a language-game in the Wittgensteinian sense. The universe itself, according to Advaitic metaphysics, is a language-game, but it is a self-transcending language game which intends to take the player to the reality underlying the game. Or, in the language of Advaita Vedānta, even Vedic authority

> does not secure for the pramāṇa itself ultimate reality, for in mokṣa where nothing but Brahman remains, even that pramāṇa as such must disappear. It signifies that a false means may lead to a true end—a position which may appear untenable; but there are many instances in life where this happens. The image of a person as reflected in a mirror is not real, but it does not therefore fail to serve as the means of showing to him so many facts about his appearance. The roaring of a lion in a dream is not real, but it may wake the dreamer to actual life. It is necessary, however, to remember in thus admitting the utility of error that nothing here is absolutely unreal so that even a false means is not without a nucleus of truth.[104]

This then is the great difference between the noncognitive theory of language-games as applied to Christian theism and as applied to Advaita Vedānta. Unlike Christian theism Advaita Vedānta can accommodate this theory within the doctrine of the *mithyātva* of the Vedas.

General Comments

After a survey of the cognitive and noncognitive theories of language John H. Hick offers the following conclusion:

101. Hiriyanna, *Essentials,* 156; see also 25.
102. Murty, *Revelation and Reason,* 35.
103. M. Hiriyanna explains the situation with great clarity; see *Essentials,* 155–56.
104. Hiriyanna, *Outlines,* 359.

> In implicit opposition to all noncognitive accounts of religious language, traditional Christian and Jewish faith has always presumed the factual character of its basic assertions. It is, of course, evident even to the most preliminary reflection that theological statements, having a unique subject matter, are not wholly like any other kind of statement. They constitute a special use of language, which it is the task of the philosophy of religion to examine. However, the way in which this language operates within historic Judaism and Christianity is much closer to ordinary factual asserting than to either the expressing of aesthetic intuitions or the declaring of ethical policies.[105]

There are two points worth noting in this passage. One is a slight tipping of the hat to the language-game theory but the other is fixing it firmly on the head in the gust of noncognitive approaches to the use of religious language in general. In a sense the position of Advaita Vedānta is curiously analogous on this point. It recognizes that Brahman-language[106] has its own special rules but insists that this does not mean that there is no ineffable reality which corresponds to Brahman.[107]

105. Hick, *Philosophy of Religion,* 94.

106. Murty, *Revelation and Reason,* chap. 4.

107. For a more recent discussion of the significance of Advaita Vedānta in relation to the nature of religious discourse, see John Grimes, *Problems and Perspectives in Religious Discourse: Advaita Vedānta Implications* (Albany: State University of New York Press, 1994), which appeared too late to be incorporated in the present discussion.

9

The Problem of Verification

The assertion that religious language is cognitive tends to fall foul of the logical positivists, who "say that since God sentences are not propositions, but symbolical expressions of certain feelings and attitudes, they cannot have any point of contact with philosophy, which is concerned with the analysis of propositions."[1]

If religious language is cognitive and makes factual assertions, how can the truth or falsehood of these propositions be established? In other words, how can they be verified? In this context John H. Hick remarks, "The basic principle—representing a modified version of the original verifiability principle of the logical positivists—that a factual assertion is one whose truth or falsity makes some experienceable difference, has been applied to theological principles."[2]

The statement needs to be unpacked. The original verifiability principle maintains that "in order to become accepted as true a proposition need only pass one test, a direct examination of its truth or falsity."[3] In the modified version it is argued that a proposition must fulfill a prior condition before being tested—it has to be meaningful; that is to say, it has to be "in principle verifiable, or at least 'probabilifiable,' by reference to human experience. This means in effect that its truth or falsity must make some possible experienceable difference. If its truth or falsity makes no difference that

1. K. Satchidananda Murty, *Revelation and Reason in Advaita Vedānta* (New York: Columbia University Press, 1959), 316.

2. John H. Hick, *The Philosophy of Religion*, 3d ed. (Englewood Cliffs, N.J.: Prentice Hall, 1983), 94.

3. Ibid.

could possibly be observed, the proposition is cognitively meaningless, it does not embody a factual assertion."[4]

John H. Hick provides two instances of cognitively meaningless cases: the instantly doubled universe and the mysterious rabbit. The example of the instantly doubled universe is cited in full below to convey its full force and impact.

> Suppose, for example, the startling news is announced one morning that overnight the entire physical universe has instantaneously doubled in size and that the speed of light has doubled. At first, this news seems to point to a momentous scientific discovery. All the items composing the universe, including our own bodies, are now twice as big as they were yesterday. But inevitable questions concerning the evidence for this report must be raised. How can anyone know that the universe has doubled in size? What observable difference does it make whether this is so or not; what events or appearances are supposed to reveal it? On further reflection, it becomes clear that there *could not* be any evidence for this particular proposition, for if the entire universe has doubled and the speed of light has doubled with it, our measurements have also doubled and we can never know that any change has taken place. If our measuring rod has expanded with the objects to be measured, it cannot measure their expansion. In order adequately to acknowledge the systematic impossibility of testing such a proposition, it seems best to classify it as (cognitively) meaningless. It first seemed to be a genuinely factual assertion, but under scrutiny it proves to lack the basic characteristic of an assertion, namely, that it must make an experienceable difference whether the facts are as alleged or not.[5]

The other example, of the rabbit, is as follows:

> For another example, consider the famous rabbit which at one time haunted philosophical discussions at Oxford. It is a very special rabbit—invisible, intangible, inaudible, weightless, and odorlesss. When the rabbit has been defined by all these negations, does it still make sense to insist that such a creature exists? It is difficult to avoid

4. Ibid., 95.
5. Ibid.

> a negative answer. It seems clear that when every experienceable feature has been removed, there is nothing left about which we can make assertions.[6]

These cases are subtly different. The rabbit seems to represent the *un*-modified verifiability principle of the logical positivists—namely, one of a direct examination of truth or falsity. The instantly doubled universe represents the modified version in the sense that the fact of its *having doubled could be true,* but because it makes no experienceable difference, it is meaningless. In the language of Advaita Vedānta, the rabbit comes closer to being a barren woman's son or a hare's horn, to being *asat* (the "totally nonexistent"), whereas the instantly doubled universe comes closer to belonging to the category of *mithyā* (what cannot be logically established even though it is perceived and experienced). In other words, Advaita Vedānta accepts the universe itself as possessing an order of reality because *it* makes an experienceable difference. If Advaitins were forced to describe the world as true or false they would be in a real quandary, but the modified version of the verifiability principle creates room for the Advaitin to acknowledge that the universe makes an experienceable difference, without accepting it as true.[7]

Some Criticisms of the Verifiability Principle

It is helpful to keep certain considerations in mind when discussing the verifiability principle in the context of religious language.

1. There is a clear distinction to be drawn between statements that are meaningful or meaningless and statements that are true or false. The statement "Pass the potatoes" conveys information and direction and yet it is neither verifiable nor falsifiable.[8]

2. Even if certain statements are false, it does not mean that they are meaningless. The statement that the sun rises in the morning is false—but it is not meaningless in the sense that it makes no experienceable difference.

3. Logical positivists tend to restrict the meaningfulness of words to *either* object-words or link-words, a practice beset with problems, however,

6. Ibid.

7. P. T. Raju, *Idealistic Thought in India* (London: George Allen & Unwin, 1953), 99–100.

8. John A. Grimes, "Advaita Vedānta and the Problem of Religious Language" (Ph.D. diss., University of Madras, 1984), 57.

since it not only consigns religious and specially metaphysical words to the limbo of semantic oblivion but also may cause problems with object-words like "photon" and link-words like "spontaneous," which also fail to meet the logical positivist criteria for meaningfulness.[9]

4. The meaning of "fact" also becomes a crucial issue. Logical positivists consider "fact" to refer "to a small class of statements containing relevance to actual or possible sense experience." This association with observability can be problematical. In a sense even air is not observed. Are not states of mind emotional facts and ideas intellectual facts?

5. Similarly, the word "experience" tends to be restricted to sense experience. But religious language makes the claim that there are facts *and* facts and experiences *and* experiences. As Murty explains:

> The Advaita school would agree with modern thinkers such as Buber, Griesbach or Bowman, who say that what is called "the experience of the self" is of an altogether different kind from the subject-object type of experience. Like Buber, Śaṅkara's school would refuse to use the word "experience" in connection with Ātman, because he who is directly aware (*aparokṣatā*) of the self can only be loosely spoken of as "experiencing"; or as Vidyāraṇya says, he who is aware of God as the inner self (*pratyagātman*) cannot "think of" God, for one thinks of only that which is aloof from or distinct from himself. The "experience" of the self is so concrete and so unanalyzable that it cannot be described as the "this." Vācaspati says it is something like the tasting of sugar, which cannot be described or differentiated in language from the experience of tasting honey. This example reminds us of Prof. Ramsey's illustration of eating a cake which cannot be expressed in abstract language.[10]

Application of the Verifiability Principle: John Wisdom

John Wisdom presents his approach to the problem through the celebrated parable of the gardener. The parable needs to be presented in some detail in order to fully grasp the philosophical point it intends to convey.

9. Ibid., 58.
10. Murty, *Revelation and Reason*, 290–91.

> Two people return to their long-neglected garden and find among the weeds a few of the old plants surprisingly vigorous. One says to the other "It must be that a gardener has been coming and doing something about these plants." Upon inquiry they find that no neighbor has ever seen anyone at work in their garden. The first man says to the other "He must have worked while people slept." The other says, "No, someone would have heard him and besides, anybody who cared about the plants would have kept down these weeds." The first man says, "Look at the way these are arranged. There is purpose and a feeling for beauty here. I believe that someone comes, someone invisible to mortal eyes. I believe that the more carefully we look the more we shall find confirmation of this." They examine the garden ever so carefully and sometimes they come on new things suggesting that a gardener comes and sometimes they come on new things suggesting the contrary and even that a malicious person has been at work. Besides examining the garden carefully they also study what happens to gardens left without attention. Each learns all the other learns about this and about the garden. Consequently, when after all this, one says "I still believe a gardener comes" while the other says "I don't" their different words now reflect no difference as to what they have found in the garden, no difference as to what they would find in the garden if they looked further and no difference about how fast untended gardens fall into disorder. At this stage, in this context, the gardener hypothesis has ceased to be experimental, the difference between one who accepts and one who rejects it is not now a matter of the one expecting something the other does not expect. What is the difference between them? The one says, "A gardener comes unseen and unheard. He is manifested only in his works with which we are all familiar," the other says "There is no gardener" and with this difference in what they say about the gardener goes a difference in how they feel towards the garden, in spite of the fact that neither expects anything of it which the other does not expect.[11]

The essence of the situation here is that "neither of the rival positions is, in principle, verifiable," as "there is no disagreement about experienceable facts." Rather, both parties are "reacting in a different way to the same set of facts." When we realize that the difference here lies not in the facts but in

11. Quoted in Hick, *Philosophy of Religion,* 96.

the understanding of those facts, "we can no longer say in any usual sense that one is right and one is wrong."[12]

The position taken by Wisdom here corresponds to the debate of Advaita Vedānta with Sāṅkhya on the nature of teleology. The Sāṅkhya school of Hindu thought accepts the view that unconscious teleology is possible, that it is possible for the garden to flourish without a gardener. In fact, an example close to that of the plants in the garden appears in the Brahma-sūtra: "Since limited products like roots, sprouts, etc. are born out of a combination of many materials, therefore all external and corporeal modifications too must have been similarly formed."[13] This would be the atheistic view of the garden. The theistic view of the garden is echoed in the following: "Palaces and pleasure gardens do not come into existence of their own accord."[14] If we refer only to the plants in the garden the statement becomes symmetrical with Wisdom's parable.

According to Advaita Vedānta, however, "unconscious teleology is unintelligible."[15] Thus it would side with the theistic version—but such taking sides makes no "experienceable difference" to the situation and therefore Wisdom's point holds.

Application of the Verifiability Principle: Antony Flew

Antony Flew converted Wisdom's parable from one of verifiability to one of falsifiability, as John Grimes explains it, in order "to illustrate that the problem of religious language lies in its unfalsifiability. His version of the parable shows that someone may dissipate his assertion completely without noticing that he has done so. A fine brash hypothesis may thus be killed by inches, the death by a thousand qualifications. Thus the challenge has shifted from verifiability to falsifiability of religious assertions. For a statement to be cognitively meaningful there must exist some conceivable event which would count against that statement."[16]

12. Ibid., 95–96.

13. Swami Gambhirananda, trans., *Brahma-Sūtra-Bhāṣya of Śrī Śaṅkarācārya* (Calcutta: Advaita Ashrama, 1977), 370.

14. S. Radhakrishnan, trans., *The Brahma Sūtra: The Philosophy of a Spiritual Life* (London: George Allen & Unwin, 1960), 366.

15. Satischandra Chatterjee and Dhirendramohan Datta, *An Introduction to Indian Philosophy* (1950; reprint, University of Calcutta, 1968), 369.

16. Grimes, "Advaita Vedānta," 22.

Thus Flew's "solution" shifts the focus from verifiability to falsifiability, and the question now posed is, "Whether there is any conceivable event which, if it were to occur, would decisively refute theism?"[17]

Antony Flew elaborates this approach as follows, in the traditional Judeo-Christian context of belief in a loving God. Could any event falsify this belief? Flew maintains that as theism is traditionally understood in Christian circles, such a proposition that "God loves us all" is unfalsifiable. He expounds his position in the following celebrated passage:

> Now it often seems to people who are not religious as if there was no conceivable event or series of events the occurrence of which would be admitted by sophisticated religious people to be a sufficient reason for conceding "There wasn't a God after all" or "God does not really love us then." Someone tells us that God loves us as a father loves his children. We are reassured. But then we see a child dying of inoperable cancer of the throat. His earthly father is driven frantic in his efforts to help, but his Heavenly Father reveals no obvious sign of concern. Some qualification is made—God's love is "not a merely human love" or it is "an inscrutable love," perhaps—and we realize that such sufferings are quite compatible with the truth of the assertion that "God loves us as a father (but, of course . . .)." We are reassured again. But then perhaps we ask: what is this assurance of God's (appropriately qualified) love worth, what is this apparent guarantee really a guarantee against? Just what would have to happen not merely (morally and wrongly) to tempt but also (logically and rightly) to entitle us to say "God does not love us" or even "God does not exist"? I therefore put . . . the simple central questions, "What would have to occur or to have occurred to constitute for you a disproof of the love of, or of the existence of, God?"[18]

From an Advaitic point of view culpability for tragedy rests not with God but with karma. God is called the overseer of karma in the Upaniṣads,[19] and according to Advaita Vedānta "Individual human beings have to suffer their karmas for His purpose. God manipulates the fruits of karma; He does not add or take away from it. The subconsciousness of man is a warehouse of

17. Hick, *Philosophy of Religion*, 97.
18. Quoted in ibid.
19. S. Radhakrishnan, ed., *The Principal Upaniṣads* (London: George Allen & Unwin, 1953), 746.

good and bad karma. Iswar [God] chooses from this warehouse what he sees will best suit the spiritual evolution at the time of each man whether pleasant or painful. Thus there is nothing arbitrary."[20] But even when the accountability is shifted to karma, it still remains unfalsifiable. This may not always be the case. Karl Potter has argued that some day the working of Karma may actually become *verifiable.*[21] But that is not, however, the case as of now.

Application of the Verifiability Principle: R. M. Hare

R. M. Hare maintains that although religious language may not be verifiable, and further that it may not be falsifiable, it may yet be useful. He coined the word *blik* to capture this quality of religious language. And thereby hangs another parable. Hare begins by admitting that "on the ground marked out by Flew, he seems to me to be completely victorious." But Hare goes on to add "I therefore shift my ground by relating another parable." Hare's parable runs as follows:

> A certain lunatic is convinced that all dons want to murder him. His friends introduce him to all the mildest and most respectable dons that they can find, and after each of them has retired, they say, "You see, he doesn't really want to murder you; he spoke to you in a most cordial manner; surely you are convinced now?" But the lunatic replies "Yes, but that was only his diabolical cunning; he's really plotting against me the whole time, like the rest of them; I know it I tell you." However many kindly dons are produced, the reaction is still the same.
>
> Now we say that such a person is deluded. But what is he deluded about? About the truth or falsity of an assertion? Let us apply Flew's test to him. There is no behaviour of dons that can be enacted which he will accept as counting against his theory; and therefore his theory, on this test, asserts nothing. But it does not follow that there is no difference between what he thinks about dons and what most of

20. Paul Brunton and Munagala Venkatramiah, *Conscious Immortality* (Tiruvannamalai: Sri Ramanasramam, 1984), 135.

21. Karl H. Potter, "The Karma Theory and Its Interpretations in Some Indian Philosophical Systems," in *Karma and Rebirth in Classical Indian Traditions,* ed. Wendy Doniger O'Flaherty (Berkeley and Los Angeles: University of California Press, 1980), 259–60.

> us think about them—otherwise we should not call him a lunatic and ourselves sane, and dons would have no reason to feel uneasy about his presence in Oxford.

On the basis of this parable Hare (1) identifies a new concept which he calls *blik* and (2) on the basis of this *blik* distinguishes his position from that of Flew as follows:

> Let us call that in which we differ from this lunatic, our respective *bliks*. He has an insane *blik* about dons; we have a sane one. It is important to realize that we have a sane one, not no *blik* at all; for there must be two sides to any argument—if he has a wrong *blik*, then those who are right about dons must have a right one. Flew has shown that a *blik* does not consist in an assertion or system of them; but nevertheless it is very important to have the right *blik*.[22]

John H. Hick, however, detects a contradiction in Hare's approach. He points out that in the "previously quoted passage" Hare has on the one hand drawn a distinction between a sane and an insane *blik* and yet has, at the same time, eliminated any basis for distinguishing between a sane and an insane *blik* by claiming "that *bliks* are unverifiable and unfalsifiable. If experience can never yield either confirmation or disconfirmation of *bliks*, there is no basis for speaking of them as being right or wrong, appropriate or inappropriate, sane or insane. These distinctions make sense only if it also makes sense to refer to tests, evidence, and verification. It is precisely this confirmation that Flew has demanded in relation to religious beliefs. It seems, then, that Hare has neither met Flew's challenge nor shown a way of avoiding it."[23]

It seems possible to maintain that Hare has shown a way to avoid the limitation imposed by the verifiability principle, contrary to the conclusion drawn by Hick. This becomes apparent if a distinction is drawn between meaningful statements and verifiable statements and if it can be shown that statements can be meaningful *without* being verifiable or falsifiable, as Hick insists. It can even be argued, from the point of view of Advaita Vedānta, that although the statement *itself* may be only meaningful, it can lead to

22. William L. Rowe and William J. Wainright, eds., *Philosophy of Religion: Selected Readings* (New York: Harcourt Brace Jovanovich, 1973), 422.
23. Hick, *Philosophy of Religion*, 98–99.

verification. In other words, one must think of language from this point of view as not merely *confirmative or disconfirmative but also transformative.* Thus in Advaita "the conception of saguṇa Brahman involves adhyāsa, and like that of Īśvara cannot be regarded as ultimate. Or to state it differently, the saguṇa Brahman includes not only reality but also appearance, which is something less than real."[24]

It should be noted here that the claim itself is muted in terms of right or wrong. In fact it is clearly stated by Advaitins that "though God as creator is only apparent, yet his importance and value should not be ignored. It is only through the lower standpoint that we can gradually mount up to the higher."[25] In Advaita in fact *efficiency has been used as a test of verifiability.* One of the grounds on which the universe is said to possess an order of reality as opposed to absolute nothingness is that "it possesses, unlike non-entity, practical efficiency or has value, being serviceable in life."[26]

This point is further strengthened if the following comment by Hare is taken into account:

> Suppose we believe that everything that happened, happened by pure chance. This would not of course be an assertion; for it is compatible with anything happening or not happening, and so, incidentally, is its contradictory. But if we had this belief, we should not be able to explain or predict or plan anything. Thus, although we should not be *asserting* anything different from those of a more normal belief, there would be a great difference between us; and this is the sort of difference that there is between those who really believe in God and those who really disbelieve in him.[27]

Advaita Vedānta regards the idea of causation as logically untenable,[28] and yet believing in it empirically is a sane *blik* because although Advaita establishes the "external world as unreal . . . it is therefore not to be taken as chaotic. From the empirical point of view it is a cosmos; and Śaṁkara speaks of it in more than one place as exhibiting spatial, temporal and causal order."[29]

24. M. Hiriyanna, *Outlines of Indian Philosophy,* 371.
25. Chatterjee and Datta, *Introduction,* 398.
26. Hiriyanna, *Essentials,* 156.
27. Quoted in Hick, *Philosophy of Religion,* 98.
28. Hiriyanna, *Essentials,* 159.
29. Ibid., 160.

Application of the Verifiability Principle: Basil Mitchell

Not to be outdone by Wisdom, Flew, and Hare, Basil Mitchell recounts a parable of his own to distinguish his position from that of Flew. As the parable covers several pages in the original, considerations of space compel one to present John Hick's abridged version:

> A member of the resistance movement in an occupied country meets a stranger who deeply impresses him as being truthful and trustworthy and who claims to be the resistance leader. He urges the partisan to have faith in him whatever may happen. Sometimes the stranger is seen apparently aiding the resistance and sometimes apparently collaborating with the enemy. Nevertheless the partisan continues in trust. He admits that on the face of it some of the stranger's actions strain this trust. However, he has faith, even though at times his faith is sorely tried, that there is a satisfactory explanation of the stranger's ambiguous behavior. "It is here [says Mitchell] that my parable differs from Hare's. The partisan admits that many things may and do count against his belief: whereas Hare's lunatic who has a *blik* about dons doesn't admit that anything counts against his *blik*. Nothing *can* count against *bliks*. Also the partisan has a reason for having in the first instance committed himself, viz. the character of the Stranger; whereas the lunatic has no reason for his *blik* about dons—because, of course, you can't have reasons for *bliks*."[30]

The extent to which the relationship between the resistance member and the resistance leader is reminiscent of the master-disciple or Guruśiṣya relationship in Advaita is striking.[31] The seeker for truth is caught in the cycle of *saṁsāra*, like the resistance fighter caught up in a war. Both want to alter and overcome the situation. Both meet someone who claims to have the solution to the problem but whose apparent behavior may not inspire such confidence. Faith is called for, and in the end it is vindicated.[32]

30. Hick, *Philosophy of Religion*, 99. For the full text, see Rowe and Wainright, eds., *Philosophy*, 424–26.

31. See Eliot Deutsch and J.A.B. van Buitenen, *A Source Book of Advaita Vedānta* (Honolulu: The University of Hawaii Press), 123ff., in which passages are translated from Śaṅkara's Upadeśasāhasrī (Classical treatise on teaching).

32. William Cenkner, *A Tradition of Teachers: Śaṅkara and the Jagadgurus of Today* (Delhi: Motilal Banarsidass, 1983), 54ff. It is interesting to note how incredible the Advaitin claim must initially

John H. Hick comments on the parable of Basil Mitchell that "Mitchell's parable is concerned with a straightforward matter of fact, which can, in principle, be definitely ascertained. The stranger himself knows on which side he is, and after the war, when all the facts are brought to light, the ambiguity of his behavior will be resolved and his true character made clear. Thus, Mitchell is concerned with stressing the similarity rather than the dissimilarity between religious beliefs and ordinary, unproblematic factual beliefs."[33] This similarity Hick alludes to toward the end of the passage is a very important element in Advaita. The propositional or cognitive bias of religious language is well illustrated by an episode described by William Cenkner: "Śvetaketu in the Upaniṣads is instructed with 'That thou art' nine times before the great axiom passes from a mere propositional statement to one fully perceived and finally caught in intuitive vision. In each of the nine stages, Śvetaketu comes to a keener understanding of reality, reality remaining always the same."[34]

Application of the Verifiability Principle: John H. Hick

Hick discusses the application of the verifiability principle in the context of Christianity in two parts: (1) a discussion of verifiability as such and (2) a discussion of verifiability in the context of Christianity. Although he offers his suggestions "based upon the fact that Christianity includes afterlife beliefs,"[35] these suggestions can also be understood and applied independently of that context.

John H. Hick identifies five points for consideration in this context. It seems best to proceed by first stating and then commenting on each from the point of view of Advaita Vedānta.

> The verification of a factual assertion is not the same as a logical demonstration of it. The central core of the idea of verification is the

---

appear to a student. Diversity of all kinds is a matter of daily experience but "if monism is the truth, no part of this diversity can be ultimate. This is the significance of the teaching of the Upanishads, so far as our common beliefs are concerned" (Hiriyanna, *Essentials,* 25). In terms of our common beliefs the Advaitin assertion is truly shocking.

33. Hick, *Philosophy of Reason,* 99.

34. Cenkner, *Tradition,* 62.

35. Hick, *Philosophy of Religion,* 100–101.

> removal of grounds for rational doubt. That a proposition, *p*, is verified means that something happens that makes it clear that *p* is true. A question is settled, so that there is no longer room for rational doubt concerning it. The way in which such grounds are excluded varies, of course, with the subject matter, but the common feature in all cases of verification is the ascertaining of truth by the removal of grounds for rational doubt. Whenever such grounds have been removed, we rightly speak of verification having taken place.[36]

Hick's position here is comparable to the doctrine of the self-validity of knowledge in Advaita Vedānta. Let the verification involve the factual assertion of a cognition. According to the Advaitic view, "whenever there is knowledge of an object, this fact is known in the very act; for nobody who has knowledge doubts whether he has it or not."[37] But does this mean that all cognitions and assertions thereof are true? False cognitions are possible but the "falsity of a cognition is due to either misapprehension, doubt, or non-apprehension."[38] "Whenever there is no awareness of any defect in the cause of a cognition, *there can be no reasonable doubt about its truth.* So every cognition attests itself as true."[39]

This is, however, true only of empirical knowledge. In relation to transcendental knowledge it could be argued that only positive experience provides verification—not the "removal of grounds for rational doubt." Once the nature of reality as determined by Advaita has been heard (*śravaṇa*), it should be reflected on. As Hiriyanna puts it, "If these are facts which are beyond the reach of reason and cannot therefore be absolutely demonstrated, philosophy should at least point to the *likelihood* of their being true."[40] But

> if reflection (*manana*) is for getting intellectual conviction, meditation (*dhyāna*) is for gaining direct experience. Without the acquisition of such immediate or intuitive experience, philosophy, even if it represents a logical certainty, will be of purely academic interest. Such theoretical knowledge may be a mental accomplishment; but, being mediate, it cannot dispel the immediate conviction in the ultimacy of diversity and will not therefore become a permanent

36. Ibid., 100.
37. Murty, *Revelation and Reason,* 13.
38. Ibid., 14.
39. Ibid.; emphasis added.
40. Hiriyanna, *Essentials,* 16.

> influence on life. The Upanishads base this part of their teaching on a fact of experience, viz. that a mediate knowledge of truth cannot overcome an immediate illusion—that seeing alone is believing.[41]

Hick's second point on the application of the verifiability principle is as follows:

> Sometimes it is necessary to put oneself in a certain position or to perform some particular operation as a prerequisite of verification. For example, one can only verify "There is a table in the next room" by going into the next room; however, it is to be noted that no one is compelled to do this.[42]

Advaita Vedānta agrees. If one wishes to verify the knowledge of Brahman, one must satisfy certain preconditions. These are spelled out in detail in Śaṅkara in his gloss on Brahmasūtra 1.1.1 and discussed in not just Advaita but all schools of Vedānta. They disagree about the exact nature of the preconditions but agree on the fact that they are required.[43]

Hick's third point is as follows:

> Therefore, although "verifiable" normally means "publicly verifiable" (i.e., capable in principle of being verified by anyone), it does not follow that a given verifiable proposition has in fact been or will in fact ever be verified by everyone. The number of people who verify a particular true proposition depends upon all manner of contingent factors.[44]

This point is also accepted within Advaita Vedānta. In Advaita Vedānta the "immediate experience or direct intuition of the Absolute is described as *vidvadanubhava* to distinguish it from lay experience."[45]

Hick's fourth point:

> It is possible for a proposition to be in principle verifiable but not in principle falsifiable. Consider, for example, the proposition that

41. Ibid., 25–26.
42. Hick, *Philosophy of Religion,* 100.
43. See Radhakrishnan, trans., *Brahma Sūtra,* 227–34.
44. Hick, *Philosophy of Religion,* 100.
45. Hiriyanna, *Outlines,* 380–81.

> "there are three successive sevens in the decimal determination of π." So far as the value of π has been worked out, it does not contain a series of three sevens; but since the operation can proceed *ad infinitum* it will always be true that a triple seven may occur at a point not yet reached in anyone's calculations. Accordingly, the proposition may one day be verified if it is true but can never be falsified if it is false.[46]

Advaita Vedānta presents us with a situation in which a proposition may be falsified if it is false but cannot be verified if it is true when it claims in "the famous statement, *brahmavid brahmaiva bhavati.* The knower of *brahman* becomes *brahman.*"[47]

Advaita Vedānta also presents a statement that may "one day be verified if it is true but can never be falsified if it is false," in terms of the following statement found in two Upaniṣads (Bṛhadāraṇyaka 4.4.7; Kaṭha 2.3.14): "When all the desires that dwell in the heart are cast away, then does the mortal become immortal, then he attains *Brahman* here (in this very body)."[48]

If a human being reaches a state of being free of desires, this statement may one day be verified as true, but it cannot be falsified if false, as *saṁsāra* is endless.

Hick's fifth point on the application of the verifiability principle is as follows:

> The hypothesis of continued conscious existence after bodily death provides another instance of a proposition that is verifiable if true but not falsifiable if false. This hypothesis entails a prediction that will be verified in one's own experience if it is true but that cannot be falsified if it is false. That is to say, it can be false, but *that* it is false can never be a fact that anyone has experientially verified. This principle does not undermine the meaningfulness of the survival hypothesis, for if its prediction is true, it will be known to be true.[49]

46. Hick, *Philosophy of Religion,* 100.

47. Radhakrishnan, trans., *Brahma Sūtra,* 267. No textual reference is provided. Grimes ("Advaita Vedānta," 179) states: "There is no knowing of Reality but only being it." He cites this as a translation of the expression *anubhavāvasānatvat* in Śaṅkara's Brahmasūtrabhāṣya 1.1.2. This does not seem to be at least the direct sense of this gloss, although Grimes's statement of the Advaitic position as such seems to be correct.

48. Radhakrishnan, ed., *Principal Upaniṣads,* 273.

49. Hick, *Philosophy of Religion,* 100–101.

In terms of the idiom of Advaita Vedānta the statement would read: rebirth is verifiable if true but not falsifiable if false.

John H. Hick developed the points discussed above in a theistic context, so they may now also be examined in that light. To make his point, he recounts the following parable:

> Two people are travelling together along a road. One of them believes that it leads to the Celestial City, the other that it leads nowhere, but since this is the only road there is, both must travel it. Neither has been this way before; therefore, neither is able to say what they will find around each corner. During their journey they meet with moments of refreshment and delight, and with moments of hardship and danger. All the time one of them thinks of the journey as a pilgrimage to the Celestial City. She interprets the pleasant parts as encouragements and the obstacles as trials of her purpose and lessons in endurance, prepared by the sovereign of that city and designed to make of her a worthy citizen of the place when at last she arrives. The other, however, believes none of this, and sees their journey as an unavoidable and aimless ramble. Since he has no choice in the matter, he enjoys the good and endures the bad. For him there is no Celestial City to be reached, no all-encompassing purpose ordaining their journey; there is only the road itself and the luck of the road in good weather and in bad.
>
> During the course of the journey, the issue between them is not an experimental one. That is to say, they do not entertain different expectations about the coming details of the road, but only about its ultimate destination. Yet, when they turn the last corner, it will be apparent that one of them has been right all the time and the other wrong. Thus, although the issue between them has not been experimental, it has nevertheless been a real issue. They have not merely felt differently about the road, for one was feeling appropriately and the other inappropriately in relation to the actual state of affairs. Their opposed interpretations of the situation have constituted genuinely rival assertions, whose assertion-status has the peculiar characteristic of being guaranteed retrospectively by a future crux.[50]

50. Ibid., 101.

The points he makes through the parable are twofold: First, "This parable, like all parables, has narrow limitations. It is designed to make only one point: that Judaic-Christian theism postulates an ultimate unambiguous existence *in patria,* as well as our present ambiguous existence *in via.* There is a state of having arrived as well as a state of journeying, an eternal heavenly life as well as an earthly pilgrimage. The alleged future experience cannot, of course, be appealed to as evidence for theism as a present interpretation of our experience, but it does apparently suffice to render the *choice between theism and atheism a real and not merely an empty or verbal choice.*"[51] Second,

> The universe as envisaged by the theist, then differs as a totality from the universe as envisaged by the atheist. However, from our present standpoint within the universe, this difference does not involve a difference in the objective content of each or even any of its passing moments. The theist and the atheist do not (or need not) expect different events to occur in the successive details of the temporal process. They do not (or need not) entertain divergent expectations of the course of history viewed from within. *However, the theist does and the atheist does not expect that when history is completed, it will be seen to have led to a particular end state* and to have fulfilled a specific purpose, namely, that of creating "children of God."[52]

Advaita Vedānta insists on the possibility, indeed the goal, of ultimate realization right here in this world. Śaṅkara's well-known comment on his gloss on Brahmasūtra 1.4.15 may be cited again here: "It should not be disputed whether the knower of *brahman* is embodied for a time or is not embodied. How can one's own intimate experience of *brahman* existing together with embodiment be denied by another?"[53]

This concept, known as that of *jīvanmukti,* is widely attested to in Advaita and to that extent Hick's idea of eschatological verification does not apply here. However, it applies to the idea of *videhamukti* or liberation coincident with the loss of the body, which is also accepted within Advaita Vedānta.

It also seems applicable to the allied doctrine of *kramamukti.* The idea here is that of progressive realization, of those who "progress from one state

51. Ibid.; emphasis added.
52. Ibid.; emphasis added.
53. Radhakrishnan, trans., *Brahma Sūtra,* 216.

of existence to a higher without returning to the world of mortals until at last they find release from the cycle of births and deaths."[54] Here the idea of eschatological verification along with the theistic parables applies, subject to the limitation that the soul is still in transit. *But Advaita Vedānta strongly subscribes to the view that liberation is possible within this very life,* and it has its own repertoire of parables to illustrate its own points. Five of them are quite well known: (1) the parable of the abandoned prince, (2) the parable of Karṇa, (3) the parable of the lost necklace, (4) the parable of the lion's cub, and (5) the parable of the tenth man.

The first parable is about a "King's Son" (*rājaputra*) who did not know that he was of royal blood. The spiritual meaning here and in the other four parables is that there is no bondage fundamentally, no release; we are by nature free. It is only an illusion that we are bound. When the yogi attains to knowledge, no fundamental change takes place in his essence; only his outlook undergoes the change—his understanding of what is "real." He dismisses the superimposed wrong notions about the underlying reality of himself and everything else, and with that comes into possession of all that he in essence is, *rājaputravat,* "like the King's Son":

The Parable of the Abandoned Prince

> There was a king's son, once upon a time, who, having been born under an unlucky star, was removed from the capital while still a babe, and reared by a primitive tribesman, a mountaineer, outside the pale of the Brahman civilization [i.e., as an outcaste, uneducated, ritually unclean]. He therefore lived for many years under the false notion: "I am a mountaineer." In due time, however, the old king died. And since there was nobody eligible to assume the throne, a certain minister of state, ascertaining that the boy that had been cast away into the wilderness some years before was still alive, went out, searched the wilderness, traced the youth, and, having found him, instructed him: "Thou art not a mountaineer; thou art the King's Son." Immediately, the youth abandoned the notion that he was an outcaste and took to himself his royal nature. He said to himself: "I am king."[55]

54. Hiriyanna, *Essentials,* 29.

55. Heinrich Zimmer, *Philosophies of India,* ed. Joseph Campbell (New York: Pantheon Books, 1951), 308.

The Parable of Karṇa

Karṇa was a hero of the Mahābhārata who was born to Kuntī while she was a virgin through the rash application of a *mantra.* She kept this fact a secret till close to the outbreak of hostilities. As Karṇa was brought up by a childless couple as their adopted foundling he did not discover his true identity till told so by Kuntī. But he was always her son. Therefore, like the case of the abandoned prince Kuntī, the mother of the Pāṇḍavas going to Karṇa on the eve of the Mahābhārata war and telling him that he is not Rādheya but a Pāṇḍava, her own son is a similar example.[56]

The Parable of the Lost Necklace

A lady had a precious necklace round her neck. Once in her excitement she forgot it and thought that the necklace was lost. She became anxious and looked for it in her home but could not find it. She asked her friends and neighbours if they knew anything about the necklace. They did not. At last a kind friend of hers told her to feel the necklace round the neck. She found that it had all along been round her neck and she was happy! When others asked her later if she found the necklace which was lost, she said, "Yes, I have found it." She still felt that she had recovered a lost jewel.

Now did she lose it at all? It was all along round her neck. But judge her feelings. She is happy as if she had recovered a lost jewel. Similarly with us, we imagine that we would realise that Self some time, whereas we are never anything but the Self.[57]

The Parable of the Lion's Cub

A lioness, who was pregnant, coming across a flock of sheep grazing, pounced upon one of them and in the exertion she gave birth to a cub. Shortly after she died. The cub found itself amongst the flock of

56. P. Sankaranarayanan, *What Is Advaita?* (Bombay: Bharatiya Vidya Bhavan, 1970), 101.

57. *Talks with Sri Ramana Maharshi* (Tiruvannamalai: Sri Ramanasramam, 1984), 565; see also 471. For another account, see Sankaranarayanan, *What Is Advaita?* 100–101: "A woman, forgetting that her necklace is round her neck goes about anxiously searching for it everywhere and querying everybody. Another woman tells her: 'It is there round your neck.' Then the first woman exclaims: 'Thank God! I have *got* my necklace back.' In truth she never 'lost' it to get it back. She was oblivious of its existence round her neck. In her ajñana she thought she had lost it. Her 'getting it now' is only getting the knowledge that it has been already and always round her neck. So too there is no 'attainment' of Brahman in moksa; it is only getting the awareness that one is Brahman already and always."

> sheep and began to live amongst them and imitate them in all possible ways. In the course of a few months it began to live like a sheep. It learnt to bleat like the sheep and live on grass and leaves. Its father who vainly searched for the lioness all over the place one day suddenly found the lion's cub in midst of sheep. It came near the flock which ran away leaving the cub behind. The cub began to bleat like the sheep and tried to run away. The lion then said to it, "Why do you bleat? You are a lion, you must roar. Why do you eat grass? That is not your food." Saying so, the lion gave the cub a piece of meat, but the cub refused to eat it. The lion then dragged the cub to a stream of water and said, "Look into the water and see whether you look like a lion or like a sheep." This convinced the cub and it ate the food given by the lion. It became transformed into its original self, began to roar like a lion and its appearance and movements from that moment became truly leonine.[58]
>
> *The Parable of the Tenth Man*
>
> Ten rustics who crossed a river in their travels . . . wished to make sure, after reaching the other shore, that all the ten of them had safely crossed over. Each one of them counted the rest and found there were only nine. They began to wail that one of them had died while crossing the river. In came a stranger who asked them the cause of their wailing. They reported that they were ten before they crossed the river, but now they were only nine and so one of them had evidently died. The stranger made all of them stand in a row and counted them "1, 2, 3 . . . 9" and pointing to the last man in the row, said "thou art the tenth" (*daśamastvamasi*). At once the rustics jumped with joy that the tenth man had been restored to them."[59]

The point of these parables is clear. Mokṣa is ever present; it remains to be realized. As Sankaranarayanan puts it,

> In these analogies, the necklace was never lost, the prince did not become a hunter's son and the tenth man was not drowned. The necklace was always on the woman's neck; by her ajñāna she imagined she had lost it. When told by another, she regained, i.e., realised

58. Swami Sambuddhananda, *Vedānta Through Stories* (Bombay: Sri Ramakrishna Ashram, 1959), 87–88.
59. Sankaranarayanan, *What Is Advaita?* 102.

> what has always been there. Due to his ajñāna of his real nature, the prince wrongly thought that he was the hunter's son. On being told by the ministers, he realised his nature as the prince that he had always been. The tenth man did not die; they all wrongly imagined in their ajñāna that they had lost the tenth man. When told by the stranger, they realised that the tenth man was always with them.[60]

Or as Ramana Maharshi has remarked: "What happens in the end? Karṇa was ever the son of Kunti. The tenth man was such all along. Rama was Vishnu all the time. Such is *jñānam.* It is being aware of That which always is."[61]

The points developed by John H. Hick in the context of a Christian eschatological verification are broadly concerned with the following questions: (1) What is the connection between afterlife and the existence of God? (2) If we achieved salvation then how would we know that it has been achieved? (3) How would we know that it is God we encounter when we do and not someone or something else?

These points may now be elaborated in the light of Advaita Vedānta. First, there is *no* direct connection between afterlife and the existence of God. John H. Hick writes:

> Even if it were granted (as many philosophers would not be willing to grant) that it makes sense to speak of continued personal existence after death, this fact cannot by itself render belief in God verifiable. Nor would an actual experience of survival necessarily serve to verify theism. It might be taken as just a surprising natural fact. The deceased atheist able to remember life on earth might find that the universe has turned out to be more complex, and perhaps more to be approved of, then he or she had realized. However, the mere fact of survival, with a new body in a new environment, would not demonstrate to such a person the reality of God. The life to come might turn out to be as religiously ambiguous as this present life. It might still be quite unclear whether or not there is a God.[62]

These remarks seem to receive interesting confirmation from the English empiricist philosopher, Sir Alfred J. Ayer, who confessed that a recent near-

60. Ibid., 102–3.
61. *Talks with Sri Ramana Maharshi,* 591. *Jñāna* means knowledge.
62. Hick, *Philosophy of Religion,* 102.

death experience had "slightly weakened my conviction that my genuine death, which is due fairly soon, [he is 88] will be the end of me though I continue to hope that it will be. [It had] not weakened my conviction that there is no God."[63] As a consequence of his experience then Ayer is prepared to concede the possibility of an afterlife but not of the existence of God. From the point of view of *Hinduism* there is no necessary connection between the two, as there are atheistic schools of Hindu thought which believe in an afterlife but not in God, for example, Sāṅkhya. However, from the point of view of *Advaita Vedānta* there is a connection, as in this system it is God who supervises the working of karma through various lives. One further point may be recognized—both Christianity and Hinduism profess postmortem survival, but in different forms. In Hinduism it takes the form of reincarnation and in Christianity of resurrection. Advaita Vedānta shares the general belief in reincarnation at the empirical level but provides two accounts of it. One applies to those who are not progressing spiritually and "are born again and again, their condition in any particular life being determined by 'the nature of their deeds' and 'the nature of their thoughts' in the past."[64] They will have an afterlife in the form of reincarnation without encountering God. But those on the high spiritual road will arrive, in due course in "*brahmaloka* or the Kingdom of God."[65] S. Radhakrishnan, who makes this equation, also identifies both *brahmaloka* and the kingdom of God with cosmic salvation (*sarvamukti*), a doctrine that is not without its problems.[66] The equation of *brahmaloka* with the Kingdom of God is, however, sustainable,[67] with this difference: that it is the worshipers of *saguṇa brahma* who reach it,[68] and those of *nirguṇa* brahma who go beyond it.

Second, how would one know that one has reached the Kingdom of God, if survival after death by itself does not involve entering it? John H. Hick offers the following explanation in a Christian context:

> The system of ideas that surrounds the Christian concept of God, and in the light of which that concept has to be understood, includes expectations concerning the final fulfillment of God's purpose for

63. John Dart, "After 'Near-Death' Experience, Prominent Atheist Warms to After Life," *The Gazette* (Montreal) 9 October 1988, B-1.

64. Hiriyanna, *Essentials*, 29. The quotation within the quotation is from Kaṭha Upaniṣad 2.2.7.

65. Radhakrishnan, trans., *Brahma Sūtra*, 218.

66. Ibid.

67. Ibid., 559.

68. Ibid., 547–48.

> mankind in the "Kingdom of God." The experience that would verify Christian belief in God is the experience of participating in that eventual fulfillment. According to the New Testament, the general nature of God's purpose for human life is the creation of "children of God" who shall participate in eternal life. One can say this much without professing advance knowledge of the concrete forms of such a fulfillment. The situation is analogous to that of a small child looking forward to adult life and then, having grown to adulthood, looking back upon childhood. The child possesses and can use correctly the concept of "being grown-up," although as a child, one does not yet know exactly what it is like to be grown-up. When one reaches adulthood, one is, nevertheless, able to know that one has reached it, for one's understanding of adult maturity grows as one matures. Something analogous may be supposed to happen in the case of the fulfillment of the divine purpose for human life. That fulfillment may be as far removed from our present condition as is mature adulthood from the mind of a little child. Indeed, it may be much further removed; but we already possess some notion of it (given in the person of Christ), and as we move toward it our concept will thereby become more adequate. If and when we finally reach that fulfillment, the problem of recognizing it will have disappeared in the process.[69]

Here we face an initial problem in comparing the Christian situation with the Advaitic, but perhaps one which can be overcome. Brahmaloka or the Kingdom of God is *not* the eventual fulfillment of Advaita Vedānta. The eventual fulfillment of Advaita Vedānta is *mokṣa* or liberation, which, in Advaita Vedānta, consists of the realization of *nirguṇa* brahman without name and form. Brahmaloka and the Kingdom of God are still within the realm of name and form.

Hence the eventual destinations of Christianity and Advaita differ but the *manner* in which this eventual destination is recognized is in some ways similar. Just as the Christian eventuality is prefigured in Christ the Advaitic eventuality is immanent in us, and when the fulfillment is achieved "the problem of recognizing it would have disappeared in the process." M. Hiriyanna's description of the process is helpful here. He explains that although it is true that *nirguṇa Brahman*

69. Hick, *Philosophy of Religion*, 103.

> cannot be grasped as an object of knowledge . . . there may be other ways of "experiencing" it; and the whole tenor of the advaitic theory of perception as well as its scheme of practical discipline . . . shows that there is such a form of experience and that we can "know" Brahman by being it. This higher type of experience is not altogether unfamiliar to us. There are moments, though all too rare, when we transcend ourselves and when even the experience that is being lived through is not cognized. We pass in it not only beyond common consciousness in which the thought of self is implicit, but also beyond explicit self-consciousness to where thought merges in experience. It may be taken as a distant analogue of the attitude of the sage who, having through long discipline learnt to feel his identity with all that exists, at last succeeds in passing beyond even that state, and losing sight of the objective world and of himself as such, is straight away installed within Reality. That constitutes the consummation of Advaitic teaching.[70]

And, third, how would we know it is God or *nirguṇa* Brahman and not something else when it is experienced? It is interesting that although Hick offers an "objective" test for the Christian example, the Advaitic counterpart is a subjective one. This "objective test" becomes feasible because, in the context of the Kingdom of God, "a further feature is added by specifically Christian theism. The New Testament expresses this in visual symbols when it says that the Lamb will be in the midst of the throne of the Kingdom. That is to say, in the situation in which the divine purpose for humanity is fulfilled, the person of Christ will be manifestly exalted. This element completes the circle of verification, linking the future fulfillment situation directly with that which is to be verified, namely, the authority of the Christ who is the source and basis of Christian faith."[71]

In the Advaitic case, the test is subjective. Murty summarizes Śaṅkara's position succinctly in this respect:

> Śaṅkara says that whether a man has knowledge of Brahman or not is to be judged by his own heart's conviction alone. So, if one knows Brahman, he is immediately liberated, though, as he has to experience the fruits of past *karmas*, he is not completely liberated till

70. Hiriyanna, *Outlines*, 376.
71. Hick, *Philosophy of Religion*, 103–4.

> death. To all outward appearances, a man may continue unchanged even after knowing Brahman; but in fact he is not the same transmigrating individual, because the realization of himself as Brahman, generated by scriptural teaching, is opposed to that. Śaṅkara explains this with the help of examples. A rich man, for whom money is everything, may be terribly grieved if he is burgled. But the same man would not be grieved if he had lost all love of money, and had taken the life of a monk. Similarly, if a man is fond of having an ear-ring, he would derive pleasure from wearing it; but once he has got over his fad, he will get no pleasure in wearing ear-rings. Even so, as long as a man thinks his body to be himself, he is subject to misery; but when he knows from Vedānta that he is Brahman, he sheds his delusion and is freed from misery. If anyone continues to be a transmigratory being, he has not yet realised Brahman; and the only one to judge whether a person has become *mukta* or not, is himself. According to Śaṅkara, the beauty of Vedānta is that once Brahman is realised, there is nothing to be sought after or done.[72]

This leads to another interesting contrast between Advaitic and Christian positions. Śaṅkara does not emphasize as much the state of trance through which Brahman may be realized as he does direct realization. But the Brahmasūtra makes it clear that when Brahman is experienced in *samādhi* all life-functions cease—only bodily warmth remains as a sign of continuing life. Thus there is an external test possible in such cases.

The discussion may now be carried further. One of the reasons Hick relies on Christ as an indicator of having encountered God is the philosophical problem associated with the claim of knowing God. He points out the relevance of Christ in this context first, before stating the philosophical difficulties:

> It is this aspect of Christian prediction that makes it possible to meet indirectly the more basic problem of recognition in the awareness of God. A number of philosophers have pointed out the logical difficulty involved in any claim to have encountered God. *How could one*

72. Murty, *Revelation and Reason*, 113–14. He cites a statement of St. Teresa in support of Śaṅkara elsewhere (ibid., 258). The statement in the quotation that he is not completely liberated till death is slightly misleading. It refers to the distinction in Advaita Vedānta between *jīvanmukti* and *videhamukti*. There is no question about *mukti* not being achievable in one's own lifetime.

> *know that it was God whom one had encountered?* God is described in Christian theology in terms of various absolute qualities, such as omnipotence, omnipresence, perfect goodness, and infinite love. Such absolute qualities cannot be observed by us, as can their finite analogues, limited power, local presence, finite goodnesss, and human love. One can recognize that a being whom one encounters has a given finite degree of power, but how does one recognize that such a being has unlimited power? How does one perceive that this being's goodness and love, although appearing to exceed any human goodness and love, are actually infinite? Such qualities cannot be given in human experience. One might claim to have encountered a being whom one presumes, or trusts, or hopes to be God; but one cannot claim to have encountered a being whom one *recognized* to be the infinite, almighty, eternal Creator.[73]

The Advaitic situation here is radically different. For the claim made in Advaita Vedānta is that the qualities Hick claims "cannot be given in human experience" are said in Advaita not to be given in human "empirical" experience but definitely given in human experience; in fact they are not demonstrative of it but constitutive of it in the ultimate sense. At this point the objection might be raised: is not such a claim a mere abstraction? "Śaṁkara recognizes the force of this objection. It is indeed the very objection he seems to have raised against another monistic view (*sattāvāda*) of Upanishadic teaching which was in vogue in his time, viz. that Brahman is universal being." But as Śaṅkara's teaching is represented by *ātmādvaita,* which regards the ultimate reality "not as objective but as identical *at bottom* with the individual self . . . it is thus eventually through something in ourselves that, according to Śaṁkara, we are able to judge of reality and unreality."[74]

Inasmuch as verification consists of the removal of rational doubt, it can be argued that such removal is achieved through the experience of Christ[75] in

73. Hick, *Philosophy of Religion,* 104; emphasis added.

74. Hiriyanna, *Essentials,* 162–63.

75. Hick, *Philosophy of Religion,* 104: "Such beliefs about God's infinite being are not capable of observational verification, being beyond the scope of human experience, but they may be susceptible to indirect verification by the exclusion of rational doubt concerning the authority of Christ. An experience of the reign of the Son in the Kingdom of the Father would confirm that authority, and therewith, by extension, the validity of Jesus's teaching concerning God's infinite transcendent nature." And again: "Even an experience of the realization of the promised Kingdom of God, with Christ reigning as Lord of the New Age, could not constitute a logical certification of his claims, nor

Christianity and our own experience in Advaita, within the eschatological context of both traditions. The clear implication of this position is the distinction between rationality and truth,[76] a distinction obscured by the positivist legacy of the Enlightenment, which identifies the two. If the truth or otherwise of certain propositions cannot be determined within the span of this life or within the course of ordinary living, then the removal of rational doubt regarding them may be substituted as the counterpart to the conventional criterion of proof, as the latter is not feasible given the circumstances of the case. This position may be accepted in its "strong version" in relation to Christianity on account of the post-morten nature of its eschatology, and in its "weak version" in relation to Advaita, which provides for pre-mortem salvation.[77]

---

of a belief in God founded upon those claims. However, it is a basic position of empiricist philosophy that matters of fact are not susceptible of logical proof. The most that can be desired is such weight of evidence as leaves no room for rational doubt; and it might well be claimed on behalf of Christianity that the eschatological verification implied in Christian theology would constitute such evidence" (105).

76. See John Hick, *An Interpretation of Religion* (New Haven: Yale University Press, 1989).

77. Hiriyanna, *Essentials*, 26, 172.

10

Existence, Reality, and Factuality

In dealing with questions of religious language, and of verification and falsification, philosophers repeatedly employ words such as "existence" (that something "exists"), "factuality" (that something is "factual" as distinguished from emotional or aesthetic), and "reality" (that something is "real" as opposed to being unreal). It would promote clearer thinking, which is often claimed to be done in their name, if they themselves were made the object of clarification.

One may begin by probing the meaning of the idea of the existence of God. To begin with, the two approaches to religious language—the cognitive and the noncognitive—attach different meanings to the expression: "God exists." John H. Hicks points out that "for those who adopt one or another of the various noncognitive accounts of religious language, there is no problem concerning the sense in which God 'exists.' If they use the expression 'God exists' at all, they understand it as referring obliquely to the speaker's own feelings or attitudes or moral commitments, or to the character of the empirical world. But what account of 'God exists' can be given by the traditional theist, who holds that God exists as the Creator and the ultimate Ruler of the universe?"[1]

In other words, whereas noncognitive accounts of religious language are prepared to accept God as a form of subjective reality or as a hypothesis in other contexts, only cognitive accounts address the question of God's actual existence. But then another question arises:

1. John H. Hick, *The Philosophy of Religion*, 3d ed. (Englewood Cliffs, N.J.: Prentice Hall, 1983), 105–6.

> Can we, then, properly ask whether God "exists"? If we do so, what precisely are we asking? Does "exist" have a single meaning, so that one can ask, in the same sense, "Do flying fish exist; does the square root of minus one exist; does the Freudian superego exist; does God exist?" It seems clear that we are asking very different kinds of questions in these different cases. To ask whether flying fish exist is to ask whether a certain form of organic life is to be found in the oceans of the world. On the other hand, to ask whether the square root of minus one exists is not to ask whether there is a certain kind of material object somewhere, but is to pose a question about the conventions of mathematics. To ask whether the superego exists is to ask whether one accepts the Freudian picture of the structure of the psyche; and this is a decision to which a great variety of considerations may be relevant. To ask whether God exists is to ask—what? Not, certainly, whether there is a particular physical object. Is it (as in the mathematical case) to inquire about linguistic conventions? Or is it (as in the psychological case) to inquire about a great mass of varied considerations—perhaps even the character of our experience as a whole? What, in short, does it mean to affirm that God exists?[2]

Theologians at one time were satisfied with distinguishing between necessary and contingent existence and stating that God's existence belongs to the former category. Hick points out, however, that it is "no answer to this question to refer to the idea of divine aseity and to say that the difference between the ways in which God and other realities exist is that God exists necessarily and everything else contingently. We still want to know what it is that God is doing or undergoing in existing necessarily rather than contingently. (We do not learn what electricity is by being told that some electrical circuits have an alternating and others a direct current; likewise, we do not learn what it is to exist by being told that some things exist necessarily and others contingently)."[3]

2. Ibid., 105.

3. Ibid. Interestingly, a similar analogy is sometimes given in modern writings on Advaita. P. Sankaranarayanan remarks: "The electric current that is carried through the wires is current, pure and simple. It does not function as such. It is nirguṇa and niṣkriya in a manner of speaking. But when mediated by appropriate mechanism, the current exhibits itself in various forms of activity as light, power, heat etc. Māyā therefore makes the pāramārthika or transcendental Reality which is one without a second into the empirical universe of multiple forms and patterns" (*What Is Advaita?* [Bombay: Bharatiya Vidya Bhavan, 1970], 62). Even here the same question could be asked. What did we really learn about Brahman?

A similar situation has emerged in the context of Advaita Vedānta. It is traditional to define Brahman in terms of a distinction between Brahman *per esse* and Brahman *per accidens.* The definition of Brahman by itself is called the *svarūpa-lakṣaṇa* of Brahman, or Brahman as is. The definition of Brahman in relation to the universe, for example, as its "creator," is called the *taṭastha-lakṣaṇa* of Brahman, or Brahman in relation to the world.[4] But as in the above case, the distinction does not help us know in what sense, exactly, it does exist. In fact the problem is more acute in the Advaitic case because although one may define Brahman "essentially," it still remains indefinable: ". . . the attribute of reality which thus characterises the essential nature of Brahman is itself an effect of *māyā* and therefore false . . . both reality and unreality are excluded. The result is that the definition of Brahman is attributeless."[5] The problem seems to be that whereas one might say "God exists," "Brahman is not an existent but existence."[6]

How are then terms like "exists," "fact," and "real" to be applied either in relation to God or Brahman? As Hick makes it clear, the terms may represent facets of the same issue: "The same question can be posed in terms of the idea of 'fact.' The theist claims that the existence of God is a question of fact rather than merely of definition or of linguistic usage. The theist also uses the term 'real,' and claims that God is real or a reality. But what do these words mean in this context? The problem is essentially the same whether one employs 'exist,' 'fact,' or 'real.' "[7]

A Proposed Solution

At least in the context of the tradition of theistic discussion in the philosophy of religion, John H. Hick, while acknowledging that "theistic thinkers will have to devote further attention" to the question "if their position is to be philosophically intelligible,"[8] offers the following suggestion:

4. S. Radhakrishnan, ed., *The Principal Upaniṣads* (London: George Allen & Unwin, 1953), 69–70. Also see R. Balasubramanian, *Advaita Vedānta* (Madras: University of Madras, 1976), 101–2.

5. R. Karunakaran, *The Concept of Sat in Advaita Vedānta* (Edakkadom, Quilon: Sri Sankara Sanskrit Vidyapeetham, 1980), 154.

6. A remark by T.M.P. Mahadevan, quoted in ibid., viii.

7. Hicks, *Philosophy of Religion,* 105.

8. Ibid., 106.

Without attempting to solve the problem here, it may be suggested that the common core to the concepts of "existence," "fact," and "reality" is the idea of "making a difference." To say that **x** exists or is real, that it is a fact that there is an **x**, is to claim that the character of the universe differs in some specific way from the character that an **x**-less universe would have. The nature of this difference will naturally depend upon the character of the **x** in question, and the meaning of "God exists" will be indicated by spelling out the past, present, and future difference which God's existence is alleged to make within human experience.[9]

Advaitic Criticism of the Solution

From the point of view of Advaita Vedānta the idea that reality is to be associated with "making a difference" is open to criticism. This has to do with how reality is conceptualized in Advaita. Simply put, according to Advaita the unreal can also make a difference. "In daily life we say that a currency note is *really* paper but *conventionally* it is money; a photograph is *really* paper but *appears* as a man; the image in a mirror *appears* as a real object but is not *really* so; and so on."[10] The currency note, though really paper, does make a difference to one's financial status; the photograph often does duty for the person himself or herself; and the "image of a person as reflected in a mirror is not real, but it does not therefore fail to serve as a means of showing to him many facts about his appearance,"[11] which may make all the difference on the evening out!

These examples may seem trivial or at least to border on the trivial, but from the point of view of Advaita they serve to illustrate that "a false means may lead to a true end"[12] "that practical utility need not rest on metaphysical validity."[13]

It is this latter point which is significant here both as a general principle and in the context of the role of God as understood in Advaita. The impres-

9. Ibid.

10. Satischandra Chatterjee and Dhirendramohan Datta, *An Introduction to Indian Philosophy* (1950; reprint, Calcutta: University of Calcutta, 1968), 398; first emphasis added.

11. M. Hiriyanna, *Outlines of Indian Philosophy* (London: George Allen & Unwin, 1964), 359.

12. Ibid.

13. Ibid., 377.

sion that the sun rises and sets or that the earth is flat is—from the higher standpoint of astronomy—erroneous, but of immense value in practical life. It makes a difference without being *really* true. Advaita makes the same claim about God, described as *saguṇa* Brahman. It can serve as a ladder to the Absolute.[14]

What then is the concept of reality according to Advaita?

Reality in Advaita

The main point to be recognized here is that whereas Western philosophical thought seems, on the whole, to contrast reality with falsity, Advaita recognizes "kinds as well as degrees of reality."[15] When these concepts are explained, the allied terms—"existence" and "fact"—appear in a new light.

One must begin by identifying "the criterion of truth and the test of reality adopted in Advaita. In order that anything may be said to be *true* or *real* it should abide in all the three periods of time, the past, the present and the future. What is seen to *exist* in only one or two of these divisions of time cannot be said to be real, i.e. it will be only partially, and not wholly, real if it can be said to be real at all."[16]

A few points deserve immediate attention: First, whereas reality, existence, and fact are used virtually synonymously in the Western philosophy of religion, in Advaita a thing may *exist* but not be *real.* "The reflection *is there,* it can be seen . . . but the reflection does not have the same reality as the object reflected; it exists but it is not real."[17]

Second, in empiricism, the objects of the universe are made the test of reality. "What can this be but some ordinary physical object perceived by the senses? But if tables and chairs and houses and peoples are accepted as paradigm cases of real objects, it becomes self-contradictory to suggest that the whole world of tables and chairs and houses and people may possibly be unreal."[18] But this is precisely what Advaita suggests. As the entire universe "came to be at a particular time, and will eventually disappear at some other

14. Ibid.

15. Ibid., 374 n. 1.

16. Sankaranarayanan, *What Is Advaita?* 1–2; second emphasis added. Technically, this condition is described as *trikālābādhita* (uncontradicted in three dimensions of time).

17. Ibid., 3.

18. Hick, *Philosophy of Religion,* 59.

time," its various objects are "all parts of a historical process, they are not eternal" and therefore not real,[19] not really.

Third, if the aseity of God is appealed to as conforming to the Advaitic criterion of reality, then Śaṅkara clearly affirms that "Brahman, does not lack existence at any time, past, present or future."[20] It is sometimes alleged that Advaita does not provide a satisfactory account of time,[21] but this should not obscure the fact that Brahman is held to be timeless or rather beyond time altogether.

Fourth, in the light of Advaita the "famous rabbit which at one time haunted philosophical discussions at Oxford" jumps differently. It was "a very special rabbit—invisible, intangible, inaudible, weightless and odorless. When the rabbit has been defined by all these negations, does it still make sense to insist that such a creature exists? It is difficult to avoid a negative answer," says John H. Hick.[22]

Similar statements have been made about Brahman, and Hiriyanna suggests in this context as well that "if an objective reality is negatively described and all knowable features are abstracted from it, we may conclude that there is nothing of it left behind. The observation that 'pure being is pure nothing' may accordingly apply to *another* form of Advaita which is named Sattādvaita, in contradistinction to the Ātmādvaita of Śaṅkara, and takes mere being (Sattāsāmānya) to be the Absolute."[23]

Fifth, we were able to distinguish between *reality* and *existence* in the light of Advaita, but what about *facts?* Now according to Advaita whatever is actually experienced in any state of *existence* is a fact—in that there is an *order* of reality (as distinguished from Reality) which corresponds to that experience. The objects experienced in both dream and waking states are *facts* in relation to that state and false in relation to the other. "Dream-water can quench dream-thirst and the dream-money can convert the dreaming pauper into a rich man during the dream. *Per contra,* waking life water cannot quench dream thirst, nor can money in his box make the dreaming 'pauper' feel that he is rich. Each is false by the standard of the other."[24]

19. Sankaranarayanan, *What Is Advaita?* 2. Technically, they are said to be subject to "birth, existence, growth, change, decay and death. These are known as sadvikāras or six ways of appearance" (ibid.).

20. Chatterjee and Datta, *Introduction,* 393; see also p. 387.

21. Karl H. Potter, ed., *Encyclopedia of Indian Philosophies: Advaita Vedānta up to Śaṃkara and His Pupils* (Delhi: Motilal Banarsidass, 1981), 88 and passim.

22. Hick, *Philosophy of Religion,* 95.

23. Hiriyanna, *Outlines,* 375 n. 3; emphasis added.

24. Sankaranarayanan, *What Is Advaita?* 46.

The Advaitic concept of reality may be clarified by a triple trichotomy: that of the *types* of reality, that of the *orders* of reality, and that of the *degrees* of reality.

Types of Reality

Advaita Vedānta distinguishes between three orders of reality: those of *sat*, *asat*, and *mithyā*.

Sat denotes the *absolutely* real, or eternal being. In Advaita Vedānta only Brahman is *sat*.[25] Moreover, just as *sat* must ever exist, *asat* can never come into existence. The two stock examples of *asat* are "a barren woman's son" and "the hare's horn." A more modern example is a "square circle." The "absolutely unreal, like 'the hare's horn' is only words."[26] The universe of our normal experience is neither the one nor the other. It is not eternal, nor is it entirely like a barren woman's son, for it is experienced as existing in a way the latter could not. This universe we experience is characterized by diversity. But, as Hiriyanna explains: "Śaṁkara regards all diversity as being an illusion (*mithyā*). But it is very important to grasp correctly the significance of so describing it. Śaṁkara's conception of the real (*sat*) is that of eternal being, and Brahman is the sole reality of that type. Similarly, his conception of the unreal (*asat*) is that of absolute nothing. The world, in all its variety, is neither of the one type nor of the other. It is not real in this sense, for it is anything but eternal. Nor is it unreal in the sense defined, for it clearly appears to us as no non-entity can. Nobody, as it is stated in advaitic works, has ever seen or is ever going to see a hare's horn or a barren woman's son. They are totally non-existent. Further it possesses, unlike non-entity, practical efficiency or has value, being serviceable in life. This is the reason why the world is described in Advaita as other than the real and the unreal (*sadasadvilakṣaṇa*) or as an illusory appearance. The serpent that appears where there is only a rope is neither existent nor non-existent. It is psychologically given (*prasiddha*), but cannot be logically established (*siddha*). In other words, the things of the world, though not ultimately real, are yet of a certain order of reality."[27]

25. Karunakaran, *Concept*, chap. 8.

26. Hiriyanna, *Outlines*, 364.

27. M. Hiriyanna, *The Essentials of Indian Philosophy* (London: George Allen & Unwin, 1948), 155–56.

The word *mithyā* is used to refer to the status of the world as "other than real or unreal." This becomes clear if the analogy of the serpent being mistakenly perceived in a rope is examined further.

> Now, what is the status of the snake? Is it "real" or "unreal"? Before this question is answered, three terms should be clearly understood. They are: *real, unreal* and *not-real.* By definition, the *real* is what *is* in all the three periods of time, the past, the present and the future. It is the *sat.* Of it, it must not be said that it *was not* at *any one of these times.* In contrast to the *real,* the *unreal* is what *is not, cannot be at any time,* the past, the present or the future. Of such nature is an impossible thing, like a square circle, or a barren woman's son or a sky flower. It is referred to as the *asat.* The *not-real* is intermediate between the *real* and the *unreal;* it is at sometimes only, not at all times. The snake *is* and is seen by the man while he is in fright. It was not before he was frightened; it ceases to be the moment he comes out of the fright by the light of correct knowledge.[28]

Thus Advaita admits three orders of Reality: *sat, mithyā,* and *asat,* or the absolutely real, the provisionally real,[29] and the totally unreal.

28. Sankaranarayanan, *What Is Advaita?* 6. "What is *not-real* has a special status. It is not 'real' or *sat* like the ultimate Reality nor is it 'unreal' *asat* like a barren woman's son. The snake which *appears* is not even *asat.* For the *asat* has no basis or substratum. Again, the snake is not *real,* because it does not satisfy the definition of the 'real,' i.e. existing at all periods of time. It disappears before the light of knowledge. It is not unreal like the barren woman's son. The latter cannot appear and cannot be seen. The snake appears to the frightened man and is seen by him. The 'real' cannot be *sublated* and the 'unreal' cannot *appear.* So the snake is neither real nor unreal; it is different from the *sat* and the *asat;* it is simply not-real. In Advaita, it is spoken of as *mithyā.* The mithyā has a mermaid sort of reality; it is really false and falsely real. In other words, it exists because it appears; but it is not *real* because it later disappears. It is real for the frightened man subject to a wrong idea but not real for the same man after the disillusionment" (ibid., 6–7).

29. It is important to note that provisional reality has a foundation. "This concept of mithyā has a special implication. In the case of the *mithyā* snake, the snake does not appear on a vacant spot. There must be rope on the ground which is wrongly seen as a snake. The deluded man as it were, 'imposes' the snake on the '*this.*' He points to something somewhere and says '*this* is a snake'; *idam sarpam.* The *idam* (this) is the basis of the wrong perception. In Vedānta, this 'basis' is called the *adhiṣṭāna;* the imposed snake is called *āropita* and the imposing is called *adhyāsa.* It is the imposition of a thing on (super-imposition) what is not that thing (*atasmin tad buddhiḥ*). The wrong perception of the mithyā snake is due to *adhyāsa* or superimposition of the snake on the 'this' effected by the man's defective understanding or *ajñāna* respecting the object. It is removed by correct knowledge or *samyakjñāna.* Then the super-imposed snake vanishes and the 'this' is seen in its true nature as the rope" (ibid., 11–12).

Orders of Reality

Let the totally unreal now be dropped from the picture. The realm of *sat* and *mithyā* or the types of reality described as "real" and "apparent" are then reduced to three orders of Reality

> usually mentioned in advaitic works. Of them, Brahman is real in the only true sense of the term (*pāramārthika*). Objects like the rope are empirically so (*vyāvahārika*) because, although by no means permanent, they endure in some form (say, as fibre if not as rope) so long as we view them from the standpoint of common experience. The being of the serpent, seen where there is only a rope, is described as illusory (*prātibhāsika*); and its distinguishing mark is that it vanishes entirely, when the illusion is dispelled. The distinction between the latter two kinds of reality may be explained in a different way also. The illusory object is given only in individual experience. When one is mistaking a rope for a serpent, others may be seeing it as a rope. Hence such objects may be described as 'private.' The empirical object, on the other hand, is 'public' inasmuch as its existence, speaking in the main, is vouched for by others also.[30]

It must be immediately noted, however, that "pain, pleasure and other modes of the antaḥ-karaṇa [the internal organ of perception] though private, are not . . . sublated," as erroneous perception such as that of mistaking a rope for a serpent is, "and are therefore not prātibhāsika,"[31] on the one hand, whereas on the other hand, from the point of view of Īśvara or God, the whole universe is "of the phenomenal or prātibhāsika type." "What is

30. Hiriyanna, *Essentials,* 167. As P. Sankaranarayanan explains: "Thus, in Advaita, there are three orders of 'reality' (*sattātraya*), the *prātibhāsika* or the reflectional, the *vyāvahārika* or the experiential and the *pāramārthika* or the transcendental. The reflection in the mirror, and the snake appearance of the rope are examples of the *prātibhāsika* existence or *sattā.* The experience of world objects in daily life is the result of their *vyāvahārika sattā* and the transcendental consciousness which sees everything as ultimate Reality *pāramārthika sattā.* Even as one knows in practical life that the reflection in the mirror is not real, so too the man of transcendent wisdom, the *jñānī,* realises that the objects of the world *as such* are not real. Even as the *prātibhāsika* is sublated in the *vyāvahārika,* so too is the *vyāvahārika* sublated in the *pāramārthika* state. The *prātibhāsika* is private to each person, the *vyāvahārika* is common to all men and the *pāramārthika* is peculiar to the jñānī alone" (*What Is Advaita?* 14–15).

31. Hiriyanna, *Outlines,* 352 n. 2.

meant by describing Īśvara's world as prātibhāsika is that its unity with himself being always realized, all variety *as such* is known to him to be a mere abstraction."[32]

Degrees of Reality

According to Advaita's overall view, "Brahman is the sole Reality, and it appears both as the objective universe and as the individual subject. The former is an illusory manifestation of Brahman, while the latter is Brahman itself appearing under the limitations which form part of that illusory universe."[33] This points to the difference in the degrees of Reality. The case of the appearance of the universe in relation to Brahman is illustrated by the example of the rope being taken for a snake and the case of the individual taking himself to be other than Brahman (Ātman) itself is illustrated by the example of mistaking a white conch to be yellow because one is looking at it through a yellow glass. "The illusion in the first case consists of mistaking a given object for another that is not given; in the second, it consists merely in attributing to an object that is given, a feature that does not really belong to it, though it also is presented at the time"[34] As Hiriyanna puts it, we may take the physical world to be an appearance of Brahman in the first degree, and the ego as an appearance of Brahman in the second.

Both the universe and individual beings are appearances, but each as "an appearance, which can never be independent, necessarily signifies a reality beyond itself."[35] Now if we apply the three orders of Reality to the two degrees of appearance we obtain an idea of how the words "existence," "reality," and "factuality" function in Advaita. The first order of reality is Reality. Both the second and third orders of Reality represent factuality, as according to Advaita even in cases of illusion there exists an object corresponding to the illusion.[36] The difference between the two levels lies in the different *kinds* of factualities involved.[37] It is also

32. Ibid., 367.
33. Hiriyanna, *Essentials,* 153.
34. Ibid., 157.
35. Hiriyanna, *Outlines,* 373.
36. Chatterjee and Datta, *Introduction,* 391.
37. Hiriyanna, *Outlines,* 373.

important to define here the meaning of the words existence, non-existence, etc., as used by the advaitin. For him, existence is the same as reality, and that identical with truth. *Sattva* and *satyam* mean the same. But what is not existence or truth or reality is not merely absolute non-existence or unreality. Unfortunately, in popular language and many systems of philosophy, both Indian and European, what is other than the real is the unreal; and that is merely what is subjectively meant or imagined. *Mithyā* is other than the real; but still it is not *asat* or unreal. That is why the advaitin says that it is *anirvacanīya,* which is explicable neither as *sat* nor as *asat,* neither as both nor as neither. Hence when interpreting the Advaita in English, we are at a disadvantage for lack of a word with the connotation of *mithyā.* We have been using the word unreal, which is very often misleading. Even the word illusion does not have this specific meaning in English. The word appearance may serve better; but it also is very often confused with the word illusion, as when it is said that the serpent is an appearance of the rope. But whatever word we use, we should bear in mind the logical and ontological difference between *mithyā* and *asat.*[38]

38. P. T. Raju, *Idealistic Thought in India* (London: George Allen & Unwin, 1953), 99–100.

11

Human Destiny: Immortality and Resurrection

The concept of a soul seems to represent a very ancient belief.[1] In any case it seems to be certainly as old as Indian history. It has even been suggested that the burial sites and rites of the Indus Valley civilization may not only indicate a belief in the existence of a soul but even in reincarnation. Reincarnation, however, will be discussed in a separate chapter because belief in a soul does not necessarily entail belief in reincarnation or vice versa. For instance, in the ṚgVeda, there does not seem to have existed "any belief in transmigration. But the survival of man after death is recognized, that is to say, the soul is conceived as immortal."[2]

The doctrine of an immortal soul—which basically posits a body-soul dualism—has played an important role in the history of Western thought. In fact it has displayed a remarkable persistence and endured through four major phases of Western intellectual history. It received its clear formulation in ancient Greece; it domiciled itself in early Christian thought; it characterized medieval thought; and it has reached the present through its modern formulation by Descartes in the seventeenth century. It is only in our own times, that is to say, in the postwar period that it has met with serious challenge and "has been strongly criticized by philosophers of the contemporary analytical school."[3]

These developments can be related to the concepts of Advaita Vedānta at virtually every stage.

1. John H. Hick, *The Philosophy of Religion,* 3d ed. (Englewood Cliffs, N.J.: Prentice Hall, 1983), 122.
2. M. Hiriyanna, *The Essentials of Indian Philosophy* (London: George Allen & Unwin, 1948), 13.
3. Hick, *Philosophy of Religion,* 123–24.

Plato is believed to be the first major Western philosopher who tried to prove the immortality of the soul. Central to an understanding of Plato's view is the distinction between the immutable and the mutable or between what is not liable to change and what is. According to Plato anything composed of parts is subject to change for that very reason. The body belongs to this category. The soul, however is indivisible and therefore immortal. Similarly, although individual acts of goodness come into and pass out of being, this, according to Plato, is not true of Goodness as such. The same is true of individual acts of justice and Justice as such, and so on. Plato thus conceived of an abiding realm where these entities exist. If, in an earthly existence, a human being contemplates these eternal verities, then at death the body is sloughed off by the soul, which then ascends to this abiding realm. As Hick puts it, "Plato painted an awe-inspiring picture, of haunting beauty and persuasiveness, which has moved and elevated the minds of men and women in many different centuries and lands."[4]

From the point of view of Advaita Vedānta Plato's picture is incomplete. First of all, the idea of a changing world is developed further into the concept of *saṁsāra* in Hindu and Buddhist thought in general and accepted, at least traditionally, within Advaita. S. Radhakrishnan remarks: "The Hindu and Buddhist systems accept the fact of *saṁsāra*, what Plato calls 'the world of coming into being and passing away.' "[5]

But this is a minor point compared to the next: that in Advaita the realm in which one experiences the kind of felicity described by Plato is not the ultimate realm—it is only the experience of Brahmaloka and, however pleasant, does not constitute the liberation of the soul. At this point three aspects of Advaita Vedānta become relevant: (1) the distinction between the *ātman* and the *jīvātman;* (2) the identity between *ātman* and *brahman;* and (3) the difference between *nirguṇa* and *saguṇa* Brahman.

Although both Plato and Advaita would agree that "we should not be bound to the cave and see the reality," they may not agree on what is bound, the nature of the cave, how one is to come out of it, and what reality might

4. Ibid., 122–23.

5. S. Radhakrishnan, trans., *The Brahma Sūtra: The Philosophy of a Spiritual Life* (London: George Allen & Unwin, 1960), 135. S. Radhakrishnan identifies some inconsistencies in Plato's description of the soul: (1) in the *Republic* Plato states "soul is substance and substance is indestructible"; (2) "yet we find in Plato the view that the soul is not quite eternal like the divine ideas" and must train for achieving eternality; (3) Plato's "proofs" in the *Phaedo* from recollection and from the soul's kinship with God prove the eternity of impersonal reason and not of the individual self (*Brahma Sūtra,* 187).

be. The points mentioned above help clarify the situation. Advaita clearly distinguishes between the *jīvātman* or the empirical self as implicated in the world and the *ātman,* the immortal soul by itself. Plato assumes a plurality of souls (*ātmans*) but Advaita, only a plurality of empirical souls (*jīvātmans*). Moreover, this *ātman* is identical with Brahman or the ultimate reality so that no room is left for the kind of blissful contemplation visualized by Plato. What Plato says may apply to a level of reality in Advaita, the Brahmaloka, a realm in which one may be reborn. "Prayer and worship of the supreme as Īśvara do not lead to final release. The devotee gets into *Brahma-loka* where he dwells as a *distinct* individual enjoying great power and knowledge. When he gains knowledge of *brahman* he obtains final release."[6]

This "distinction between rebirth (*punarjanma*) and release (*mokṣa*) is familiar to all systems of Hindu thought." According to Radhakrishnan: "We find it also in some of the philosophies of the West. In Plato, for example, we have these two conceptions. There is the doctrine of the *Symposium* which is not of a future life but of timeless existence, attainable here and now by an escape from the flux of time. There is the other doctrine of the *Phaedo* involving pre-existence and post-existence which are concepts possessing meaning only with regard to the temporal life of the soul."[7] John H. Hick described Plato's vision in terms of the *Phaedo;* it is the doctrine of the *Symposium* which seems closer to the position of Advaita Vedānta.[8]

The inclusion of the concept of the immortal soul in Christian theology is best illustrated by the following statement of Jacques Martin:

> A spiritual soul cannot be corrupted, since it possesses no matter; it cannot be disintegrated, since it has no substantial parts; it cannot lose its individual unity, since it is self-subsisting, nor its internal energy, since it contains within itself all the sources of its energies. The human soul cannot die. Once it exists, it cannot disappear; it will necessarily exist for ever, endure without end. Thus, philosophic reason, put to work by a great metaphysician like Thomas Aquinas, is able to prove the immortality of the human soul in a demonstrative manner.[9]

6. Ibid., 39; emphasis added.
7. Ibid., 185.
8. Another Advaitic criticism of Plato would be that it is not so much that the soul contemplates reality but rather that it is identical with it; the soul does not contemplate but is goodness, and so on.
9. Quoted in Hick, *Philosophy of Religion,* 123.

The basic argument here rests on the monadic nature of the soul. But this has been criticized on both metaphysical and psychological grounds. The philosophical argument is that "although it is true a simple substance cannot disintegrate, consciousness may nevertheless cease to exist through the diminution of its intensity to zero."[10] This would imply that consciousness is an attribute of the substance soul, a position identifiable within Hindu thought but opposed by Advaita Vedānta, on the ground that the relationship between consciousness and soul is itself a distinct entity, which introduces a third entity to explain the connection between substance and attribute and requires additional relationships to explain the relation of the original relationship to substance and attribute and leads to infinite regress.[11]

The psychological argument challenges the notion that the "mind is a simple entity."[12] Advaita Vedānta would seem to be rather sympathetic to this position at the *empirical* level. For it regards what is normally regarded as the soul (*ātman*) as only an element that as the "witness" (*sākṣī*) is "the implication of empirical thought. It is involved in all such thought, but is not identical with it."[13] This mental activity is carried out not by a simple but a complex (*viśiṣṭa*)[14] entity called *antaḥkaraṇa* (the internal organ), which constitutes the limiting adjunct of the soul and is called in different places by different names such as *manas* (mind), *buddhi* (intelligence), *vijñāna* (knowledge), *citta* (thought). This difference in nomenclature is something made dependent on the difference in the modifications of the internal organ which is called *manas* when in a state of doubt, e.g., *buddhi* when it is in a state of determination and the like.[15] Its complex character, however, is as much metaphysical as psychological. At the metaphysical level it is "only the unity of the passive sākṣin and the active antaḥ-karaṇa which is real for all practical purposes. That is what knows, feels and wills. In this complex form it is known as the jīva or the empirical self,"[16] also called *jīvātman.*

Descartes's redefinition of the body-soul distinction is also significant in the context of Advaita, especially when viewed in the context of the distinction between mind and matter. Descartes "could be certain of nothing save his own mind," which led to the formulation of "idealism as mentalism or

10. Ibid.
11. William M. Indich, *Consciousness in Advaita Vedānta* (Delhi: Motilal Banarsidass, 1980), 30.
12. Hick, *Philosophy of Religion,* 123.
13. Hiriyanna, *Essentials,* 165.
14. Ibid., 158.
15. M. Hiriyanna, *Outlines of Indian Philosophy* (London: George Allen & Unwin, 1964), 343.
16. Ibid.

subjectivism."[17] It is a matter of considerable interest that although Advaita emphasizes the certainty of the existence of one's self in a way analogous to that of the mind in Descartes, like Descartes it also felt exposed to mentalism and subjectivism, which again, like Descartes, it combatted.[18] Hick points out that Descartes fixed such a wide gulf between matter and mind that it had to be bridged by invoking "the instrumentality of God"[19] through the doctrine of Occasionalism, which allowed indirect contact between mind and matter. Readers of Hindu philosophy will recall that *atheistic* Sāṅkhya, according to most scholars, never quite succeeded in solving the difficulty plausibly.[20] Advaita solves it by ultimately aligning matter itself with spirit.[21] P. T. Raju goes on to note that even when God was invoked as a *deus ex machina* "then the difficulty was only pushed back, not solved. For the problem took on a new form: How can God make a material event an occasion for a corresponding mental event in knowledge? What is His relation to matter on the one hand, and to mind on the other? In the question, How can there be any connection between matter which is unconscious and God who is a spirit? we see the old problem again."[22]

The old problem is actually older—it goes right back to the heart of Advaita Vedānta in the form of the issue of the "self" and the "not-self" and how they can come into any relation at all. The Advaitin suggests that in fact they do *seem* to establish a relation, but questions whether they actually do so. As Hiriyanna puts it,

> The Advaita definitely denies that there can be any relation at all between two such disparate entities as spirit and matter. But at the same time, it cannot be forgotten that our investigation of experience leads us to the conclusion that they are not only together but are often identified with each other as implied, for example, when a person says "I am walking." Here the act of walking is obviously a feature characterizing the physical body; and yet it is predicated of the person's self which is spiritual. The only explanation conceivable is that their association must be a mere appearance or, in other words, that the relation between them is ultimately false. A necessary

17. P. T. Raju, *Idealist Thought in India* (London: George Allen & Unwin, 1953), 46–47.
18. Hiriyanna, *Outlines*, 351.
19. Raju, *Idealistic Thought*, 46–47.
20. Hiriyanna, *Essentials*, 115–16, 126–27, 160.
21. Hiriyanna, *Outlines*, 342.
22. Raju, *Idealistic Thought*, 47.

> corollary to this conclusion is that one of the relata is unreal. Both, of course, cannot be regarded as unreal, for in that case, since all the three elements—the two relata and the relation—become false, and since the idea of falsehood necessarily points to a standard of truth, we shall have to postulate another reality from the viewpoint of which we declare them to be false. The advaitin therefore takes for granted that it is matter which is false.[23]

Hence the movement of thought from Śaṅkara toward idealism and that from Descartes toward determinism, although for both "the ultimate presupposition which was indubitable," that of self-awareness, was "not a proposition to be proved true or false by scientific tests."[24] Whereas for Śaṅkara the self becomes a counterpart of spirit, for Descartes it becomes "a counterpart of the body. Spinoza felt that if bodily states were strictly determined, mental states were also subject to a strict determinism. Mind and body became objects of scientific treatment only on the condition of a universal determinism. Freud and Marx adopt a similar objective view of the human self, that it is determined ultimately by unconscious impulses or relations of economic production."[25]

Criticism of the Concept of an Immortal Soul

Modern trends in philosophy have undermined the idea of the immortality of the soul. The basic argument is that characteristics earlier ascribed to the soul, such as compassion, can be described as behavioral dispositions without straining one's credulity by implying belief in a mysterious entity like the soul.[26]

On this point the position of Advaita Vedānta is complex. On the one hand it would accept the description of all mental activity as characteristic of the "empirical individual"—but would question the belief that the individual is merely an empirical being. Here its concept of *sākṣī* is of key importance. Whatever empirical characteristics described earlier pertained to the

23. Hiriyanna, *Essentials,* 160–61.
24. Radhakrishnan, trans., *Brahma Sūtra,* 104.
25. Ibid., 152. Was Descartes a Western Śaṅkara who failed only because of the theism his times and culture obliged him to adhere to?
26. Hick, *Philosophy of Religion,* 125.

jīva, and the *sākṣīn* and the *jīva* are, as Hiriyanna puts it, "not identical, though at the same time they are not quite different either. While the jīva may become the object of self-consciousness on account of the objective element it includes, it is wrong to speak of the sākṣīn as knowable, for it is the pure element of awareness in all knowing; and to assume that it is knowable would be to imply another knowing element—a process which leads to the fallacy of infinite regress. But the sākṣīn does not therefore remain unrealized, for being self-luminous, by its very nature, it does not require to be made known at all."[27]

Such an assumption is, of course, not acceptable to modern philosophy. In view of this situation it might be of interest to review the Advaitin arguments for the existence of the *ātman.*

Proofs of the Existence of the Soul

Advaita Vedānta offers the following main arguments to establish the existence of a soul, though modern Advaitins concede that "theoretically the position of the Materialists, it must be admitted, is irrefutable. It cannot be *demonstrated* that the soul or ātman in the accepted sense *is.* That indeed is recognized by some orthodox thinkers themselves, who accordingly lay stress in their refutation . . . upon the indemonstrability of the opposite position that the body and the soul are *not* distinct."[28]

The following points are worth noting in this connection:

1. Consciousness as a property of the body must be either essential or accidental. If essential, its absence in swoon or deep sleep is not explained; if accidental, some other factor must be invoked.
2. Consciousness as we know it is always found in association with a physical organism, but there is nothing to prevent it from continuing in *another form* after its dissolution.
3. Constant association does not make one element the property of another. The eye cannot see without light but vision is a property of the eye, not light.

27. Hiriyanna, *Outlines,* 343. "In other words, the jīva is spirit as immanent in the antaḥkaraṇa, while the sākṣin is spirit as transcendent" (344).

28. Ibid., 192. Cārvākas were Indian materialists.

4. The body can be seen by one who possesses it as well as by others. But our thoughts and feeling are not thus known. "The knowledge which a philosopher has of his toothache is different from that of the dentist who treats it."[29]
5. A person dreams of being a tiger. On waking up he disowns the dream *body* of the tiger but not the dream *consciousness.* "If the one were the property of the other, both should be avowed or disavowed together."[30] Moreover, "consciousness cannot be a quality of the body, because there are many dream-cognitions during sleep, when the body becomes inactive."[31]

Two arguments especially advanced in Advaita may be presented in more detail. One of them is based on the observation that consciousness and body are not concomitant. In deep sleep, swoon, death—the body exists without consciousness. "If it were a natural quality of the body, it would persist in it in deep sleep, swoon, and death. But it is never found in these cases."[32] Moreover, "love, hate, and other modifications of consciousness are not always preceded by modifications of the body."[33] The more challenging argument, however, is one with a cosmic ramification as well. In a well-known comment on the Brahmasūtra Śaṅkara says that "in the world we see that from the sentient human body insentient things, like hair and nails, are born—and from insentient rotten matter, like cowdung, etc. insects and worms, which are sentient are born."[34] Śaṅkara thus clearly shows an awareness of both the possibilities—to put it most generally—of matter arising from mind, and mind from matter. The essential Advaitin position here reflects the priority it accords to consciousness. It is maintained that consciousness

> cannot be generated by the material elements because it apprehends them and their products as objects. Colour cannot apprehend itself or the colour of any other thing. But consciousness apprehends the internal qualities of the self and the external material elements and

29. Ibid., 193.
30. Ibid., 192.
31. Jadunath Sinha, *A History of Indian Philosophy* (Calcutta: Sinha Publishing House, 1956), 258.
32. Ibid., 257.
33. Ibid., 263.
34. Raju, *Idealistic Thought,* 122. "In Śaṅkara's days such a theory was believed, but Pasteur's experiments have exploded such theories" (K. Satchidananda Murty, *Revelation and Reason in Advaita Vedānta* [New York: Columbia University Press, 1959], 174). The main point here is not the accuracy of the theory but the anticipation of the materialist thesis.

> their products. A quality of matter is insentient, and cannot apprehend itself as an object of consciousness. But consciousness apprehends matter and its qualities, and must therefore be different from them. Consciousness is self-luminous, but objects are manifested by consciousness. Therefore consciousness can never be identical with its objects.[35]

However, with the general climate of opinion in the West turning toward greater recognition of the reality of the body as opposed to the soul, the idea of resurrection has received renewed emphasis. As John H. Hick remarks: "As a result of this development, much mid-twentieth-century philosophy has come to see the human being as in the biblical writings, not as an eternal soul temporarily attached to a mortal body, but as a form of finite, mortal, psychophysical life. Thus, the Old Testament scholar J. Pedersen said of the Hebrews that for them 'the body is the soul in its outward form.' This way of thinking has led to quite a different conception of death from that found in Plato and the Neoplatonic strand in European thought."[36]

The Case for Resurrection

John H. Hick has argued that a credible case for resurrection can be made on the basis of biblical material. He does so by affirming the "religious difference between the Platonic belief in the immortality of the soul and the Judaic-Christian belief in the resurrection of the body" in that "the latter postulates a special divine act of re-creation . . . only through the sovereign creative love of God can there be a new existence beyond the grave,"[37] otherwise death is final; by relying on Paul's vision that the resurrection "has nothing to do with the resuscitation of corpses in a cemetery" but "concerns God's re-creation or reconstitution of the human psychophysical individual, not as the organism that has died but as *soma pneumatikon,* a 'spiritual body' inhabiting a spiritual world as the physical body inhabits our present material world";[38] by "ignoring Paul's own hint" that the resurrected body may

35. Sinha, *History,* 258.
36. Hick, *Philosophy of Religion,* 124. "Tertullian takes the extreme position that the soul is nothing if it is not body" (Radhakrishnan, trans., *Brama Sūtra,* 190).
37. Hick, *Philosophy of Religion,* 125.
38. Ibid.

be "as unlike the original body as a full grain of wheat differs from the wheat seed"; and "by relying on the Patristic belief of the correspondence between the physical and the resurrected body."[39]

According to Hick a "major problem confronting any such doctrine is that of providing criteria of personal identity to link earthly life and the resurrection life."[40] He takes a hypothetical case of one John Smith and illustrates the problem by making John Smith undergo a case of sudden geographical disappearance and appearance; a case of reincarnation; and a case of resurrection, which he then describes as follows:

> Now suppose, third, that on John Smith's death the "John Smith" replica appears, not in India, but as a resurrection replica in a different world altogether, a resurrection world inhabited only by resurrected persons. This word occupies its own space distinct from that with which we are now familiar. That is to say, an object in the resurrection world is not situated at any distance or in any direction from the objects in our present world, although each object in either world is spatially related to every other object in the same world.[41]

An Advaitic Viewpoint

From an Advaitic point of view eternal life, in the form of *jīnvanmukti,* is possible right here. For the Advaitin, John 11.23–26 would be especially interesting, since it has been suggested that in this passage

> Jesus substitutes the idea of the present eternal life of individuals for the hope of a general resurrection of the righteous. When Martha says about her brother "I know that he shall rise again in the resurrection at the last day," Jesus said to her "I am the resurrection and the life; he that believeth in me, though he die, yet shall he live; and whosoever liveth and believeth in me, shall never die." He apparently substitutes the conception of a present eternal life which is unaltered by death for a resurrection at some future date, "the last day." According to Jesus we can have eternal life while still in the flesh.[42]

39. Ibid., 126.
40. Ibid., 125.
41. Ibid., 126.
42. Radhakrishnan, trans., *Brahma Sūtra,* 185.

Advaita Vedānta is even prepared to accept cases of literal resurrection. Ramana Maharshi (1879–1950), a modern Advaitin,

> cited the story of Parikshit. He was a still-born child. The ladies cried and appealed to Sri Krishna to save the child. The sages round about wondered how Krishna was going to save the child from the effects of the arrows (*apandavastra*) of Asvatthama. Krishna said, "If the child be touched by one eternally celibate (*nityabrahmachari*) the child would be brought to life." Even Suka dared not touch the child. Finding no one among the reputed saints bold enough to touch the child, Krishna went and touched it, saying, "If I am eternally celibate (*nityabrahmachari*) may the child be brought to life." The child began to breathe and later grew up to be Parikshit.[43]

In general, however, Advaitins are not impressed by feats of resuscitation or even resurrection partly because elements of it are associated with the process of reincarnation and partly because of its limited franchise. "It is said of some saints that they revived the dead. They, too, did not revive all the dead."[44] Ramana Maharshi offers his own interpretation of resurrection as follows:

> Christ is the Ego.
> The Cross is the Body.
> When the Ego is crucified, and it perishes,
> What survives is absolute being (God).[45]

Concepts of Heaven and Hell

That Jesus Christ could offer eternal life here on earth in this life is connected with the Christian idea of the Second Coming, which for the early believers seemed to be just around the corner. In this respect the position of the early Church needs to be fully appreciated. J. G. Davies has argued in

43. *Talks with Sri Ramana Maharshi* (Tiruvannamalai: Sri Ramanasramam, 1984)), 423. Part of the point of the story is that although Kṛṣṇa had several wives he could claim to be celibate because his psyche was free of carnal desires. The sage Śuka mentioned in the story was unmarried. Thus virtue conforms to internal psychic states rather than outward appearance.

44. Ibid., 311.

45. Ibid., 86.

relation to the return of Christ that apostolic preaching transformed "a prophecy of a return into a prophecy of an *immediate* return."[46] This would then have enabled salvation, of course in Christian terms, to be achieved in this very life, a situation which would then parallel the Advaitic idea of living liberation.

But the Second Coming did not materialize, and consequently a postponed eschatology had to be evolved, requiring greater emphasis on the ideas of Heaven and Hell. In respect to these ideas John H. Hick makes the following observations: First, Heaven constitutes the fulfillment of the Christian religious expectation. When discussing the belief in resurrection Hick asks:

> What is the basis for this Judaic-Christian belief in the divine recreation or reconstitution of the human personality after death? There is, of course, an argument from authority, in that life after death is taught throughout the New Testament (although very rarely in the Old Testament). More basically, though, belief in the resurrection arises as a corollary of faith in the sovereign purpose of God, which is not restricted by death and which holds us in being beyond our natural mortality. In a similar vein it is argued that if it be the divine plan to create finite persons to exist in fellowship with God, then it contradicts both that intention and God's love for the human creatures if God allows men and women to pass out of existence when the divine purpose for them still remains largely unfulfilled.[47]

He goes on to say: "It is this promised fulfillment of God's purpose for the individual, in which the full possibilities of human nature will be realized, that constitutes the 'heaven' symbolized in the New Testament as a joyous banquet in which all and sundry rejoice together."[48] Second, Hick suggests that it is "questionable whether any theodicy can succeed without drawing into itself this eschatological faith in an eternal, and therefore infinite good which thus outweighs all the pains and sorrows that have been endured on the way to it."[49] Third, the idea of heaven has to be balanced with that of hell, in the interests of the same theodicy. But Hick here distinguishes

46. J. G. Davies, "Christianity: The Early Church," *The Concise Encyclopedia of Living Faiths*, ed. R. C. Zaehner (Boston: Beacon Press, 1987), 55.

47. Hick, *Philosophy of Religion*, 126.

48. Ibid.

49. Ibid., 126–27.

between an eternal hell which might itself become "a major part of the problem of evil"[50] and hell as "purgatorial suffering" of the kind experienced in life which may pave the way for heaven. Fourth, Hick even suggests that the "idea of hell may be deliteralized and valued as a powerful and pregnant symbol of the grave responsibility inherent in our human freedom in relation to our Maker."[51]

The response from Advaita Vedānta on these points would run mainly along the following lines: First, in Advaitic thought the soul always possesses a "body" of some kind, physical or ethereal. Again, this is not an act of special grace from God but how the universe functions in general under God's supervision.[52] Second, the Advaitic view on this point would be that theodicy does seem to presuppose eschatology—but not necessarily of the kind visualized in Christianity. Rather it is concerned with the time horizon required for karma to work itself out. Here again God is not directly involved—one's deeds are. God supervises the working of karma (*karmādhyakṣa*).[53]

Third, the Advaitic position in general is similar to Hick's suggestion on a temporary hell; but according to it heaven is also temporary. In Advaita, as in Hinduism, "heaven and hell are temporary states and heaven therefore

50. Ibid., 127.

51. Ibid.

52. This point is often not sufficiently recognized. The following remarks by M. Hiriyanna possess special relevance at this point: "The Indian schools of thought postulate, as the support and condition of all psychical life, a physical vesture for the self, which is other and subtler than the visible body and which, though its existence is not commonly realised, accompanies the self until it finds release. Release, in fact, is only release from it. Whether the self should not necessarily remain embodied even in that condition is a question which we need not discuss, for we are concerned here with the problem of reincarnation and not with that of final release. This vesture serves as a link between the real self and its fleshly envelope which alone changes with each life, giving rise to the notions of death and re-birth. It is conceived differently in different systems, but all of them acknowledge it in some form or other. Speaking generally, it is in this intermediary that the dispositions of former lives are stated to be treasured up; and, since it does not change from one birth to another, there is no point in the criticism that man's soul must cease to be or, at least, change with the dissolution of his body at death. It is true that the visible body also is intimately connected with the self, but the contention is that its loss or replacement by another will not affect the *inner* life of the individual" (M. Hiriyanna, *Popular Essays in Indian Philosophy* [Mysore: Kavyalaya Publishers, 1952], 44–45).

53. Śvetāśvatara Upaniṣad 6.11. S. Radhakrishnan suggests a parallel with Romans 11.22: "Behold therefore the goodness and severity of God" (*The Principal Upaniṣads* [London: George Allen & Unwin, 1953], 114). In some schools of Hindu thought even God is dispensed with: "So orthodox a philosopher as Jaimini looked upon the doctrine of God as a heresy, and affirmed in its place the doctrine of the autonomy of *Karma*. Even systems like the Vedanta, which believe in God, take care to represent the destiny of the individual as depending virtually on himself" (Hiriyanna, *Popular Essays*, 47).

never appears as man's final goal: it can only be a prelude to a better incarnation which will bring a man nearer to final liberation."[54] An exception, however, has to be made in the case of devotional Hinduism in which theistic heavens such as those of Viṣṇu and Śiva are lasting abodes. But Advaita does not seem to allow such exceptions.

The suggestion has been made, however, that some verses of the Bhagavadgītā, one of the texts accepted as authoritative within Advaita Vedānta, imply eternal damnation. This is a view held by R. C. Zaehner, among others, who writes:

> It is usually alleged that hell in Hinduism is, like heaven, a temporary state, and yet in the sixteenth chapter of the Gītā Krishna describes the state of those men who inherit a "devilish destiny" in terms so strong as to make one wonder how salvation can be possible for them. Liberation, the final release from the round of birth and death, is frequently referred to as the "highest way": it is final and definitive. Similarly in 16.20 Krishna speaks of the "lowest way," and if we read this passage without any preconceptions we can scarcely avoid the conclusion that this too is final: such men have reached a point of no return. They have deliberately chosen enmity to God, and for such, Krishna makes abundantly clear, divine grace is not available.
>
> > Selfishness, force, and pride, desire and anger—[these do] they rely on, envying and hating Me who dwell in their bodies as I dwell in all. Birth after birth in this revolving round, these vilest among men, strangers to [all] good, obsessed with hate and cruel, I ever hurl into devilish wombs. Caught up in devilish wombs, birth after birth deluded, they never attain to Me: and so they tread the lowest way. Desire—Anger—Greed: this is the triple gate of hell, destruction of the self: therefore avoid these three (16.18–21).
>
> This would seem to be final.[55]

The school of Advaita Vedānta, however, does *not* interpret the verses in this manner. The "hurling into devilish wombs" is taken to mean that "such men are reaping the inevitable fruit of their actions," Kṛṣṇa "merely dis-

54. R. C. Zaehner, *The Bhagavad-Gītā* (Oxford: Clarendon Press, 1969), 23.
55. Ibid., 23–24.

penses their deserts"; their case is considered hopeless *while* they work out the evil karma in devilish wombs and it is incumbent on man, a free agent, especially while still a man, to "try to shake off the *asura* nature," as Ānandagiri explains while commenting on Śaṅkara's commentary on the verses.[56]

And fourth, a deliteralized view of hell is possible in Advaita but as symbolic of human freedom in relation to human beings themselves and not so much God. This is suggested by a deliteralized view of heaven; as when it is observed: "Heaven, it has been remarked, is first a temperament and then anything else."[57]

Parapsychology and Postmortem Existence

Ever since the founding of the Society for Psychical Research in 1802 in London, and similar societies in other parts of the world, the study of paranormal phenomena has been placed on a sounder scientific basis. What was once a fad, and now sometimes gives the appearance of a fashion, also has a more serious side to it—as represented by the development of parapsychology.

Hick refers in this context to the "spiritualist movement," which "claims that life after death can be proved by well-attested cases of communication between the living and the 'dead.' "[58] Now it is obvious that if it could be shown incontrovertibly that the dead had communicated with the living, the case for postmortem existence could be taken as established. After careful examination of the evidence Hick concludes that these instances of communication between the living and the dead are really cases of telepathy, when the term refers to the "fact that sometimes a thought in the mind of one person apparently causes a similar or associated thought to occur to someone else when there are no normal means of communication between them, and under circumstances such that mere coincidence seems to be excluded."[59]

The significance of Hick's conclusion is not that the explanation he offers

56. W. Douglas P. Hill, *The Bhagavad-Gītā*, 2d ed. (London: Oxford University Press, 1966), 194.

57. Hiriyanna, *Outlines*, 25.

58. Hick, *Philosophy of Religion*, 127.

59. Ibid., 128.

of communication between the living and the dead is unprecedented,[60] but rather that as a philosopher of religion he is prepared to accept the reality of parapsychological phenomenon such as telepathy and then is willing to use it to question evidence for survival after death through another apparently parapsychological phenomenon such as communication from the dead. In other words, his approach is not reductionistic; but he explains evidence of one kind within parapsychology with the help of evidence of another kind from within the same field to question the survival hypothesis.

When one examines the question of survival after death[61] in the context of parapsychology and asks the question, "Is there proof that I will survive?" two additional questions immediately arise, What do I mean by "I"? and, What constitutes proof?

Raynor C. Johnson, after a careful examination of the questions, offers the following answers. On the question, Will "I" suvive? he remarks:

> By "survival of the change called death" in our initial question we therefore mean: will the whole hierarchy of the self continue in its richness of being when the body disintegrates? Shall I, this centre of consciousness which I know myself to be, with all my higher faculty of Love, of Creativity, of passionate hunger for Beauty and Truth, with my essential memories and my gathered harvest of wisdom (small though it be): shall I continue in unbroken communion with those I love and with these values? This is at heart the question we really want answered—and put in this form it takes us far beyond the realm where psychical research alone can give us complete information.[62]

On this point, of course, Advaita Vedānta would concur, for the determination of the "I" according to it is a metaphysical and not a psychological or parapsychological matter.

On the question of proof, Johnson writes:

> What do we mean by "proof" of survival? It would be well if we asked ourselves precisely what sort of evidence we should be prepared to accept as proof, and then we can see if it is obtainable.

60. Ibid., 140; see also Raynor C. Johnson, *The Imprisoned Splendour* (New York: Harper & Brothers, 1953), chap. 9.

61. The major work in the field in this area is F.W.H. Myers, *Human Personality and Its Survival of Bodily Death* (London: Longmans, Green, 1903).

62. Johnson, *Imprisoned Splendour,* 273–74.

> Suppose an honest medium claimed that he (or she) was in communication with an intimate friend of ours who had died, what would satisfy us that the claim was true? Let us take the much simpler case: a friend is believed to be on one side of an impenetrable screen and we are on the other. It is opaque, and somewhat distorts the voice, although conversation is still possible. How should we identify our friend? We should undoubtedly be able to do so through the myriad subtle emotional, intellectual and moral distinctions which make each individual unique. I think we should particularly make use of (a) mannerisms or idiosyncrasies of thought, speech or action; (b) specific memories and interests which were shared; (c) reactions, emotional, intellectual and spiritual, to circumstance—which would reveal the underlying character.[63]

Precisely such confirmation is offered by mediums but Johnson points out, as noted earlier, that other parapsychological phenomena such as telepathy cannot be ruled out. He remarks, almost ruefully,

> It is rather an ironical situation, for the evidence of psychical research has brought to us a recognition of the vast sweep of Mind, of its extraordinary powers not tied down to one point of time and space, and in doing this has shown it to be most improbable that Mind depends on matter for its ability to exist and function. Never has the survival by Mind of the death of the body seemed so probable, on the basis of evidence, yet never has conclusive experimental proof of survival been so difficult to secure. If we knew definitely what are the limits beyond which extra-sensory faculty cannot operate, it would be possible to devise a conclusive experiment; but we do not know these limits.[64]

After sifting through the evidence Johnson himself is personally inclined to accept the thesis of postmortem survival but offers his formal conclusion more objectively:

> Each student of the evidence must decide for himself what is his verdict about Survival. He is not limited to two contrasting judgments

63. Ibid., 274.
64. Ibid., 275.

> "proven" or "not proven." He may think it not proven and improbable; he may think it not proven but probable—in which case he will adopt it as a working hypothesis—or he may be confident it is proven—in which case he has found for himself an answer to one of Life's most heart-searching questions and should feel both relief and gratitude.[65]

Evidence from Near-Death Experiences

The evidence from near-death experiences consists of the accounts of those who were resuscitated after being pronounced clinically dead. Interestingly, evidence of this kind goes as far back as the Greeks if one takes into account the myth of Er, a Greek soldier, found in Book X of the *Republic.* Er, a soldier apparently killed in battle, saw his own body being collected along with those of others who had perished. When it was about to be cremated, however, he revived and told of a journey in the world beyond, which involved three stages. In the first, once his soul had relinquished the body, he was joined by other souls until they came to what seemed like a passage to other realms. In this second stage the souls were judged by divine beings who could read their lives in a glance as it were. Er, however, was spared such judgment and in its stead was offered the assignment to go back to the living and tell them what he had experienced. Er returned and woke "up to find himself upon the funeral pyre." He had no idea of how he got there.[66]

Plato narrates this as consisting of "probabilities, at best" and hedges it with numerous caveats,[67] but the reader will notice its family resemblance to many modern cases. On the basis of his study of several such cases Dr. Raymond A. Moody, Jr., has drawn the following typical picture of what was experienced by the subjects who underwent near-death experiences, "which embodies all the common elements, in the order in which it is typical for them to occur." Moody's integrated account may be presented as consisting of the following ten elements:

1. The person dies, or is at least pronounced dead.
2. The person experiences two phenomena more or less simultaneously,

65. Ibid., 288.
66. Raymond A. Moody, Jr., *Life After Life* (New York: Bantam Books, 1975), 118.
67. Ibid., 119.

one sensory, namely, a ringing or buzzing noise and the other motor, that of passing through a dark tunnel.

3. The person finds himself or herself outside the physical body but in the same physical environment.
4. The person witnesses his or her own body and the attempts to revive it.
5. The person soon becomes conscious of the new "body" he or she possesses, "of a very different nature and with very different powers."
6. In this new environment new things begin to happen, such as the appearance of the dear departed.
7. Of far greater moment however, is the appearance of a being of light. "This being asks him [or her] a question, nonverbally, to make him [or her] evaluate his life and helps him along by showing him [or her] a panoramic, instantaneous playback of the major events of his life."
8. Next, some kind of a barrier is encountered which represents a limit between two realms, which indicates that it is not yet time for the person to pass on.
9. The person resists having to return but to no avail and finds himself or herself back in the body.
10. Finally, when he or she tries to tell others what transpired, nobody believes it.[68]

Again, as in other instances, the exact implication of these cases is not clear. "Do these accounts describe the first phase of another life, or perhaps a transitional stage before the connection between the mind and body is broken; or do they describe only the last flickers of dream activity before the brain finally loses oxygen? It is hoped that further research may find a way to settle this question."[69]

Advaita Vedānta, however, has been familiar for centuries with the concept of a subtle body or *liṅga-śarīra.*[70] The overall process of death and reincarnation as visualized within Advaita Vedānta from the point of view of the *liṅga-śarīra* may be summed up as follows. The soul is never without a body or a vehicle as it were. Although we are only conscious of our physical body, this is not the only body we possess. At the time of death the gross

68. Ibid., 21–23.

69. Hick, *Philosophy of Religion,* 132.

70. Hiriyanna, *Outlines,* 348; Radhakrishnan, trans., *Brahma Sūtra,* 205; Karl H. Potter, "The Karma Theory and Its Interpretation in Some Indian Philosophical Systems" in *Karma and Rebirth in Classical Indian Traditions,* ed. Wendy Doniger O'Flaherty (Berkeley and Los Angeles: University of California Press, 1980), 259.

body is shed but a subtle body survives and serves as a vehicle of the soul. This subtle body possesses several characteristics:

1. Although material in nature it is transparent and invisible.
2. It is associated with consciousness and memory.
3. In particular, Śaṅkara regards it as consisting of (a) *prāṇa* or vital breath, (2) *manas* or mind, (c) *indriyas* or senses, both sensory and motor, (d) *avidyā* or primal ignorance, and of course (e) *karma.*
4. In general Śaṅkara associates it "with determinate consciousness due to *vāsanā* and *vidyā, karma* and *pūrva janma,*" that is, as determined by mental impressions based on habitual tendencies, knowledge, the quality of actions and deeds of former lives.
5. There is also the suggestion that its size might resemble that of the thumb. There are some statements in the Upaniṣads to that effect, and in the Mahābhārata, in the "story of Sāvitrī, it is said that Yama [the Lord of Death] extracted from the gross body of Satyavān the self which is of the size of a thumb."
6. It possesses form. "At the point of death, as servants of a king gather round him when he starts on a voyage, so all the vital functions and faculties of an individual gather around the living soul, when it is about to withdraw from its bodily form. The *ātman* or the Universal Self which is present as *sākṣīn* throughout successive experiences is a mere spectator."[71]

Resurrection and reincarnation are two modes of immortality—one more somatic in nature, the other more spiritual. Western thought focuses more on the first; Advaita focuses more on the second. But while in the Western context immortality carries with it an implication of salvation in some form, it is not so in the case of Advaita, wherein salvation implies being freed from the occurrence of resurrection as well as from the recurrence of reincarnation.

71. Radhakrishnan, trans., *Brahma Sūtra,* 205.

12

Human Destiny—An Alternative Vision: Karma and Reincarnation

On the whole, the Western religious tradition, including Islam, has viewed human destiny in terms of resurrection; but the Indian religious tradition, including Buddhism, has viewed human destiny in terms of rebirth. Both visions of human destiny include some sort of afterlife; they simply don't agree on what it might be. John H. Hick discusses three versions of the concept of reincarnation, identified by him as (1) the popular concept, (2) the Vedantic concept, and (3) a demythologized interpretation.

The Popular Concept

John H. Hick first presents the basic idea of reincarnation—that "we have all lived before and that the conditions of our present life are a direct consequence of our previous lives"[1]—then goes on to say that in "its more popular form in both East and West the doctrine of reincarnation holds that the conscious character-bearing and (in principle) memory-bearing self transmigrates from body to body."[2] Hick refers to the problem of "memory" across lives[3] but seems prepared to accept the well-known case of Shanti Devi, who was born in 1926 and claimed to be a reincarnation of a person named Lugdi, who was born earlier in 1902, dying later.

1. John H. Hick, *The Philosophy of Religion*, 3d ed. (Englewood Cliffs, N.J.: Prentice Hall, 1983), 134.

2. Ibid.

3. See also S. Radhakrishnan, trans., *The Brahma Sūtra: The Philosophy of a Spiritual Life* (London: George Allen & Unwin, 1960), 198ff.

Hick basically addresses the problem of continuity between lives and within a life and identifies three strands in this connection: memory, bodily continuity, and the pattern of mental dispositions.

How individual identity is sustained within a lifetime might be examined first. Hick points out that if he compares himself as he was at age two with how he is at age fifty-eight, the physical *and* psychological differences are so great that it is not possible to identify the child and the man as the same person. However, "he remembers being told when his sister, who is two years younger than himself, was born. Thus there is a tenuous memory link . . . despite all the dissimilarities that we have noted. . . . This fact reminds us that it is possible to speak of memory across the gap of almost any degree of physical and psychological difference."[4]

This, however, is not usually the case across two lives. Within one life body and memory provide continuity, but these identifiers are missing in the context of several lives. Only the third strand, that of psychological continuity, is available, but its use for the purpose of identification according to Hick "is beset with the most formidable difficulties." Character traits as markers of identity are just too vague to be of any practical help in establishing continuity through more than one life. Character traits, such as introversion and extroversion or egotism and altruism, may be found throughout a population and across the span of several centuries. A "male Tibetan peasant of the twelfth century B.C." may share one or more of these traits with "a female American college graduate of the twentieth century A.D." Yet it would hardly be reasonable to regard one of them as the incarnation of the other on that ground alone. This difficulty is not removed when the time span is reduced. The case of Lugdi who was believed to have reincarnated as Shanti Devi was alluded to earlier. If this identification was based on character traits alone, one would encounter a serious problem, for by this criterion Shanti Devi could be a reincarnation of any of the many people with whom her character exhibited similarity. Thus according to Hick "this criterion of character similarity is far too broad and permissive; if it establishes anything, it establishes much too much and becomes self-defeating."[5]

At this point it is useful to cite the remarks with which John H. Hick introduces the concept of karma as an explanation of the *differentia* in the human condition. He writes that in criticism of the Western "religious assumption that human beings are divinely created" the Indians

4. Hick, *Philosophy of Religion*, 135.
5. Ibid., 137.

> point to the immense inequalities of human birth. One person is born with a healthy body and a high IQ, to loving parents with a good income in an advanced and affluent society, so that all the riches of human culture are open to one who then has considerable freedom to choose his or her own mode of life. Another is born with a crippled body and a low IQ, to unloving, unaffluent, and uncultured parents in a society in which that person is highly likely to become a criminal and to die an early and violent death. Is it fair that they should be born with such unequal advantages? If a new soul is created whenever a new baby is conceived, can the Creator who is responsible for each soul's unequal endowment be described as loving?[6]

It is my suggestion that by opposing the doctrine of karma and reincarnation to theism—*which is not how the situation is perceived either in Hinduism in general or Advaita Vedānta in particular,* a vital point is overlooked. The doctrine of karma and reincarnation is used to explain the *differentia* in the human condition and the individual's *responsibility* for it on the basis of previous actions rather than the individual's *similarity* with the past incarnation. Often the moral used to adorn a reincarnatory tale is in the contrast between a protagonist's life and a past incarnation. In fact, as M. Hiriyanna remarks: "So deep is the conviction of some of the adequacy of karma to account for the *vicissitudes* of life and the *diversity* of the human conditions that they see no need . . . to acknowledge the existence of even God, conceived as the creator of the world and the controlling judge."[7] If the expression "vicissitudes of life" in the above quotation is read as "vicissitudes of lives," the point becomes clearer. It must be added that Advaita Vedānta does not dispense with God as some Hindu systems do, but the point to emphasize is that it is the empirical variety of the universe which Advaita challenges at another level, and it uses karma to explain that *variety* and continuity of creatures rather than to explain *similarity* in this sphere.

Hence, from the point of view of Advaita, memory must be the criterion of identity. "The variety of the world is born of *Karma,*"[8] and the person's identity in this variety, both in terms of the various forms the person assumes and the various forms among which the person finds him- or herself,

6. Ibid., 133.

7. M. Hiriyanna, *The Essentials of Indian Philosophy* (London: George Allen & Unwin, 1948), 48; emphasis added.

8. Radhakrishnan, trans., *Brahma Sūtra,* 192.

are to be connected, in terms of Hick's portrayal, by the thread of memory, which can be recovered once the veil of *avidyā* or nescience is penetrated.[9]

The Vedantic Concept

John H. Hick presents a synopsis of Advaita Vedānta in the context of reincarnation. This synopsis can be presented in the form of six distinct but related statements: (1) the ultimate reality according to Advaita Vedānta is one undifferentiated homogeneous consciousness called Brahman; (2) the universe is a creative expression of this Brahman under the influence of *māyā;* (3) this association of Brahman with *māyā* not only creates the universe but also leads to the emergence of several souls representing individuated units of consciousness; (4) this sense of separation or alienation of the souls from Brahman is ultimately illusory, just as differences in the space contained within different jars is illusory, as they all merely enclose a preexisting pervasive space; (5) once the barriers constituting the illusory differences are removed, the souls become one with Brahman just as the jar-spaces all become one once the jars are broken; (6) thus although there is a plurality of souls, this plurality is ultimately illusory; (7) this illusion must be overcome to attain consciousness of one's liberative identity with Brahman; and (8) the "doctrine of karma and rebirth is concerned with the soul and its evolution from the state of illusion to true self-consciousness."[10]

He further points out that if the Hindus are asked why this account is true, they appeal to (1) revelation, (2) the possibility of recalling past lives, and (3) reincarnation to explain the existence of inequalities. In a work on the philosophy of religion the first may be overlooked, but the next two arguments deserve serious consideration.

9. See Śaṅkara's comment on Bhagavadgītā 5.5.

10. Hick, *Philosophy of Religion,* 137–38. The choice of the jar by Hick to illustrate the confinement of Brahman as an individual soul is a happy one as, with a slight modification, it enables one to illustrate two views within Advaita Vedānta on how such finitizing comes about and how its removal may exemplify liberation. These two views are known as the doctrine of delimitation (*avacchedavāda*) and the doctrine of reflection (*pratibimbavāda*). In his presentation Hick employs the former. The latter may be illustrated as follows. Imagine that all the jars are filled with water and the single moon is reflected in each of them, creating the illusion of many moons. Once the jar is broken and the water drains away the moon-image disappears or, if you please, merges back into the original image. Śaṅkara employs both metaphors; see William M. Indich, *Consciousness in Advaita Vedānta* (Delhi: Motilal Banarsidass, 1980), 50–52.

Hick finds the idea of past-life recall beset with problems. He raises the following points: (1) "Now, what exactly does reincarnation mean when it is thus given factual anchorage by a claimed retrospective yogic memory of a series of lives that were not linked by memory while they were being lived? The picture before us is of, say, a hundred distinct empirical selves living their different lives one after another and being as distinct from each other as any other set of a hundred lives; and yet differing from a random series of a hundred lives in that the last member of the series attains a level of consciousness at which he or she is aware of the entire series."[11] (2) Even when in a higher state of consciousness previous lives are recalled, Hick continues, "There is something logically odd about such 'remembering,' which prompts one to put it in quotation marks. For this higher state of consciousness did not experience those earlier lives and therefore it cannot in any ordinary sense be said to remember them. Rather, it is in a state *as though* it had experienced them, although in fact it did not."[12] (3) Even if the new ontological status is overlooked there is the following problem: "Let us name the first person in the series A and the last Z. Are we to say that B–Z are a series of reincarnations of A? If we do, we shall be implicitly stipulating the following definition: given two or more noncontemporaneous human lives, if there is a higher consciousness in which they are all 'remembered,' then each later individual in the series is defined as being a reincarnation of each earlier individual. But reincarnation so defined is a concept far removed from the idea that if I am A, then *I* shall be repeatedly reborn as B–Z."[13] (4) Hick's next objection shifts the axis of argument from a temporal to a spatial grid:

> Further, there is no conceptual reason why we should even stipulate that the different lives must be non-contemporaneous. If it is possible for a higher consciousness to "remember" any number of different lives, there seems in principle to be no reason why it should not "remember" lives that have been going on at the same time as easily as lives that have been going on at different times. Indeed, we can conceive of an unlimited higher consciousness in which "memories" occur of all human lives that have ever been lived. Then *all* human lives, however different from their own several points of view, would

11. Ibid., 141.
12. Ibid.
13. Ibid.

> be connected via a higher consciousness in the way postulated by the idea of reincarnation. It would then be proper to say of *any* two lives, whether earlier and later, later and earlier, or contemporaneous, that the one individual is a different incarnation of the other.[14]

Advaita Vedānta's point-by-point response to Hick's questions would likely run as follows:

1. It is not correct to claim that because the various lives are not linked by conscious memory they are the same as any other random series. It is a fairly common human experience that we may behave in similar ways without remembering having behaved so earlier (all the while the previous behavior influencing the present) with the repetitive pattern becoming clear to us through the force of a revelation at a certain point in our life. This may result from introspection or from psychoanalysis. The *last* incident of the type may well throw the whole habitual pattern into focus.

2. The expression, "higher state of consciousness" needs to be clarified. "Śaṅkara admits that extraordinary powers . . . can be obtained by Yoga; but he denies the capacity of Yogic practices to vouchsafe the knowledge of the oneness of the self."[15] Two states of consciousness above the normal, therefore, are involved here: one in which one possesses clairvoyant vision regarding previous lives but has *not* achieved realization and another in which one has. The higher state of consciousness Hick refers to seems to correspond to realization, and the rest of his remarks are based on that assumption.

The relevant question to ask at this stage is, What happens to a person's karma when the higher state of consciousness is achieved or when the person achieves realization or *mokṣa?* The answer to this question may be summarized as follows: "*Mokṣa* may be realized during one's life and when so realized one is a *jīvanmukta.* All the accumulated action which has not yet borne fruit (*saṁcita-karman*) and all action which would otherwise take place in the future (*āgāmi-karman*) is obliterated; action done in the past which has already begun to bear fruit (*prārabdhakarman*) must, however, be carried out. The *jīvanmukta* carries this out though without its affecting him, for he is unattached to it."[16]

It should be further recognized that the "jīvan-mukta's life has two

14. Ibid.

15. K. Satchidananda Murty, *Revelation and Reason in Advaita Vedānta* (1959; reprint, New Delhi: Motilal Banarsidass, 1974), 136.

16. Eliot Deutsch and J.A.B. van Buitenen, *A Source Book of Advaita Vedānta* (Honolulu: The University of Hawaii Press, 1971), 312.

phases: It is either samādhi or mystic trance when he turns inwards and loses himself in Brahman; or the condition known as vyutthāna or reversion to common life when the spectacle of the world returns but does not delude him since he has once for all realized its metaphysical falsity. Diversity continues to appear then as the sun, we may say, continues to appear as moving even after we are convinced that it is stationary."[17]

3. When the person is in higher consciousness there is no duality or any sense of empirical life as we live it; when the person reverts to common life he sees this present life in the *same* series as previous ones, in whatever light the entire series is viewed. The higher consciousness is not implicated in the series.

4. So long as one is functioning at the level of diversity one is not in higher consciousness or *nirguṇa* Brahman. It is only when the Ultimate is viewed along with Māyā[18] that one functions in the realm described by John H. Hick. The picture he has painted is at the level of Īśvara or God as understood in Advaita Vedānta. The confusion he fears is avoided by the fact that "God arranges things so that the resulting experiences match the merit and demerit characterizing the agent's past acts."[19]

The question of inequality associated with the doctrine of karma and rebirth may now be addressed. It has been claimed by Advaitin scholars that the doctrine of karma and rebirth offers an adequate explanation of the inequalities observed in life. Thus M. Hiriyanna remarks that "the law of karma is essentially ethical"[20] and goes on to say:

> It is this conviction that there are in reality no inequities in life which explains the absence of any feeling of bitterness—so apt to follow in the wake of pain and sorrow—which is noticeable even among common people in India when any misfortune befalls them. They blame neither God nor their neighbour, but only themselves for it. In fact, this frame of mind, which belief in the karma doctrine produces, is one of the most wholesome among its consequences. Deussen refers

17. M. Hiriyanna, *Outlines of Indian Philosophy* (London: George Allen & Unwin, 1964), 381. See also Murty, *Revelation and Reason*, 128.

18. Hiriyanna, *Essentials*, 163–64.

19. Karl H. Potter, "The Karma Theory and Its Interpretations in Some Indian Philosophical Systems," in *Karma and Rebirth in Classical Indian Traditions*, ed. Wendy Doniger O'Flaherty (Berkeley and Los Angeles: University of California Press, 1980), 258.

20. Hiriyanna, *Essentials*, 48.

> thus to the case of a blind person whom he met once during his Indian tour: "Not knowing that he had been blind from birth, I sympathized with him and asked by what unfortunate accident the loss of sight had come upon him. Immediately and without showing any sign of bitterness, the answer was ready to his lips, 'By some crime committed in a former birth.' "[21]

John H. Hick disputes the fact that the doctrine of karma and reincarnation offers an adequate solution for the problem of inequality. He argues that the doctrine fails to provide an adequate explanation whether or not the process of reincarnation and the karmic concatenation is accepted as beginningless (*anādi*). In Advaita it is.[22] It is interesting that Hick argues the untenability of the position under *both* assumptions, thereby presenting a very strong case that the doctrine of karma and reincarnation per se cannot explain inequality. In the context of Advaita Vedānta, however, both parts of the argument are relevant in different contexts. Hick first argues that if we assume there is no first life but a "beginningless regress of incarnations,"[23] then

> the explanation of the inequalities of our present life is endlessly postponed and never achieved, for we are no nearer to an ultimate explanation of the circumstances of our present birth when we are told that they are consequences of a previous life, if that previous life has in turn to be explained by reference to a yet previous life, and that by reference to another, and so on, in an infinite regress. One can affirm the beginningless character of the soul's existence in this way, but one cannot then claim that it renders either intelligible or morally acceptable the inequalities found in our present human lot. The solution has not been produced but only postponed to infinity.[24]

To this the Advaitin response is based on scriptural authority and reason. The argument based on the authority of revealed scripture may be ignored, but the argument based on reason should be considered. The logic of Advaita Vedānta may be presented thus:

21. Ibid., 48–49.
22. Murty, *Revelation and Reason,* 5.
23. Hick, *Philosophy of Religion,* 142.
24. Ibid.

> The beginninglessness of the world can be known through reason. If the world had a sudden and definite beginning, then even liberated souls would be liable to birth. Further, if the world had a definite beginning, how are the evil and the inequalities accounted for? For whose faults do souls suffer? It cannot be said that nescience is the cause of the world, because nescience which is of uniform nature cannot be the cause of inequalities. So the fruits of one's own actions in previous births must be the cause of one's happiness and unhappiness in the present birth. God only sees that each one reaps the rewards of his actions—whether good or bad. Unless the world of transmigration is beginningless, there cannot be an ever-present causal relation between *karmas* and inequalities. Reason (says the Advaitin) forces us to assume the world's beginninglessness.[25]

In other words, it is precisely to invariably connect karma and inequality that the beginninglessness of the universe is established; that is to say, Hick's argument on this point is, as it were, reversed. Thus the Advaitin response here is that the doctrine of karma and reincarnation, far from *perpetually postponing* the explanation of inequality, *continually supplies* it.

Hick then makes the alternative assumption that there is a first life and says:

> If instead we were to postulate a first life (as Hinduism does not), we should then have to hold either that souls are created as identical psychic atoms or else as embodying, at least in germ, the differences that have subsequently developed. If the latter, the problem of human inequality arises in full force at the point of that initial creation; if the former, it arises as forcefully with regard to the environment that has produced all the manifold differences that have subsequently arisen between initially identical units. Thus if there is a divine Creator, it would seem that that Creator cannot escape along any of these paths from an ultimate responsibility for the character of the creation, including the gross inequalities inherent within it.[26]

Hick uses the postulation of a first life as an argument against theism. It is interesting that Advaita uses even the presumption of a beginningless series

25. Murty, *Revelation and Reason,* 180.
26. Hick, *Philosophy of Religion,* 142.

of reincarnations as an argument against *rational* theism. The misery observed in the world can, of course, be attributed to karma but it is pointed out that actions by themselves are inert and an intelligence is required to effectively connect them with results. Thus the blame cannot be thrown on the karma of the creatures for "How can the fruits of actions, which are unintelligent, move God to create in a particular way?"[27] Moreover, if God is omnipotent, why are creatures allowed to perform bad actions at all? It is in this context that Advaita Vedānta points out how even the beginninglessness of the world cannot negate divine culpability. "The beginninglessness of the world cannot be invoked to explain this difficulty; because however far back we may push this, the defect of reciprocal dependence (i.e. that God acts in accordance with *karmas* and that these are productive of results when moved by God) is not removed."[28]

A Demythologized Interpretation

As indicated earlier, John H. Hick refers to three versions of the doctrine of karma: (1) a popular concept, (2) a Vedantic conception, and (3) a demythologized version. According to this last interpretation, the doctrine of karma and reincarnation is to be understood, according to Hick, as "a mythological expression of the fact that all our actions have effects on some part of the human community."[29] Hick is pursuing here a line of interpretation proposed by J. C. Jennings.[30] In interpreting "karma, with reincarnation as its mythological expression" as "a moral truth, a teaching of universal human responsibility" Hick offers an interpretation of the doctrine which is attractive in at least four ways. (1) It takes the odium out of the doctrine of karma and reincarnation as "an unverifiable and unfalsifiable metaphysical idea." (2) It provides a corporate vision of karma in which our lives can be seen as affected by those who came before us and affecting those who come after. Hick develops this idea in terms of the successive effects of preceding generations on succeeding ones rather than on interaction among peoples in the present. (3) It develops the doctrine of karma and reincarnation in a

27. Murty, *Revelation and Reason,* 143.
28. Ibid., 144.
29. Hick, *Philosophy of Religion,* 142.
30. Ibid.

contemporary rather than historical sense by indicating how in the context of international problems "the actions of each individual and group affect the welfare of all."[31] (4) It further proposes how "both the popular idea of the transmigration of souls and the more philosophical idea of the continuity of a 'subtle body' from individual to individual in succeeding generations can be seen as mythological expressions of this great moral truth."[32]

From the point of view of Advaita Vedānta, such an interpretation, however attractive, appears a bit forced. The doctrine of karma and reincarnation is accepted in Advaita as valid only at the *empirical* level.[33] The pedagogy of Advaita, through the succession of teachers, does involve a generational dimension but this is not connected with the doctrine of karma as such.[34] In the contemporary context, it is the individual who is liberated, hence the corporate dimension, though not entirely absent, is hardly emphasized.[35] The doctrine of karma and reincarnation is not viewed in Advaita as a mythological expression of moral truth but as a moral truth in itself. Hence it is difficult to extend Hick's demythologized interpretation to Advaita.

Another attempt to demythologize the doctrine of karma and reincarnation has been made by Eliot Deutsch. Deutsch has argued that the doctrine of karma may be just a convenient fiction to pacify the mind when it is disturbed by the vicissitudes of life, thus making it easier for it to remain detached and thereby ensure progress on the spiritual path.[36] This is an attractive interpretation from within an Advaitic framework, but the Advaitin position would tend to be that this is not just a convenient fiction but a convenient fact!

There is, however, one sense in which karma and reincarnation is "demythologized" within Advaita itself. One well-known doctrine within Advaita known as the *ajātivāda* of Gauḍapāda, a predecessor of Śaṅkara. This extreme position is articulated by Gauḍapāda thus in his Māṇḍūkya-Kārikā:

> II, 31. As dream and illusion or a castle in the air are seen (to be unreal), so this whole universe is seen by those who are wise in Vedānta.

31. Ibid., 143.
32. Ibid.
33. Deutsch and van Buitenen, *Source Book*, 127.
34. See William Cenkner, *A Tradition of Teachers: Śaṅkara and the Jagadgurus of Today* (Delhi: Motilal Banarsidass, 1983).
35. Radhakrishnan, trans., *Brahma Sūtra*, 21, 39, 214, 218, 220, 497.
36. Deutsch and van Buitenen, *Source Book*, 120–22.

> II, 32. There is no dissolution and no creation, no one in bondage and no one who is striving for or who is desirous of liberation, and there is no one who is liberated. This is the absolute truth.
>
> III, 15. The creation which has been set forth in different ways by illustrations of earth, metal, sparks is only a means for introducing the truth. In no manner are there any real distinctions.
>
> III, 19. The birthless One is differentiated only through illusion, and in no other way. For if differentiation were real then the immortal would become mortal (which is absurd).
>
> III, 28. There is no birth for a non-existent thing either through illusion or in reality. The son of a barren woman is not born either through illusion or in reality.
>
> III, 46. When the mind does not disappear nor again is dispersed, when it is motionless and without sense-images, then it becomes Brahman.
>
> III, 48. No individual is born, for there is nothing to cause (its birth). This (Brahman) is that highest truth—where nothing is born.[37]

The argument underlying these verses, which conclude the chapter, may be summarized as follows. A *re*birth must be preceded by an original birth. Although empirically the phenomenon of rebirth is accepted as a matter of course in Advaitic discourse, the metaphysically penetrating question to ask is whether such an *original* birth is even possible. In other words, is one really born to begin with if the universe into which one is born is merely an appearance? In that case, the original birth can only be apparent. It is then equally apparent that the subsequent rebirths can be no more real than the original birth, which itself is ontologically dubious, for if Brahman is the only Reality, then how could anything *really* come into being beside it? And if one cannot thus really be born, how could one possibly be reborn?[38] This, however, is a doctrine that is hard to bear *and* forbear, and Advaitins realize this.

37. Ibid., 120–21.

38. See Arvind Sharma, *The Experiential Dimension of Advaita Vedānta* (Delhi: Motilal Banarsidass, 1993), 31–35.

13

The Conflicting Truth Claims of Different Religions

Introduction

It is sometimes claimed that whereas in the past great movements of religious expansion such as those of Buddhism, Christianity and Islam did involve contact among followers of different religions, such contact for the most part represented "conflicts rather than dialogues."[1] It is only during the past few centuries that such contact has stimulated inquiry into the actual beliefs and practices of various religions in a less combative atmosphere and has "brought home to an increasing number of us the problem of the conflicting truth claims made by different religious traditions."[2]

Although this may be true globally, it seems that India had to face the issue of religious pluralism—and that of the conflicting truth claims inherent in such a situation—at least as far back as the sixth century B.C.E. This may or may not be what Heinrich Zimmer had in mind when he wrote: "We of the Occident are about to arrive at a crossroads that was reached by the thinkers of India some seven hundred years before Christ,"[3] but conflicting truth claims were certainly an element in the situation Indian thinkers had to reckon with at the time. This point is well illustrated by the following parable:

1. John H. Hick, *The Philosophy of Religion*, 3d ed. (Englewood Cliffs, N.J.: Prentice Hall, 1983), 107.
2. Ibid.
3. Heinrich Zimmer, *Philosophies of India*, ed. Joseph Campbell (New York: Pantheon Books, 1951), 1.

Buddha, the Blessed One, gives of the blind men and the elephant to illustrate that partial knowledge always breeds bigotry and fanaticism. Once a group of disciples entered the city of Śrāvasti to beg alms. They found there a number of sectarians holding disputations with one another and maintaining 'This is the truth, that is not the truth. That is not truth, this is the truth." After listening to these conflicting views, the brethren came back to the Exalted One and described to him what they had seen and heard at Śrāvasti.

Then said the Exalted One:

"These sectarians, brethren, are blind and unseeing. They know not the real, they know not the unreal; they know not the truth, they know not the untruth. In such a state of ignorance do they dispute and quarrel as they describe. Now in former times, brethren, there was a Rājā (king) in this same Śrāvasti. Then, brethren, the Rājā called to a certain man, saying: 'Come thou, good fellow! Go, gather together all the blind men that are in Śrāvasti!'

" 'Very good, Your Majesty,' replied that man, and in obedience to the Rājā, gathered together all the blind men, took them with him to the Rājā, and said: 'Your Majesty, all the blind men of Śrāvasti are now assembled.'

" 'Then, my good man, show the blind men an elephant.'

" 'Very good, Your Majesty,' said the man and did as he was told, saying: 'O ye blind men, such as this is an elephant.'

"And to one he presented the head of the elephant, to another, the ear, to another a tusk, the trunk, the foot, back, tail and tuft of the tail, saying to each one that was the elephant.

"Now, brethren, that man, having presented the elephant to the blind men, came to the Rājā and said: 'Your Majesty, the elephant has been presented to the blind men. Do what is your will.'

"Thereupon, brethren, the Rājā went up to the blind men and said to each: 'Have you studied the elephant?'

" 'Yes, Your Majesty.'

" 'Then tell me your conclusions about him.'

"Thereupon those who had been presented with the head answered 'Your Majesty, an elephant is just like a pot.' And those who had only observed the ear replied: 'An elephant is just like a winnowing basket.' Those who had been presented with the tusk said it was a ploughshare. Those who knew only the trunk said it was a plough.

> 'The body,' said they, 'is a granary; the foot, a pillar; the back, a mortar; the tail, a pestle; the tuft of the tail, just a besom.'
>
> "Then they began to quarrel, shouting, 'Yes, it is!' 'No, it isn't!' 'An elephant is not that!' 'Yes it is like that!' and so on, till they came to fisticuffs about the matter.
>
> "Then, brethren, that Rājā was delighted with the scene.
>
> "Just so are these sectarians who are wanderers, blind, unseeing, knowing not the truth, but each maintaining it is thus and thus."[4]

The parable is significant in that it follows a direction opposite to the one taken by the Western philosophy of religion, which has evolved on the principle laid down by Hume "that, in matters of religion, whatever is different is contrary."[5] The parable here illustrates that whatever is contrary is not necessarily contradictory. John H. Hick elaborates Hume's point made in relation to miracles—that while it constitutes the proof of one religion it must constitute the disproof of another—thus: "By the same reasoning, any ground for believing a particular religion to be true must operate as a ground for believing every other religion to be false; accordingly, for any particular religion there will always be far more reason for believing it to be false than for believing it to be true."[6]

Advaita Vedānta takes a different view on this point because it emphasizes experience rather than belief. "To say that God exists means that spiritual experience is attainable."[7] Because it is attainable in different forms, each attainment confirms rather than contradicts attainment or expression of it. It is Hume's assumption that different attainments represent different and contradictory beliefs but "Hindu thinkers warn against rationalistic self-sufficiency"[8] in these matters which takes the form of dogma and maintain that different attainments represent different apprehensions of the one Reality, which is infinite, so that "toleration is the homage which the finite mind pays to the inexhaustibility of the Infinite."[9] This is recognized by Śaṅkara,

4. See T. M. P. Mahadevan, *Outlines of Hinduism* (1960; reprint, Bombay: Chetana, 1971), 18–20.

5. Cited in Hick, *Philosophy of Religion,* 109.

6. Ibid., 108.

7. S. Radhakrishnan, *Eastern Religions and Western Thought* (New York: Oxford University Press, 1959), 22.

8. Ibid.

9. Ibid., 317.

who contended with other schools of thought but also proclaimed the insufficiency of any one school of thought in relation to the divine.[10]

The key points to be noted here in the Advaitic vision of Reality are as follows: (1) The Absolute is beyond human words and may be brought within the limits of comprehension in many diverse but not necessarily mutually negating ways.[11] (2) This Absolute or the Real is one, which explains the "attitude of acceptance of other cults."[12] In this context the following line of the ṚgVeda (1.164.46) is often invoked: "The Real is one, the learned call it by various names, Agni, Yama, Mātariśvan."[13] (3) The Real is known through experience, and the experience of a modern Hindu mystic such as Rāmakṛṣṇa (1836–86) confirms the view that various religions represent different approaches to the same Reality.[14] Thus the Advaitin position tends to be very different from that of Hume, as is obvious from the statement of S. Radhakrishnan on this very point.

> It is sometimes urged that the descriptions of God conflict with one another. It only shows that our notions are not true. To say that our ideas of God are not true is not to deny the reality of God to which our ideas refer. Refined definitions of God as moral personality, and holy love may contradict cruder ones which look upon him as a primitive despot, a sort of sultan in the sky, but they all intend the same reality. If personal equation does not vitiate the claim to objectivity in sense perception and scientific inquiry, there is no reason to assume that it does so in religious experience.[15]

W. A. Christian's Analysis

W. A. Christian analyzes religious disagreements among world religions as consisting of basically two kinds: (1) "doctrinal disagreements," in which "different predicates are affirmed of the same subject"—for example, Jesus was "the One whom God promised to send to redeem Israel," a statement

10. S. Radhakrishnan, trans., *The Brahma Sūtra: The Philosophy of a Spiritual Life* (London: George Allen & Unwin, 1960), 37–38.
11. Ibid., 38.
12. Radhakrishnan, *Eastern Religions and Western Thought,* 308.
13. Ibid.
14. Ibid., 312.
15. S. Radhakrishnan, *The Hindu View of Life* (New York: Macmillan, 1927), 20.

about which Jews and Christians substantially differ, as over the statement that "Jesus is the Messiah," over which they may be seen to only nominally differ on account of different conceptions of the Messiah, and (2) "basic religious disagreements," in which "different subjects are assigned to the same predicate," as when the *ultimate* is regarded as God in Christianity, Brahman in Hinduism, and Tao in Taoism.[16]

The Advaitin response to Christian's analysis is basically consistent with its position described earlier: that whether it is a case of affirming different predicates of the same subject or of assigning different subjects to the same predicate, the language-barrier in relation to Brahman is never overcome.

Within this broad limitation, however, in Advaita Vedānta "doctrinal disagreements" play a more important role than "basic religious disagreements." Advaita has little difficulty with different predicates being assigned to the same subject. Thus Śaṅkara quotes the following text in his Aitareya-Upaniṣad Bhāṣya: "Some speak of it as Agni, some as Manu, Prajāpati, Indra, others as Prāṇa, yet others as the eternal Brahman."[17]

But the situation is different in the case of doctrinal disagreements. Just as one can speak of the Messiah in the context of Judaism and Christianity, one can speak of Brahman in the context of the Vedantic tradition. Advaita accords primacy to *nirguṇa* Brahman, but some other schools of Vedānta accord primacy to *saguṇa* Brahman. In fact, "The main issue that was debated by the Vedantins who came after Śaṅkara was whether *Brahman* is *nirguṇa* or *saguṇa.*"[18] Troy Wilson Organ graphically illustrates the difference involved in the two approaches: water is water, no doubt, but it is quite different when experienced as H_2O or as a cold splash on one's face.[19]

This doctrinal disagreement within Vedānta, however, has characterized it from the earliest times to the present,[20] and has continued through the centuries *without compromising tolerance* within it in any marked degree. This is because the issue arises at the level of the ultimate. No school of Vedānta rejects the validity of either the *saguṇa* or *nirguṇa* formulation: the issue is of relative priority rather than absolute truth. Indeed, Gauḍapāda, a famous predecessor of Śaṅkara, says that Advaita Vedānta "is pleasing to all, has no dispute with anyone, and is not hostile to anyone."[21]

16. See Hick, *Philosophy of Religion,* 108–11.
17. Mahadevan, *Outlines of Hinduism,* 17.
18. Ibid., 150.
19. During a talk at the World Philosophy Congress, Brighton, 1988.
20. Mahadevan, *Outlines of Hinduism,* 251.
21. Radhakrishnan, trans., *Brahma Sūtra,* 29.

W. C. Smith's Analysis

Just as W. A. Christian probed the nature of belief in the context of conflicting truth claims, W. C. Smith probes the nature of religion itself. He concludes that it represents the Western habit of "turning good adjectives into bad substantives"[22] through "illicit reification,"[23] which manifested itself after the Enlightenment in the form of raising the question about the truth or falsity of a religion as an intellectual system. Religions should really be viewed as cumulative traditions. As he puts it, "It is not appropriate to speak of a religion as being true or false, any more than it is to speak of a civilization as being true or false."[24]

It seems that Smith is arguing against a religion being related to theories of truth on the one hand and advocating a Wittgensteinian "culture-game" theory on the other. Both of these are questionable from an Advaitin point of view. The correspondence theory is hard to verify in relation to religions, but even if it is accepted that the various religions represent distinct "truth-systems" in accordance with the coherence theory, so to speak, and are "relative," even then what is true of one may not be true of another. It is true that Smith blunts this last point by arguing that religions are to be viewed as culture-systems rather than truth-systems. However, the followers of the religions regard them as making truth claims, and from that point of view the problem persists.

The "culture-game" theory on the model of the "language-game" does have the merit of avoiding the truth-falsehood issue but opens up the Santayanan point that "religions are not true or false but better or worse." Here again Smith would not like to force the issue—but the Advaitin would—of whether the issue is veridical or functional. If the question of whether religion is true or false is *not* asked, then the question of whether it is good (useful) or bad (useless) needs to be asked. A modern Advaitin, S. Radhakrishnan, for instance, states: "Let us frankly recognize that the efficiency of a religion is to be judged by the development of religious qualities such as quiet confidence, inner calm, gentleness of the spirit, love of neighbour, mercy to all creation, destruction of tyrannous desires, and the aspiration for spiritual freedom, and there are no trustworthy statistics to tell us that these qualities are found more in efficient nations."[25]

22. Hick, *Philosophy of Religion,* 112.
23. Ibid.
24. Ibid., 113.
25. Radhakrishnan, *Eastern Religions and Western Thought,* 323.

The point here is not that these virtues cannot be quantitatively measured but rather that they form the qualitative propaedeutic for the study of Advaita according to Śaṅkara.[26]

John H. Hick's Analysis

John H. Hick distinguishes among three kinds of differences among the religions of the world: (1) differences in modes of experiencing the divine Reality, especially as personal or impersonal; (2) philosophical and theological differences; and (3) differences in the "key or revelatory experiences that unify a stream of religious experience and thought."[27] Hick seems to think that differences in the first two categories are not hard to overcome. He writes, for instance, that the personal and impersonal modes of encountering reality could be "understood as complementary rather than as incompatible."[28] Similarly, in the philosophical and theological realms the various religions may converge in the future as they face the challenges of critical scholarship, science, and globalization together and overcome or moderate their historical specificities. It is the differences of the third kind which Hick sees as constituting "the largest difficulty in the way of religious agreement. Each religion has its holy founder or scripture, or both, in which the divine Reality has been revealed—the Vedas, the Torah, the Buddha, Christ and the Bible, the Qur'an. Wherever the Holy is revealed, it claims an absolute response of faith and worship, which thus seems incompatible with a like response to any other claimed disclosure of the Holy."[29]

Advaita Vedānta seems to confirm Hick's view on the first point—that the personal and impersonal approaches to the divine may be viewed as complementary.[30] It also seems to confirm his second point—that modernity will reduce religious differences. In this matter Advaita Vedānta may well have anticipated modern developments.[31] We may now examine the third kind of difference, which according to Hick may prove to be a major obstacle in

26. Radhakrishnan, trans., *Brahma Sūtra,* 227.

27. Hick, *Philosophy of Religion,* 116.

28. Ibid.

29. Ibid., 117.

30. Radhakrishnan, trans., *Brahma Sūtra,* 126–27; P. Sankaranarayanan, *What Is Advaita?* (Bombay: Bharatiya Vidya Bhavan, 1970), 69, and passim.

31. K. Satchidananda Murty, *Revelation and Reason in Advaita Vedānta* (1959; reprint, New Delhi: Motilal Banarsidass, 1974), 312.

resolving conflicting truth claims. The issue here turns on the founder and scripture of the tradition.

Advaita Vedānta dispenses with the issue of the founder in accepting the Vedas as *apauruṣeya;* that is, as possessing neither a human nor divine author.[32] But what about its claim that only the Vedas can supply humanity with saving knowledge?[33]

Some scholars, K. Satchidananda Murty among them, have argued very strongly that salvation must be mediated through the Vedas in the context of Advaita Vedānta.[34] This does seem to be the general position, despite problems,[35] but it is not entirely clear whether this is a substantial or a nominal position and even whether the position within Advaita Vedānta might not be more charitable than it has been made out to be.[36]

In this context Brahmasūtra 1.1.4 is significant, as it declares that the Upaniṣads, are to be interpreted *tat tu samanvayāt* (on the principle of harmony).[37] The well-known modern thinker, S. Radhakrishnan has suggested that "today the *samanvaya* or harmonization has to be extended to the living faiths of mankind"[38]—and, one might add, to the *scriptures* of all the living faiths of mankind. Such an approach might have the effect of rendering the third difficulty identified by Hick more tractable.

A Philosophical Framework for Religious Pluralism in John H. Hick and Advaita Vedānta: A Comparison

John H. Hick then goes on to propose a philosophical framework for religious pluralism, the basic principle of which is that we can "think in terms of a single divine noumenon and perhaps many diverse divine phenomena."[39] In elaborating this position Hick makes several remarks that are quite signifi-

32. Ibid., chap. 3.
33. Ibid., 51–52, 326, and passim.
34. Ibid., 10, 119, 134, 254, and passim.
35. Ibid., 138–39; P. V. Kane, *History of Dharmaśāstra* (Poona: Bhandarkar Oriental Research Institute, 1977), vol. 5, part 2, p. 921; William Cenkner, *A Tradition of Teachers: Śaṅkara and the Jagadgurus of Today* (Delhi: Motilal Banarsidass, 1983), 49 n. 3.
36. Murty, *Revelation and Reason,* 163; M. Hiriyanna, *The Essentials of Indian Philosophy* (London: George Allen & Unwin, 1948), 173.
37. Radhakrishnan, trans. *Brahma Sūtra,* 246.
38. Ibid., 249.
39. Hick, *Philosophy of Religion,* 120.

cant from the point of view of Advaita Vedānta: (1) Hick identifies the "similar (though not identical) distinctions"[40] found within the major religious traditions between the Real as such and the Real as experienced by human beings.

> In the west the Christian mystic Meister Eckhart drew a parallel distinction between the Godhead (*Deitas*) and God (*Deus*). The Taoist scripture, the *Tao Te Ching,* begins by affirming that "the Tao that can be expressed is not the eternal Tao." The Jewish Kabbalist mystics distinguished between En Soph, the absolute divine reality beyond all human description, and the God of the Bible; and among the Muslim Sufis, Al Haqq, the Real, seems to be a similar concept to En Soph, as the abyss of Godhead underlying the self-revealing Allah. More recently Paul Tillich has spoken of "the God above the God of theism." A. N. Whitehead, and the process theologians who follow him, distinguish between the primordial and consequent natures of God; and Gordon Kaufman has recently distinguished between the "real God" and the "available God."[41]

Hick draws on Immanuel Kant's concept of "the world as it is *an sich,* which he called the noumenal world, and the world as it appears to human consciousness, which he calls the phenomenal world." Taking his cue from this, Hick forms "the hypothesis that the Real *an sich* is experienced by human beings in terms of one of the two basic religious concepts" ("the Real as such and the Real as experienced by human beings"), which when experienced are "made more concrete (in Kantian terminology, schematized) as a range of particular images of God or particular concepts of the Absolute."[42] Thus, on the one hand, are the *different* images of God as found in the various theistic religions explained and on the other the different forms of nontheistic religions which refer to the Absolute—"Brahman, Nirvana, Sunyata, the Dharma, the Dharmakaya, the Tao."[43]

Hick further maintains that although it is sometimes claimed of the absolutistic experience that it is unmediated, unlike the theistic, by the human mind, "our hypothesis will have to hold that even the apparently direct and unmediated awareness of the Real in the Hindu *moksha,* in the Buddhist

40. Ibid., 118.
41. Ibid., 118–19.
42. Ibid., 120.
43. Ibid.

satori, and in the unitive mysticism of the West, is still the conscious experience of the human agent and as such is influenced by the interpretative set of the cognizing mind."[44] Ultimately, Hick concludes that "it is a possible, and indeed an attractive hypothesis—as an alternative to total skepticism—that the great religious traditions of the world represent different human perceptions of and response to the same infinite divine Reality."[45]

The reader will recognize that this position is very similar to the one developed by modern Advaitin thinkers. However, the difference between the position advocated by John H. Hick and the position of the Advaitin on these points needs to be clarified.

1. The reader will notice, and Hick specifically mentions,[46] the similarity of the distinctions between Godhead and God, and so on, to the distinction drawn between *nirguṇa* and *saguṇa* Brahman in Advaita. Here the point to be kept in mind from the Advaitic point of view is that "God as immanent (saguṇa) and God as transcendent Reality (nirguṇa) are not two any more than the man on the stage and the man outside the stage are two."[47] This is an allusion to Śaṅkara's analogy of the actor—a shepherd who appears on the stage in the *role* of a king is not two people, a shepherd and a king. In other words, Advaita would insist, the *nirguṇa* and *saguṇa* refer to two aspects of the *same* Reality.

2. Immanuel Kant's concept of *Ding an sich* must be used with some caution in the context of Advaita. This becomes clear from certain observations made by M. Hiriyanna while concluding a discussion of *nirguṇa* Brahman:

> Here naturally arises the question whether such an entity is not a sheer abstraction. Śaṁkara recognizes the force of this objection. It is, indeed, the very objection he seems to have raised against a certain other monistic view (*sattādvaita*) of Upanishadic teaching which was in vogue in his time, viz. that Brahman is universal Being. Śaṁkara's monism differs from it in that it views the ultimate reality not as objective, but as identical *at bottom* with the individual self (*ātmādvaita*). This altered conception secures the maximum certainty to the reality of Brahman, for nothing can possibly carry greater certitude

44. Ibid., 121.
45. Ibid.
46. Ibid., 118.
47. Satischandra Chatterjee and Dhirendramohan Datta, *An Introduction to Indian Philosophy* (1950; reprint, Calcutta: University of Calcutta, 1968), 398.

> with it than one's belief in the existence of oneself. "A man," it has been said, "may doubt of many things, of anything *else;* but he can never doubt of his own being," for that very act of doubting would affirm its existence. It is thus eventually through something in ourselves that, according to Śaṁkara, we are able to judge of reality and unreality. Such a view does not mean that the self is known to us completely. Far from it. But, at the same time, it does not remain wholly unknown, being our own self—a fact which distinguishes the advaitic ultimate from not only the universal Being referred to above, *but also (to mention a Western parallel) the thing-in-itself of Kant.*[48]

In Advaita, the thing-in-itself is knowable in a metempirical way, as the *ātman,* though there is considerable controversy surrounding the issue of how it is known.[49] In this debate the role of the *mind* is one of the points at issue. According to one school, for instance, *direct* knowledge of the ultimate Reality, Brahman, is possible because as "Brahman, which is to be known, is not different from the knower (the subject) immediate knowledge is possible."[50] Another view is that "though the knowledge of Brahman derived from scripture is not itself immediate, Brahman is immediate; and Brahman is immediately experienced by mind only."[51]

Although the latter position is closer to Hick's, neither position would agree with his statement that the experience is "*influenced* by the interpretative set of the cognizing mind,"[52] as the dispute between them is over the mechanics of Realization alone. What is crucial to note here is the possibility of "immediate knowledge not involving sense-perception. The empirical self, for instance, is immediately known, but it cannot be said to be *presented* to any sense. Hence the word pratyakṣa, which literally means 'presented to a sense,' is here replaced by the wider term aparokṣa or 'not mediate.' "[53] It is also important to note, in a broader context, the pervasive significance of the Ātman = Brahman identity in Advaita.

However, although the *experience* as such is not influenced by the cognizing mind—because, in the technical jargon of Advaita, the internal organ (*antaḥkaraṇa*) is merged with nescience (*avidyā*), *of which it is a prod-*

48. Hiriyanna, *Essentials,* 162; emphasis added.
49. Murty, *Revelation and Reason,* 103–11.
50. Ibid., 107.
51. Ibid., 111.
52. Hick, *Philosophy of Religion,* 121.
53. M. Hiriyanna, *Outlines of Indian Philosophy* (London: George Allen & Unwin, 1964), 345.

uct, before the latter is sublated, leading to Brahman-*experience*—our *knowledge* of it may be influenced by the internal organ "for no knowledge, whether mediate or immediate, is possible in the absence of the internal organ,"[54] although the self, *ātman,* is ontologically prior to the "false identity of the self and the not-self," which presupposes *avidyā* or ignorance."[55]

3. The previous discussion clarifies the view whether, from the point of view of Advaita, one can agree with Hick that "even the apparently direct and unmediated awareness of the Real . . . is still the conscious experience of the human subject and as such is influenced by the interpretative set of the cognizing mind."[56] The Advaitic position would seem to suggest that the awareness of the Real is unmediated and direct, but when it becomes recognized *as* the conscious experience of the subject it is influenced by the mind-set. On the analogy of sleep it may be pointed out that our personality has nothing to do with the *state* of deep sleep; "None of the features of sleep . . . is 'known' at the time, for no knowledge, whether mediate or immediate, is possible in the absence of the internal organ. But they are nevertheless realized then as shown by the fact of their being recalled afterwards."[57] At the stage of recall the internal organ is again active and the mind-set now comes into play.

4. The Advaitin philosophical framework, nevertheless, for religious pluralism, is very similar to Hick's and shares its attractive features. It is, however, capable of an extension that is possible while one is functioning from within an Advaitic framework but perhaps not possible if one is operating within the framework suggested by Hick. Nor is it entirely clear whether the new position represents any advance or possesses any advantage over that advocated by John H. Hick. It, however, needs to be taken into account as it does actually appear in the history of Advaita Vedānta. It is rooted in the Advaitic position that in the final analysis only one ultimate reality exists, which is called *Brahman* or *ātman.* But if there is really only one reality, are we left with any other position to even contend with? Thus a modern exponent of Advaita Vedānta can affirm that

> Advaita is *non-dual-ism.* Reality, according to its insight, is non-dual, not-two. Advaita does not profess to formulate conceptually what

54. Ibid., 349.
55. Hiriyanna, *Essentials,* 165.
56. Hick, *Philosophy of Religion,* 121.
57. Hiriyanna, *Outlines,* 349.

> Reality is. It is not, therefore, a system of thought, an *ism.* It is not a school among schools of philosophy. It does not reject any view of Reality; it only seeks to transcend all views, since these are by their very nature restricted, limited, and circumscribed. The pluralisms, theistic or otherwise, imagine that they are opposed to Advaita. But Advaita is not opposed to any of the partial views of Reality.[58]

Such an affirmation is in keeping with the tradition of Advaita Vedānta, for an early exponent of it, Gauḍapāda (seventh century C.E.) declared: "The dualists (i.e. pluralists) are conclusively firm in regard to the status of their respective opinions. They are in conflict with one another. But, Advaita is in no conflict with them. Advaita, verily, is the supreme truth; dvaita is a variant thereof. For the dualists, there is duality either way (i.e. both in the Absolute and in the phenomenal manifold). With that (duality) this (non-duality) is not in conflict."[59]

Such a view has the merit of being nonconflictual, but at the cost of dismissing the other party out of hand. This is apparent in a remark Śaṅkara makes in his commentary on the verses of Gauḍapāda quoted above. Śaṅkara writes: "As one who is mounted on a spirited elephant does not drive it against a lunatic who stands on the ground and shouts, 'Drive your elephant against me who also am seated on an elephant,' because he (the former) has no notion of opposition, even so (is the case with the non-dualist). Thus, in truth, the knower of *Brahman* is the very self of the dualists. For this reason, our view is not in conflict with theirs."[60]

In point of fact, however, Śaṅkara did engage other schools in debate and dialogue. Perhaps if it is realized that Śaṅkara is talking here from a metempirical point of view, whereas all discourse is carried on within the empirical realm, the contradiction is converted into a paradox.

5. The founder and the scriptures loom large as an issue in Hick's agenda, but Advaita Vedānta deals in the eternal rather than the historical. It could be argued that it apotheosizes the Veda; however, the Veda also belongs to the realm of *mithyā*;[61] moreover, some say that the Vedas are endless, which creates room for the acceptance of other scriptures.[62] Finally, experience takes precedence over the Vedas, on which their own claim

58. T.M.P. Mahadevan, *The Insights of Advaita* (Mysore: University of Mysore, 1970), 4.
59. Ibid., 4–5.
60. Ibid., 6.
61. Murty, *Revelation and Reason*, 99.
62. Mahadevan, *Outlines of Hinduism*, 39.

to validity really rests.[63] Thus what John H. Hick identifies as the main obstacles to the accommodation of conflicting truth claims turn out to be less problematical in the case of Advaita Vedānta.

Conclusion

Despite these divergences there is little doubt that there exists a very strong family resemblance in the philosophical frameworks offered by John H. Hick and Advaita Vedānta for resolving conflicting truth claims. This becomes quite clear from such Advaitic statements as the following found in the Yogavāśiṣtha (III.1.12; III.5, 6, 7; V.8.19):

> Many names have been given to the Absolute by the learned for practical purposes such as Law, Self, Truth.
>
> It is called Person by the Sāṁkhya thinkers, Brahman by the Vedāntins, pure and simple consciousness by the Vijñānavādins, Śūnya by the Nihilists, the Illuminator by the worshippers of the Sun. It is also called the Speaker, the Thinker, the Enjoyer of actions and the Doer of them.
>
> Śiva for the worshippers of Śiva, and Time for those who believe in Time alone.[64]

63. Eliot Deutsch, *Advaita Vedānta: A Philosophical Reconstruction* (Honolulu: East-West Center Press, 1969), 75.
64. Radhakrishnan, *Eastern Religions and Western Thought,* 318–19.

Bibliography

Apte, V. M., trans. *Brahma-Sūtra Shānkarabhāshya.* Bombay: Popular Book Depot, 1960.

Balasubramanian, R. *Advaita Vedānta.* Madras: University of Madras, 1976.

Basham, A. L. *The Wonder That Was India.* New York: Grove Press, 1954.

Bhattacharyya, Haridas, ed. *The Cultural Heritage of India.* 4 vols. Calcutta: The Ramkrishna Mission Institute of Culture, 1969.

Bolle, Kees W. *The Bhagavadgītā: A New Translation.* Berkeley and Los Angeles: University of California Press, 1979.

Bowes, Pratima. *The Hindu Religious Tradition: A Philosophical Approach.* London: Routledge & Kegan Paul, 1977.

Braithwaite, R. B. *An Empiricist's View of the Nature of Religious Belief.* Cambridge: Cambridge University Press, 1955.

Brunton, Paul, and Munagala Venkatramiah. *Conscious Immortality.* Tiruvannamalai: Sri Ramanasramam, 1984.

Burch, George Bosworth, ed. *Search for the Absolute in Neo-Advaita.* Honolulu: The University of Hawaii Press, 1976.

Cenkner, William. *A Tradition of Teachers: Śaṅkara and the Jagadgurus of Today.* Delhi: Motilal Banarsidass, 1983.

Chatterjee, Satischandra, and Dhirendramohan Datta. *An Introduction to Indian Philosophy.* New edition. Calcutta: University of Calcutta, 1968.

Dart, John. "After 'Near-Death' Experience, Prominent Atheist Warms to After Life." *The Gazette* (Montreal), 9 October 1988, B–1.

Dasgupta, Surendranath. *A History of Indian Philosophy.* Vol. 1. Delhi: Motilal Banarsidass, 1975.

Datta, D. M. *The Six Ways of Knowing.* Calcutta: University of Calcutta, 1972.

Davies, J. G. "Christianity: The Early Church." In *The Concise Encyclopedia of Living Faiths,* ed. R. C. Zaehner. Boston: Beacon Press, 1967.

Deutsch, Eliot. *Advaita Vedānta: A Philosophical Reconstruction.* Honolulu: East-West Center Press, 1969.

Deutsch, Eliot, and J.A.B. van Buitenen, eds., *A Source Book of Advaita Vedānta.* Honolulu: The University of Hawaii Press, 1971.

Devaraja, N. K. *Hinduism and the Modern Age.* New Delhi: Islam and The Modern Age Society, 1975.

Hill, W. Douglas P. *The Bhagavad-Gītā.* 2d ed. London: Oxford University Press, 1966.

Gambhirananda, Swami, trans. *Brahma-Sūtra-Bhāṣya of Śrī Śaṅkarācārya.* Calcutta: Advaita Ashrama, 1977.

Godman, David, ed. *The Teachings of Sri Ramana Maharshi.* London: Arkana, 1985.

Grimes, John A. "Advaita Vedānta and the Problem of Religious Language." Ph.D. diss., University of Madras, 1984.

Gupta, Bina. *Perceiving in Advaita Vedānta: An Epistemological Analysis and Interpretation.* Lewisburg, Pa.: Bucknell University Press, 1991.

Herman, Arthur L. *The Problem of Evil and Indian Thought.* Delhi: Motilal Banarsidass, 1976.

Herring, Herbert. *Reflections on Vedānta.* Madras: University of Madras, 1978.

Hick, John H. *The Philosophy of Religion.* 3d ed. Englewood Cliffs, N.J.: Prentice Hall, 1983.
Hiriyanna, M. *The Essentials of Indian Philosophy.* London: George Allen & Unwin, 1948.
———. *Popular Essays in Indian Philosophy.* Mysore: Kavyalaya Publishers, 1952.
———. *Indian Philosophical Studies.* Mysore: Kavyalaya Publishers, 1957.
———. *Outlines of Indian Philosophy.* London: George Allen & Unwin, 1964.
Hume, Robert Ernest, trans. *The Thirteen Principal Upanishads.* 1877. 2d ed. London: Oxford University Press, 1968.
Indich, William M. *Consciousness in Advaita Vedānta.* Delhi: Motilal Banarsidass, 1980.
Jacob, Colonel G. A. *A Manual of Hindu Pantheism: The Vedāntasāra.* 1881. Reprint. Varanasi: Bharat-Bharati, 1972.
Jayatilleke, K. N. *Early Buddhist Theory of Knowledge.* London: George Allen & Unwin, 1963.
Johnson, Raynor C. *The Imprisoned Splendour.* New York: Harper & Brothers, 1953.
Kane, P. V. *History of Dharmaśāstra.* 5 vols. Poona: Bhandarkar Oriental Research Institute, 1977.
Karunakaran, R. *The Concept of Sat in Advaita Vedānta.* Edakkadom, Quilon: Sri Sankara Sanskrit Vidyapeetham, 1980.
Madhavananda, Swami. *Vedānta-Paribhāṣā of Dharmarāja Adhvarindra.* Belur Math, Howrah: The Ramakrishna Mission, Saradapitha, 1963.
———. *Vivekachudamani of Shri Shankaracharya.* Calcutta: Advaita Ashrama, 1966.
Mahadevan, T.M.P. *The Philosophy of Beauty with Special Reference to Advaita Vedānta.* Bombay: Bharatiya Vidya Bhavan, 1969.
———. *Outlines of Hinduism.* 1960. Reprint. Bombay: Chetana, 1971.
———. *The Insights of Advaita.* Mysore: University of Mysore, 1970.
Moody, Raymond A., Jr. *Life After Life.* New York: Bantam Books, 1975.
Murty, K. Satchidananda. *Revelation and Reason in Advaita Vedānta.* New York: Columbia University Press, 1959. Reprint. New Delhi: Motilal Banarsidass, 1974.
Myers, F.W.H. *Human Personality and Its Survival of Bodily Death.* London: Longmans, Green, 1903.
O'Flaherty, Wendy Doniger, ed. *Karma and Rebirth in Classical Indian Traditions.* Berkeley and Los Angeles: University of California Press, 1980.
Organ, Troy Wilson. *Hinduism: Its Historical Development.* Woodbury, N.Y.: Barron's Educational Series, 1974.
Pattanayak, P. M. *A Graphic Representation of Vedanta Sara.* New Delhi: Harman Publishing House, 1987.
Payne, Robert. *The Life and Death of Mahatma Gandhi.* New York: E. P. Dutton, 1969.
Potter, Karl H., ed. *Encyclopedia of Indian Philosophies: Advaita Vedānta up to Śaṃkara and His Pupils.* Delhi: Motilal Banarsidass, 1981.
Radhakrishnan, S. *The Hindu View of Life.* New York: Macmillan, 1927.
———. *Indian Philosophy.* Vol. 2. London: George Allen & Unwin, 1927.
———, ed. *The Principal Upaniṣads.* London: George Allen & Unwin, 1953.
———. *Eastern Religions and Western Thought.* New York: Oxford University Press, 1959.
———, trans. *The Brahma Sūtra: The Philosophy of a Spiritual Life.* London: George Allen & Unwin, 1960.
———. *Indian Philosophy.* 2 vols. London: George Allen & Unwin, 1962.
Raju, P. T. *Idealistic Thought in India.* London: George Allen & Unwin, 1953.
Rambachan, Anantanand. *Accomplishing the Accomplished: The Vedas as a Source of Valid Knowledge in Śaṅkara.* Honolulu: University of Hawaii Press, 1991.
Randall, J. H. *The Role of Knowledge in Western Religion.* Boston: Beacon Press, 1958.

Rowe, William L., and William J. Wainright, eds. *Philosophy of Religion: Selected Readings.* New York: Harcourt Brace Jovanovich, 1973.
Sambuddhananda, Swami. *Vedānta Through Stories.* Bombay: Sri Ramakrishna Ashram, 1959.
Sankaranarayanan, P. *What Is Advaita?* Bombay: Bharatiya Vidya Bhavan, 1970.
Sastry, Alladi Mahadeva, trans. *The Bhagavad Gita with the Commentary of Sri Sankaracharya.* 1979. Reprint. Madras: Samata Books, 1985.
Seshagiri Rao, K. L. *The Concept of Śraddhā.* Patiala: Roy Publishers, 1971.
Sharma, Arvind. "Śaṅkara's Attitude to Scriptural Authority as Revealed by His Gloss on Brahmasūtra 1.1.3." *Journal of Indian Philosophy* 10 (1982): 179–86.
———. *The Experiential Dimension of Advaita Vedānta.* Delhi: Motilal Banarsidass, 1993.
———. "Feature Review: *Accomplishing the Accomplished: The Vedas as a Source of Valid Knowledge in Śaṅkara* by Anantanand Rambachan." *Philosophy East & West* 43, no. 4 (1993): 737–44.
Sharma, Chandradhar. *A Critical Survey of Indian Philosophy.* London: Rider, 1960.
Sharma, R. K., and V. B. Dash, trans. *Caraka Saṁhitā.* 2 vols. Varanasi: Chowkhamba Sanskrit Series Office, 1976.
Sinha, Jadunath. *A History of Indian Philosophy.* Calcutta: Sinha Publishing House, 1956.
Smart, Ninian. *Doctrine and Argument in Indian Philosophy.* London: George Allen & Unwin, 1964.
Swahananda, Swami, trans. *Pañcadaśī of Śrī Vidyāraṇya Swāmī.* Madras: Sri Ramakrishna Math, 1967.
Talks with Sri Ramana Maharshi. Tiruvannamalai: Sri Ramanasramam, 1984.
The Cultural Heritage of India. Calcutta: The Ramakrishna Mission Institute of Culture, 1958.
Tillich, Paul. *Dynamics of Faith.* New York: Harper & Row, 1957.
———. *Systematic Theology.* 3 vols. Chicago: University of Chicago Press, 1951–63.
Tripathi, R. K. *Problems of Philosophy and Religion.* Varanasi: Banaras Hindu University, 1971.
Walker, Benjamin. *Hindu World.* 2 vols. London: George Allen & Unwin, 1968.
Zaehner, R. C. *The Bhagavad-Gītā.* Oxford: Clarendon Press, 1969.
Zimmer, Heinrich. *Philosophies of India.* Edited by Joseph Campbell. New York: Pantheon Books, 1951.

Index